Opening Doors

MENA DEVELOPMENT REPORT

Opening Doors

Gender Equality and Development in the Middle East and North Africa

THE WORLD BANK
Washington, D.C.

Contents

Tables

Foreword

Since the early 1990s, countries in the Middle East and North Africa (MENA) Region have made admirable progress in reducing the gap between girls and boys in areas such as access to education and health care. Indeed, almost all young girls in the Region attend school, and more women than men are enrolled in university. Over the past 2 decades, maternal mortality declined 60 percent, the largest decrease in the world. Women in MENA are more educated than ever before. Nevertheless, as recent popular calls for greater social and economic inclusion illustrate, these achievements have not yet translated into a more equal role for women in political and economic life. Women in MENA clearly yearn to put their hard-won skills into action now.

It is not only in the protest squares that we have seen women whose aspirations are changing rapidly but increasingly unmet. The worldwide average for the participation of women in the workforce is approximately 50 percent. In MENA, their participation is half that at 25 percent. Young women especially have high rates of unemployment. This fact is surely an important one to grapple with as the Region undergoes a profound transformation in which young citizens, who already make up the bulk of the population, are at the forefront of calls for change.

This, then, is the context for our new report, *Opening Doors: Gender Equality and Development in the Middle East and North Africa*. In this report, we argue for urgent reform on multiple fronts to secure equal opportunities for women alongside men. A complex set of constraints inhibits women's choice and mobility. Legal and social barriers limit where and how long women can work. The lack of relevant skills in demand by the market narrows their opportunities. Finally, there are limited private sector and entrepreneurial prospects not only for jobs but also for those women who aspire to create and run a business. These constraints present multiple challenges for reform.

Each country in MENA will, of course, confront these constraints in different contexts. However, inherent in many of these challenges are rich opportunities as reforms unleash new economic actors. For the private sector, the challenge is to create more jobs for young women and men. However, therein lies opportunity, too, because many of these young candidates are technology savvy and tuned in to current trends. For policymakers, undoing the inequalities that women face invites a complex mix of bold policy shifts, legal change, and education to help women achieve the appropriate skills. The World Bank has been pursuing an exciting pilot program in Jordan to assist young women graduates in preparing to face the work environment. Initial results are promising but also point to attitudinal shifts that may need to be quite significant to make a real difference.

My hope is that this report presents more than a useful diagnostic. For the World Bank, it will be the analytical basis for our renewed commitment and strategy to support gender equality in MENA. We want to ensure that our country dialogues and Bank-supported programs and policies are informed by a gender perspective. We also want to continue to learn what works through carefully designed policy pilots, and to share these lessons with countries around the world. As MENA countries set out toward a more inclusive development path, there is a tremendous opportunity for women and men to be equal partners in this new era.

Inger Andersen
Vice President
Middle East and North Africa Region
The World Bank

Acknowledgments

This report is a regional companion piece to the *World Development Report 2012: Gender Equality and Development*, and was completed under the guidance of Inger Andersen, Vice President, Middle East and North Africa Region, World Bank.

The overview of the report greatly benefited from a series of consultations with stakeholders in the MENA Region. Early consultations were held with Kuwait and Tunisia followed by in-country consultations in October 2011 in the Arab Republic of Egypt, Jordan, Lebanon, Tunisia, and the Palestinian Territories. By and large, the gender challenges identified in the overview and the report were endorsed. The salience of legal constraints to women's participation outside the home was a recurring theme. The team would like to gratefully acknowledge the inputs and feedback of all participants, and hope that these are reflected in the full report.

This report has benefited from the time and efforts of many. Led by Tara Vishwanath (Task Team Leader and Lead Economist, MNSED), the core team comprises Gabriela Inchauste Comboni (Senior Economist, PRMPR), Quy-Toan Do (Senior Economist, DECPI), Nandini Krishnan (Economist, MNSED), Nga Nguyen (Consultant, MNSED), and Thomas Walker (Economist, SASHD). Patti Petesch (independent consultant) conducted the analysis of qualitative data, Tazeen Hasan (Consultant, DECDP), with support from Talajeh Livani (Consultant, MNSED), provided inputs for the analysis of the legal framework; and Radu Ban (Bill and Melinda Gates Foundation) contributed to the analysis of civic and political participation. The report has benefited from the support of the Women, Business and the Law team, who contributed data for the legal analysis. The analysis on labor markets was supported by Matthew Groh (Consultant, DECFP), Umar Serajuddin (Economist, MNSED), Alejandro Hoyos Suarez (Consultant, PRMPR) and Hernan Winkler (Consultant, PRMPR). Kevin Carey (Senior Economist,

MNSED) provided significant contributions to the analysis of GCC economies. We thank Faythe Calandra (Program Assistant, MNSPR) for substantial support in formatting this report. Alicia Hetzner (Senior Editor) edited the book. Paola Scalabrin, Rick Ludwick, and Nora Ridolfi, Office of the Publisher, managed the final production.

The team would like to take this opportunity to gratefully acknowledge the support from the PREM Poverty Reduction and Equity group, especially Jaime Saavedra (Sector Director). At various stages of its preparation, the report gained from comments and advice from Jishnu Das (Senior Economist, DECHD) and Jean-Michel Marchat (Lead Private Sector Development Specialist, AFTFW). The team gratefully acknowledges peer reviewers Ritva Reinikka (Sector Director, AFTHD) and Sudhir Shetty (Co-Director, *World Development Report 2012*, now Sector Director, EASPR) for their comments and support. The team also thanks individuals and teams within and outside the Region for taking the time to provide detailed comments, especially Jeni Klugman (Sector Director, PRMGE), Nadereh Chamlou (Senior Adviser, MNACE) and the MNA Human Development and Sustainable Development teams.

Finally, the team would like to thank Manuela V. Ferro (Sector Director, MNSPR), Bernard Funck (Sector Manager, MNSPR) and Caroline Freund (Chief Economist, MNA) for their support throughout the entire process.

Abbreviations

ACS	American Community Survey
ADR	Alternative dispute resolution
AFR	Africa Region, World Bank
AFTFW	Africa Region, Finance and Private Sector Development, World Bank
AFTHD	Africa Region, Human Development, World Bank
ALG	Algeria
ALMP	Active Labor Market Policy
BBL	Billion barrels
BBO	Billion barrels of oil
BHR	Bahrain
BPO	Business process outsourcing
CCT	Conditional cash transfer
CEDAW	Convention on the Elimination of All Forms of Discrimination against Women
CIJD	Chief Islamic Justice Department (Jordan)
COHRE	Centre for Housing Rights and Eviction
COMTRADE	Commodity Trade statistics database
CSO	Community service organization
DECHD	Development Economics Group, Human Development Unit, World Bank
DECOS	Development Economics Group, Operations and Strategy Unit, World Bank
DECPI	Development Economics Group, Poverty and Inequality Unit, World Bank
DECWD	Development Economics Group, *World Development Report*, World Bank
DJI	Djibouti
EAP	East Asia and Pacific Region, World Bank

EASPR	East Asia and Pacific Region, Poverty Reduction and Economic Management, World Bank
ECA	Eastern Europe and Central Asia Region, World Bank
EdStats	Education statistics (World Bank)
EGY	Egypt, Arab Republic of
EITC	Earned income tax credit
ELMPS	Egypt Labor Market Panel Survey
ERF	Economic Research Forum (Egypt)
GCC	Gulf Cooperation Council
GDP	Gross domestic product
GEME	Gender Equity Model in Egypt
GNI	Gross national income
ICT	Information and communication technology
IFC	International Finance Corporation
IHSES	Iraq Household Socio-Economic Survey
ILO	International Labour Organization
IMF	International Monetary Fund
IPA	Innovations for Poverty Action
IRQ	Iraq
IZA	Institute for the Study of Labor
JICA	Japan International Cooperation Agency
JOR	Jordan
Jordan NOW	Jordan New work Opportunities for Women
KWT	Kuwait
LAC	Latin America and the Caribbean Region, World Bank
LBN	Lebanon
LE	Egyptian Pound
LIC	Low-income country
LFP	Labor force participation
LMI	Low and middle income
LMRA	Labour Market Regulatory Authority (Bahrain)
MAR	Morocco
MENA, MNA	Middle East and North Africa Region, World Bank
MHYS	Morocco Household and Youth Survey
MNACE	Middle East and North Africa Region, Chief Economist's Office, World Bank
MNSED	Middle East and North Africa Region, Social and Economic Development Unit, World Bank
MNSPR	Middle East and North Africa Region, Poverty Reduction and Economic Management, World Bank
NBER	National Bureau of Economic Research
n.e.c.	Not elsewhere classified
NGO	Nongovernmental organization
NSP	National Solidarity Program (Afghanistan)
OECD	Organisation for Economic Co-operation and Development

OMN	Oman
OSS	One-stop shop
PEKKA	Perempuan Kepala Keluarga (Female-Headed Household Program)
PRMGE	Poverty Reduction and Economic Management, Gender Unit, World Bank
PRMPR	Poverty Reduction and Economic Management, Poverty Reduction Unit, World Bank
PSD	Private sector development
PSF	Price Stabilization Fund
PT	Palestinian Territories
QAT	Qatar
SA	South Asia Region
SAU	Saudi Arabia
SR	Saudi Riyal
SSA	Sub-Saharan Africa
SSC	Social Security Corporation
SYPE	Survey of the Young People of Egypt (Population Council)
SYR	Syria
TTL	Task team leader
TUN	Tunisia
UAE	United Arab Emirates
UIS	Institute for Statistics (UNESCO)
UK	United Kingdom
UNDP	United Nations Development Programme
UNESCO	United Nations Education, Scientific and Cultural Organization
UNFPA	United Nations Population Fund
UNIDO	United Nations Industrial Development Organization
UNIFEM	United Nations Development Fund for Women
UNSTAT	United Nations Statistics Division
UNU-WIDER	United Nations University World Institute for International Development Economics Research
US	United States
US$	United States dollar
WBG	World Bank Group
WDR	*World Development Report*
WHO	World Health Organization
WVS	World Values Survey
YEM	Yemen, Republic of

Note: All dollar amounts are US dollars unless otherwise indicated.

Overview

Many countries in the Middle East and North Africa (MENA) Region are undergoing a profound transformation. From Morocco to the Republic of Yemen, popular movements have called for reforms to make governments more inclusive and more accountable, extend social and economic freedoms, and increase employment opportunities. Young women and men have been at the forefront of these calls for change, reflecting their desire to participate actively in the political sphere. How the Region's societies will change in the wake of these popular movements remains an open question.

Facing popular pressure to be more open and inclusive, some governments in the Region are considering and implementing electoral and constitutional reforms to deepen democracy. These reforms present an opportunity to enhance economic, social, and political inclusion for all, including women, who make up half the population. However, the outlook remains uncertain. In 2011, Tunisia mandated that an equal number of women and men run as candidates on the electoral list, and women have secured one-quarter of the seats in the constituent assembly. In the Arab Republic of Egypt, millions of women turned out to vote in the 2011–12 parliamentary elections but, ultimately, made up only 2 percent of the lower house of parliament.

The world has acknowledged the power of Arab women as catalysts of change, awarding the 2011 Nobel Peace Prize to Tawakel Karman. She is the first Yemeni, the first Arab woman, and the youngest recipient of this honor. At the same time, across the Region, many are expressing concern that efforts to advance women's rights and access to opportunities may be halted, and even reversed. In this context, it may become increasingly important to safeguard and advance the gains from past reforms.

Across the Region, young women and men are full of aspirations (box O.1). Education is seen as a pathway to meaningful careers, through which young people can build their identities and contribute to their

---

BOX O.1

A Younger Generation Full of Aspirations

Rahma[1] comes from a region of the Republic of Yemen in which it often is said, "To educate a woman is wrong because she has no place but her husband's house."[2] Nevertheless, over the objections of her neighbors and community leaders, Rahma became the first female in her town to complete high school. She also was the first to take a job at a private medical clinic and the first to participate in a one-year health-care training program in Sana'a. Rahma since has returned to her town, married, and delivers babies in a special room added to her house. The community has grown to respect and admire her, and other girls are following in her footsteps. Rahma's younger sister is attending the Health Institute in nearby Ibb City.

Very few women in Rahma's mountainside town work for pay. Yet, when asked in focus groups what they hoped to be when they were 25 years old, adolescent girls declared, "A teacher," "A lawyer," "An engineer," "A broadcaster." The girls plan to marry and raise families, but many also aspire to work in professional settings in which they can apply their "hard work, diligence, excellence [and] morals, with confidence and with education and responsibility." Similarly, in their focus groups, the boys hoped to "get married, make my wife happy, and find a good job." They also expected to have to "work hard and persevere" to realize their dreams.

In a Gaza neighborhood, a 24-year-old who graduated from university said she wants to earn "a Master's degree and then open a private enterprise with my friend." A young man from the same community reports, "I want to be an architect."

Sources: World Bank 2012b, 44, forthcoming.
Notes:
1. Pseudonym.
2. In January 2011, nearly 500 adolescents, youths, and adults from the Republic of Yemen and the Palestinian Territories participated in small discussion groups on a wide range of gender issues. This data collection was part of a 20-country rapid qualitative assessment conducted in 2010 and 2011 as background for the *World Development Report 2012: Gender Equality and Development*. For the global companion report that draws on the qualitative dataset, see Munoz Boudet, Petesch, and Turk (forthcoming).

---

communities (box O.2). Through work, young women and men alike aspire to achieve great things and, in turn, inspire their peers. Their stories demonstrate that success in economic and political life does not need to come at the cost of family life and household responsibilities.

Complementing the World Development Report 2012: Gender Equality and Development (WDR 2012), this report, Opening Doors: Gender Equality in the Middle East and North Africa, focuses on the challenges and reform priorities for gender equality in the MENA Region. Following the approach of the 2012 WDR, the current report argues that "gender equality is smart economics" in MENA, as it is around the world. The report draws on economic analysis of quantitative data from MENA, qualitative research, and other international evidence to analyze gender challenges and identify the priority areas for policy action to promote gender equality in the Region.

The report argues that the MENA Region exhibits a gender equality paradox. Although, most MENA countries have made admirable progress in closing their gender gaps in education and health outcomes, these investments in human development have not yet translated into commensurately higher rates of female participation in economic and political life.

Worldwide, women remain disadvantaged relative to men. In developing countries, women typically have higher mortality rates, particularly in infancy, in early childhood, and in the reproductive ages (the "missing women" syndrome); lower levels of education and literacy; and lower pay in formal employment. Women also are underrepresented in politics and often lack the same legal rights that men have. While women in developed countries enjoy similar outcomes as men in the arenas of education and health, they continue to be paid less than men and have lower levels of representation in politics and senior management. Development does not automatically guarantee equality of outcomes so special attention by policymakers often is necessary to create change.

Gender gaps are worth addressing for both intrinsic and instrumental reasons. First, gender equality is intrinsically important. Freedom from absolute deprivation—in education and health care, for instance—is a basic human right that applies equally to women and men. Second, gender equality is an instrument for development: it can enhance economic efficiency and improve development outcomes. As the 2012 WDR argues, ". . . gender equality is smart economics" and matters for development. Providing women and men with equal access to education, economic opportunities, and assets has the potential to boost productivity. Furthermore, gender equality benefits the welfare of future generations. For example, improved education and employment opportunities for women have been shown to increase women's bargaining power, resulting in greater investment in children's health and education. Finally, when women and men have equal chances to be socially and politically active and to influence laws, politics, and policymaking, institutions and policies are more likely to be fair and representative of society as a whole.

With higher levels of education and lower fertility rates than ever before, women in the Region increasingly are looking for work. The public sector long has been the dominant source of employment, especially for women in the Region, who typically earn significantly more there than they would in the private sector. Indeed, women's typical fields of study, such as education, health services, and humanities, are geared toward employment in the public sector, thus reinforcing their preference and suitability for government jobs. However, further expansion of the public sector is increasingly fiscally unsustainable, especially in the labor-abundant, oil-poor countries.

Moreover, job creation in the private sector so far has been too limited to absorb the large and growing number of young jobseekers. In addition, within this limited sphere, women are unable to compete on an equal footing due to several interrelated factors. First, women in the Region continue to face significant restrictions on mobility and choice. These constraints are held in place by legal frameworks, including regulations that restrict work and political participation; and by social and cultural norms. A second constraint is the poor quality of education and critical skills mismatches between what is studied in school, especially for girls, and what the private sector demands. Third, employers often perceive women as more costly and less productive than men. For their part, women have concerns about their reputations and safety in private sector jobs. This report focuses on the incentives and constraints generated by the economic and institutional structures that prevail in MENA countries.

The economic and political environment arising from the Arab Spring has created an unprecedented window of opportunity for change. Given the growing labor, demographic, and fiscal constraints, and the changing aspirations in the Region, policy reforms urgently are needed to boost job creation for all.

For women, these reforms alone will not suffice. Even as jobs are created, additional measures will be required to address the myriad constraints to women's participation in the workforce. Targeted, coordinated efforts are needed on multiple fronts to increase women's participation in the economic and political spheres, and these efforts must be specific to country context. These efforts include changes in policies to secure women's equality under the law, to bridge the remaining gender gaps in health and education, to redress the skills mismatch in the job market, and to promote women's civic and political participation.

Changes in laws alone will do little if jobs are insufficient, or, as noted above, if few women possess the requisite skills that jobs demand. Furthermore, a continuation of policies that increase subsidies, public sector pay and benefits, or public sector employment will not help. On the contrary, these policies will further distort the incentives for private sector job creation and for women to seek work in this sector.

In consultations held across the Region to prepare the report, women affirmed their desire to work and highlighted the lack of job opportunities, reiterating the constraints posed by the legal and regulatory framework and conservative social norms. A recurrent theme in the discussions was the role played by laws that govern women's ability to exercise choice, move freely, and access opportunities. These powerful social and political

---

BOX O.2

Importance of Education for a Girl

"Education is very important because it builds the future. It's the best weapon for a girl these days. Education develops the girl and the society as a whole. It also makes the girl able to take a decision. And school is the ladder that leads a girl to higher positions in society after . . . finishing [university]."

—Young women's focus group, West Bank farming village,
Background Assessment for WDR 2012
(World Bank 2011b, 2012b, forthcoming)

---

sentiments will have important implications for those who seek to govern in the next several years. As these issues are being debated and decisions taken, MENA has a unique opportunity to improve economic productivity and social cohesion by enabling women to participate fully in the economy and society.

Impressive Achievements in Human Development Have Yet to Translate into Commensurate Participation in Economic and Political Life

Over the past 4 decades, MENA countries have made impressive strides in achieving gender parity in education and health outcomes (figures O.1 and O.2). Since 1970, countries in the Region have recorded the world's fastest progress in human development (UNDP 2010b). In this period, 5 MENA countries (Algeria, Morocco, Oman, Saudi Arabia, and Tunisia) were among the top 10 fastest movers. During the same period, the average growth rates of key indicators—such as female literacy, infant mortality, and life expectancy—exceeded those of most other developing Regions. MENA as a whole is close to achieving gender parity in primary and secondary enrollment rates, comparing favorably to low and middle income (LMI) countries worldwide. Maternal mortality in the Region is one-half the world average; and in the past decade, fertility rates have declined rapidly.

Gender gaps remain in some dimensions of human development—particularly in school completion rates—and gender differences in educational specialization remain significant. Nevertheless, most MENA countries are well on their way to achieve gender parity in key human

FIGURE O.1

MENA's Progress in Female Literacy, 1985–2010

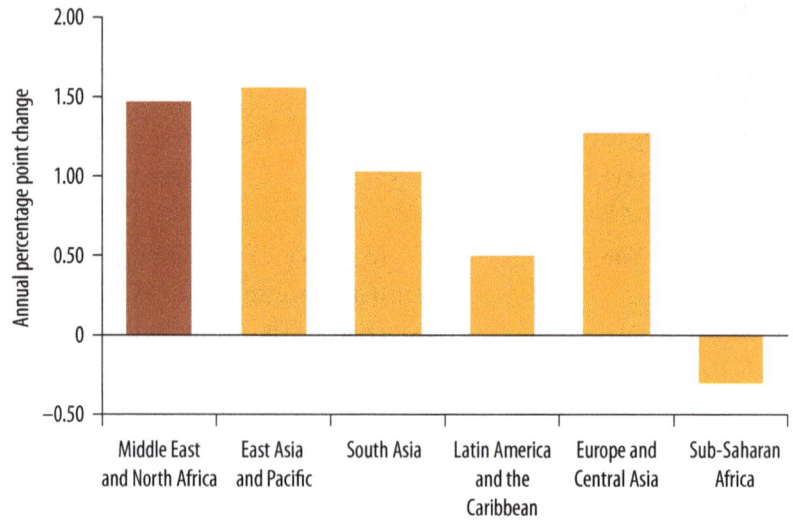

Source: Staff calculations based on WDI 2011 (World Bank multiple years).

FIGURE O.2

MENA's Progress in Women's Health and Education, 1985–2010 (Average Annual Growth Rates in Key Indicators)

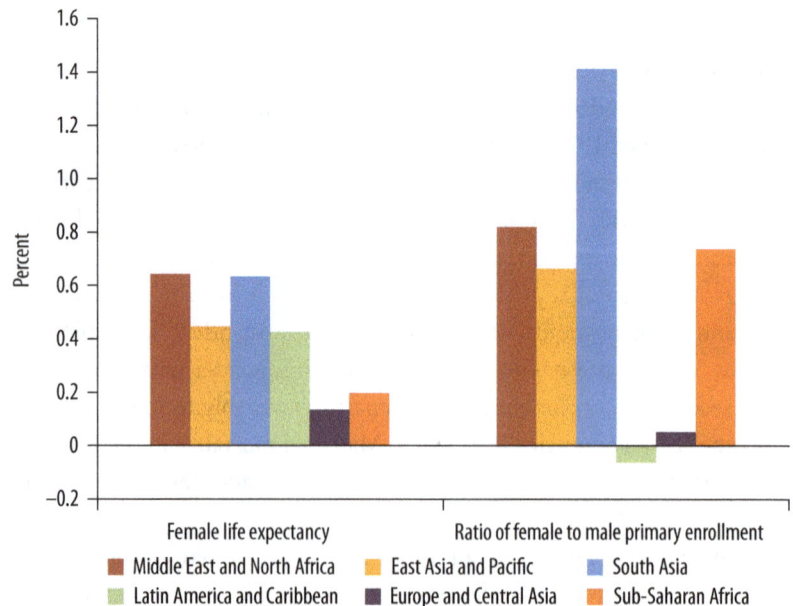

Source: Staff calculations based on WDI 2011 (World Bank multiple years).

development indicators (World Bank 2010). Indeed, more girls than boys now enroll in tertiary education. This "reverse gender gap" also is evident in learning outcomes. Contrary to global patterns, girls in the MENA Region outperform boys in mathematics in grade 4. In some MENA countries, this trend continues through grade 8 (Fryer and Levitt 2009).

Across the world, higher per capita incomes have been accompanied by progress in human development. MENA is no exception. For instance, MENA countries have, on average, female life expectancy at birth that is 9.1 percentage points higher than other non-OECD (Organisation for Economic Co-operation and Development) countries, a difference explained primarily by wealth. This correlation between human development outcomes and per capita incomes also is evident within MENA. For example, just as they have relatively lower per capita incomes, Djibouti and the Republic of Yemen have lower human development outcomes than the rest of the Region. Progress has been uneven within countries as well. For instance, in Upper Egypt, the rate of illiteracy among youth is higher than the national average: 17 versus 11 percent. Female youth in Upper Egypt have illiteracy rates of 24 percent—twice those of their male counterparts and 10 percentage points higher than the national average for young women (World Bank 2011a).

Paradoxically, these considerable investments in human capital have not yet been matched by increases in women's economic participation. While gaps in economic opportunities for women persist in all countries in East Asia and Pacific, Europe and Central Asia, Latin America and Caribbean, and Sub-Saharan Africa, more than 50 percent of the women aged 15 and above participate in the labor market. In contrast, the corresponding figure in MENA is only 25.2 percent. Almost all MENA countries have female labor force participation rates below the average for lower and middle income (LMI) countries (figure O.3). Not surprisingly, the lowest participation rates are in fragile or conflict-affected countries, including Iraq, the Palestinian Territories, and the Republic of Yemen, where concerns about women's safety and mobility clearly are more salient. For the Region as a whole, female labor force participation has increased slowly: by an average of only 0.17 percentage points annually over the last 3 decades.

Women across the world, especially young mothers, face difficulties balancing work and family life. Similar difficulties affect women in MENA. Household responsibilities may be one explanation for the low rates of female labor force participation. While the decision to work clearly is guided by an individual's preferences, the high rates of female unemployment observed in the Region indicate the influence of important constraints to women who do want to work. These constraints also

FIGURE O.3

Female and Male Labor Force Participation across MENA, Ages 15–64

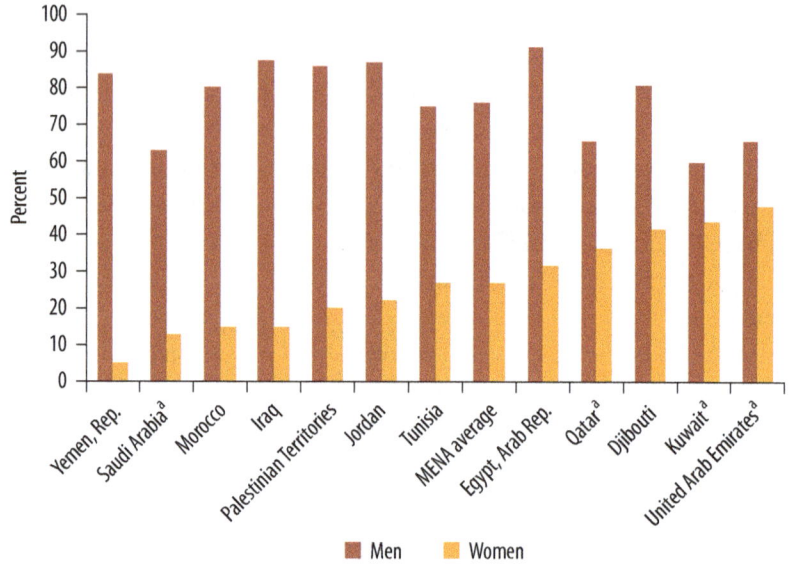

Source: Household surveys (appendixes A and C).

a. Official estimates for national nonimmigrant population.

are reflected in MENA's wide gap between female and male unemployment rates. Over the last 25 years, this gap doubled from 5.5 percent (1985) to more than 10.0 percent (2010). Unemployment rates are especially high among young people. In many countries in the Region, unemployment rates among young women aged 15–24 approach 50 percent (figure O.4), compared to 10–20 percent for males of the same ages.

Furthermore, these high rates of unemployment understate the true degree to which women in the Region lack economic opportunities. A look at data from Tunisia provides evidence that participation rates are lower in regions with higher unemployment, suggesting that many women have become discouraged from looking for work, so they are no longer are counted in the ranks of the unemployed. This effect appears stronger among women with lower levels of education, perhaps because tertiary-educated women often are willing to remain unemployed for longer in the hope of obtaining a public sector job. Moreover, jobs in the informal sector may mask significant underemployment and often involve few benefits and limited job security. Such jobs may underutilize the skills of educated women who were unsuccessful in securing formal sector work. Finally, opportunities for self-employment also are limited. As in the rest of the world, women entrepreneurs are a minority in MENA. Of

FIGURE O.4

Gender Gaps in Youth Unemployment Rates, Ages 15–24

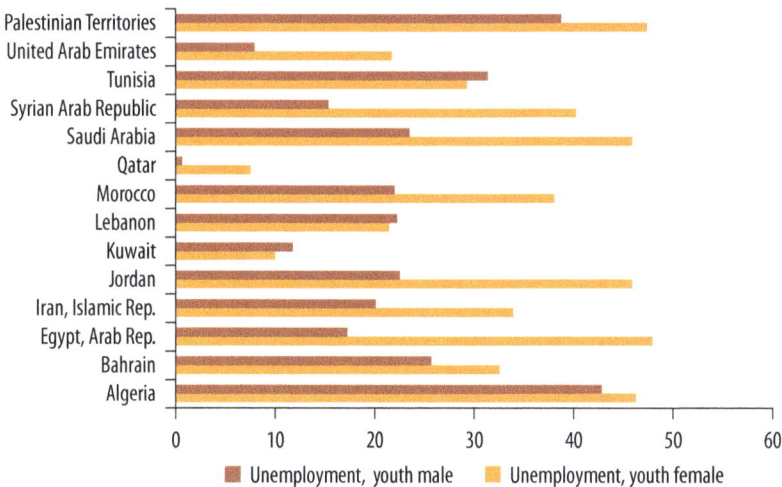

Source: WDI 2011 (World Bank multiple years).

the 5,887 firms in 10 MENA countries surveyed by the World Bank between 2003 and 2010, only 15 percent were female owned.

In the last half-century, many parts of the world have witnessed an expansion of female participation in civil society and politics. Nevertheless, on average worldwide, women make up less than 20 percent of representatives to legislatures. Women in the developing world face common constraints to political participation. These constraints often include stereotypes about their ability as politicians and leaders, norms about the appropriateness of women in public office, and limited access to financial and social capital. Inclusive political processes and institutions not only better represent the preferences of the population as a whole but also tap the talents and innate abilities of hitherto underrepresented sections of society. In MENA, women remain heavily underrepresented in politics, holding approximately only 7 percent of parliamentary seats.

During the last decade, a number of MENA countries have made progress in extending women's rights to vote and to run for political office. In 2005, women in Kuwait were granted the same political rights as men. In other countries in the Gulf Cooperation Council (GCC), including Bahrain, Oman, and the United Arab Emirates, women are being appointed or elected to political office (Kelly and Breslin 2010). In Tunisia, women now fill 25 percent of the seats in the new Constituent Assembly. In the Palestinian Territories, 5 of 21 cabinet members are women, and all major political parties have minimum quotas for women in their governing bodies. Iraq and Jordan have introduced electoral quo-

FIGURE O.5

Women in Legislatures (Lower or Single Houses)

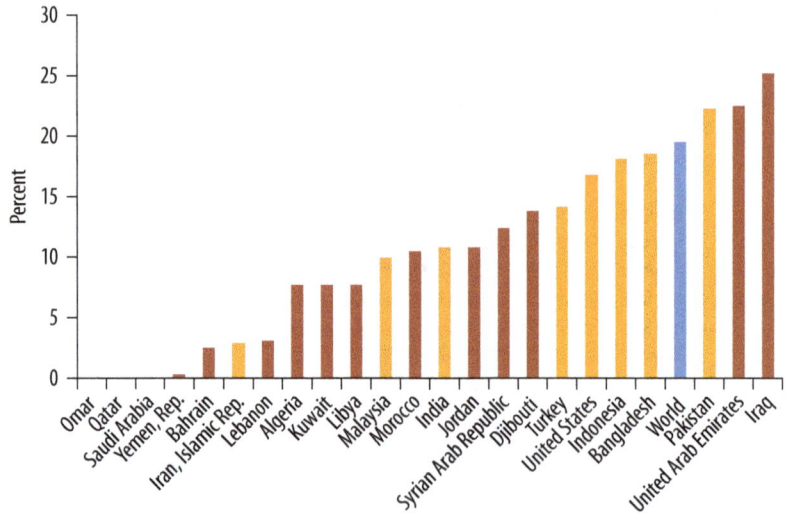

Source: IPU 2011.

tas for women in parliamentary and municipal elections (figure O.5). Saudi Arabia has granted women the right to vote and run for office, beginning with the next round of municipal elections scheduled for 2015. These advances bode well for creating more inclusive and representative institutions across the Region.

This report argues that the Region's conservative gender norms, its legal and institutional framework, and the incentives and opportunities generated by its economic structure lie at the heart of the puzzle of low rates of female participation in politics and the economy.

The Answer Lies within: MENA's Gender Norms and Economic and Legal Structures Drive Low Rates of Women's Participation in Public Sphere

Education and basic health care have come to be considered as universal rights. In contrast, participation in the labor force—looking for work and being employed—remains very much influenced by preferences and opportunities. Worldwide, only 50 percent of women participate in the labor force, although there is a wide variation across Regions: from 25 percent in MENA to 65 percent in low-income countries (LICs). As may be expected, low-income countries have the highest rates of female participation in the workforce: many women have no choice but to work and help earn a living. High-income countries, with rates of female labor

FIGURE O.6

Female Labor Force Participation, 1980–2009

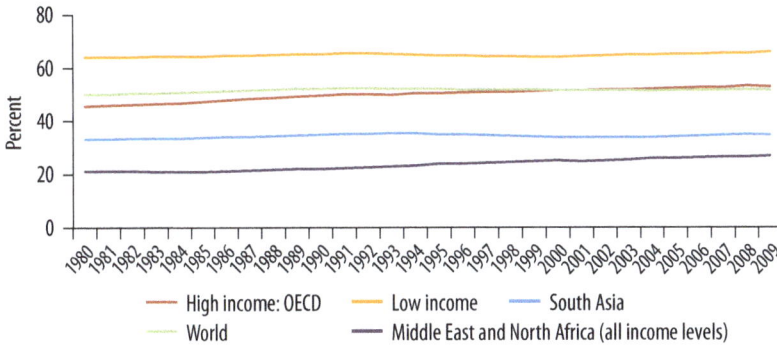

Source: WDI 2011 (World Bank multiple years).

force participation of approximately 50 percent, have developed sophisticated systems to bring women into the workplace and help them balance their dual roles of work and family. These systems comprise incentives and social security, including flexible work hours and generous maternity and paternity benefits. The question remains: What explains MENA's very low female participation in the workforce and political life?

It is striking how slowly the global female labor force participation rate changed over 30 years (figure O.6). One possible explanation is that norms concerning women's roles outside the home can be slow to change. However, over time, they do evolve. For instance, in the United States during the 1930s, only 10 percent of married women participated in the labor force, and an overwhelming majority of husbands disapproved of their wives working. Today, the married female labor force participation in the US is upwards of 70 percent, and more than 80 percent of husbands approve of their wives working. The subsequent shift in norms for married women working in the US evolved over a century and through the creation of opportunities for women to participate in the economy.

Indeed, there are examples of countries in which female workforce participation has increased substantially fueled by an economic transformation that pulls women into jobs in an environment that supports their ability to exercise choice. During the 1980s, female labor force participation in Greece, Ireland, and Spain was approximately 30 percent, well below the world average. Over the next 3 decades, the participation of women in the workforce in these countries increased by 15–20 percent. In each of these countries, economic growth created new opportunities for women, while the legal and institutional frameworks created flexible work options and a conducive work environment for them.

In MENA also, gender norms and the economic and institutional framework are important. A burgeoning and dynamic academic literature cites the role of these factors in explaining the Region's relatively low rates of female labor force participation. Researchers point to the importance of (a) religion, (b) the Region's oil endowment, and (c) patriarchal norms as explanatory factors.

Religion unquestionably has played a significant role in the evolution of customs, social norms, and laws in MENA. However, attributing gender outcomes to Islam is too simplistic, as there is a great diversity of outcomes for women in the Muslim world. This diversity can be attributed in part to the interpretation of religious law and its interaction with local cultures and legal history, factors that vary considerably across Muslim countries. These varied interpretations, in turn, have resulted in varying norms and regulations governing women's rights and opportunities.

With more than 50 percent of the world's proven oil reserves concentrated in only five MENA countries (the Islamic Republic of Iran, Iraq, Kuwait, Saudi Arabia, and the United Arab Emirates), MENA's low rates of female labor force participation often are attributed to oil. It has been argued that the economic structure, social norms, and institutional characteristics of oil-rich economies discourage women from formal sector work (Moghadam 2004b). Ross (2008) argues that oil production "reduces the number of women in the labor force, which in turn reduces their political influence."[1] Oil-rich countries tend to have undiversified private sectors characterized by male-dominated employment and large public sectors. Consequently, employment opportunities for women often are highly concentrated in the public sector.

Oil is a significant source of income for some MENA countries and undeniably has limited the growth of nonoil sectors. Nevertheless, it is notable that many countries in the Region are net oil importers but still have rates of female labor force participation as low as those of oil-rich MENA countries. In contrast, oil producers outside MENA such as Norway and the Russian Federation have higher rates of female labor force participation.

The academic consensus on what explains MENA's low female labor force participation has yet to emerge. This lack of agreement reflects the multiplicity of issues at work, their complicated interplay, and the inability of any one factor to explain the MENA puzzle. Across the world, Region-specific factors such as gender norms, the legal framework, and the structure of the economy are important determinants of female labor force participation. These Region-specific factors can have a powerful influence on the incentives, preferences, opportunities, and ability of women to participate in work and politics. Nowhere is this effect as strong as in MENA. Relative to the OECD, and taking into account any role of oil and religion, living in MENA powerfully dampens women's economic participation, lowering female labor force participation by 47 percent, or by almost half relative to the OECD.

Gender Norms Constrain Women's Roles outside the Home

Social and cultural norms dictate the "do's" and "don't's" of individual everyday conduct (Portes 2011). In many parts of the world, these norms reflect elements of a patriarchal society in which women's primary sphere of influence is within the home (Moghadam 2004a), whereas men are the breadwinners and decision makers in the political and economic spheres (Offenhauer 2005).

Restrictive patriarchal elements are not unique to MENA society. Similarly, just as they are across the world, MENA's norms, although relatively more traditional, are changing with time, as education increases, opportunities arise, and the demographic balance shifts.

The value placed on women's role within the household is evident in data from five MENA countries: Egypt, Iraq, the Islamic Republic of Iran, Jordan, and Morocco (WVS 2005). In these countries, perceptions of women's roles in the home, education, employment, and politics are distinctly more traditional than the global average. Despite these perceptions, in these countries, women are more likely than men to disagree with statements such as "When jobs are scarce, priority should be given to men." Respondents who are younger and more educated also tend to be more supportive of women's involvement. Nevertheless, compared with the rest of the world, MENA citizens overall hold less favorable views about women in leadership positions, as business executives, or as politicians (chapter 2, figure 2.4).

The qualitative literature on gender in the MENA Region brings to life the diverse social and cultural norms that influence women in many dimensions of their lives. Focus group research by Miles (2002) reveals how gender norms surrounding women's restricted mobility, household care burdens, occupational segregation, and son preference constrain women's economic participation in communities in and around Amman, Jordan. Miles reports, for example, how families more often reserve their scarce wasta (special connections) to help their educated sons, rather than their educated daughters, to secure good jobs. In their report on the major challenges related to youth employment in Egypt, Assaud and Barsoum (2007) draw on evidence to illustrate the increased occupational segregation along gender lines since the oil boom (and the damp-

BOX O.3

Little Mercy for Working Women

In early 2011 focus group discussions in the Palestinian Territories, women and men widely agreed that it would be quite unlikely for a woman to take any kind of work requiring a distant commute. They felt that the travel would interfere with women's household duties and expose them to risks of harassment unless chaperoned. In contrast, in the men's focus group in an urban community of the West Bank, a 39-year-old trader confided how other important pressures having to do with men's maintaining a dominant status and the low priority accorded to women's economic roles also may keep women from entering the labor force:

"A man can go anywhere to work and . . . gets jealous of his sister if she goes to a nearby place to work. So how do you think it will happen that she can go to a faraway place? . . . But the man's responsibilities are different.

He has to work. Otherwise, he will never build his home or get married. But for the girl it is different. . . ."

A man from another urban neighborhood in the West Bank argued that the lack of public safety for women is a troubling consequence of the transition underway in gender norms: "Women have just started entering society, so the man is still trying to maintain his control." A young men's group from this same neighborhood similarly posited that a woman was likely to encounter ongoing harassment and low wages because she is "not able to speak up and defend herself because she is weak." "And, as you know," added a 21-year-old university student, "our customs and traditions don't have mercy."

—Background Assessment for WDR 2012 (World Bank 2011b, 2012b, 44, forthcoming)

ening effects that segregation has had on female wages). They also illustrate how fears of workplace harassment, especially in smaller workplaces, discourage many women from working in less traditional jobs (box O.3).

Despite gender norms in the MENA Region, and irrespective of marital status, women aspire to be employed. In a 2010 World Bank survey of Jordanian female community college graduates entering the workforce,[2] 92 percent said that they plan to work after graduation, and 76 percent reported that they expect to be working full time. These numbers are consistent with attitudes reflected in the 2005 World Values Survey in which 80 percent of women in Egypt and Jordan disagreed with the statements, "A woman with a full-time job cannot be a good mother" and

"Having a full-time job interferes with a woman's ability to have a good life with her husband."

In environments in which the influence of conservative norms is more muted, women are better able to translate their aspirations into reality. This is evident in analysis of labor market outcomes for immigrants in France and the United States. Labor force participation rates of MENA women who immigrate to the United States are much higher than those of nonmigrants, and fall by less after marriage. Furthermore, women of MENA origin who immigrated to France as youngsters have participation rates more similar to their male counterparts than do women who immigrated as adults. These findings point to the important influence of gender norms in explaining low rates of participation in the Region.

Equality under the Law and Its Enforcement Are Critical for Women's Agency

Laws institutionalize social norms and, in turn, reinforce them. When the institutional framework formalizes unequal rights for women, the state condones male authority over women's everyday decisions, actions, and movements, limiting their choices and participation in society. Almost all MENA countries have constitutional clauses that set out the equality of citizens, and many have ratified international conventions that affirm gender equality. Nevertheless, laws often differentiate between the sexes, thus reinforcing traditional gender roles within the househld and in the wider community. Reforms of these laws often have been piecemeal, thus exhibiting progress in certain areas but stagnation (or even regression) in others.

Legal systems within the Region differ widely and derive from multiple sources: religious law, customary law, colonial legislation (French Napoleonic codes, English common law and statutes), constitutional law, international conventions, and Regional treaties.[3,4] For instance, citizenship laws in many MENA countries were derived from British and Napoleonic codes (Hijab 2002). This plurality also extends to the implementation and enforcement of laws.

Unequal rights and treatment under the law are not unique to the MENA Region. In the US, before 1920, women did not have the right to vote; and until the 1930s, married women could travel only on their husbands' passports. Unequal treatment of women in jobs, pay, and promotion was made illegal in the United States only 20 years after the end of World War II. However, in many other countries, inequality under the law is still active (box O.4). In Spain, spousal permission continued to be a precondition for a wife to work until 1979; and in Switzerland until

MENA Not Unique: Constraints Faced by Women Elsewhere as Well

In Swaziland, due to the supremacy of customary personal law, women are regarded as legal minors. Cameroon, Côte d'Ivoire, and the Democratic Republic of Congo all follow the French legal tradition. These three countries have head of household laws and legal restrictions on wives' ability to work based on a 1950s version of the French Civil Code (Hallward-Driemeier and Hasan 2011).

In Latin America in the mid-1980s, Chile and Peru reformed their laws that required spousal permission to work. In Europe, Greece and Switzerland also were late reformers and repealed their laws regarding permission only in the 1980s.

1984. In MENA, Tunisia repealed spousal permission to work in 1959, and Morocco did so in 2004 (box O.5).

In determining women's participation outside the home, certain aspects of the letter, interpretation, and implementation of the law are particularly salient. Some laws directly affect and limit women's agency within their households. In several MENA countries,[5] the legal minimum age of marriage for girls is lower than for boys. In some other countries, including Saudi Arabia (UNSTAT 2012) and the Republic of Yemen,[6] a legal minimum marriage age for girls does not exist.[7] Delaying marriage could improve a woman's decision making power within her household, especially with respect to education, choice of partner, and the decision to work. Although some progress has been made to protect women from domestic violence in Egypt, Jordan, and Morocco (UN Women 2011), implementation remains weak. In many MENA countries, including the Islamic Republic of Iran and the Syrian Arab Republic, citizenship laws prevent women married to foreign men from accessing welfare and educational benefits for their children and employment opportunities for their husbands. In much of the Region, married women retain control over their own separate property but have limited access to property acquired during the marriage.[8] If they did not enter the marriage with significant personal assets and did not work while married, women could be vulnerable if they are divorced or widowed.

Guardianship laws in many countries also restrict women's mobility and occupational choices. These laws require a woman to obtain permission from her husband or a male relative to obtain a passport, travel outside the country, apply for a job, and get married.[9] For instance, in Jordan, an unmarried woman over the age of 18 does not need permission to

---

BOX O.5

Political Economy of Reform in Tunisia and Morocco: Momentum for Change

Tunisia still faces gender disparities in outcomes. Nevertheless, the country is recognized in the Arab world for its early legal reforms that advanced gender equality. The first phase of reforms came immediately at independence in 1956 and was perceived as government driven. The Personal Code was overhauled, giving women the right to file for divorce, establishing the principle of alimony, and enabling married women to travel and work without the permission of their husbands. It was women's organizations that played an active role in shaping the second wave of reforms in 1993. The main foci of the campaign were discriminatory citizenship laws, which then were reformed. The first, top-down phase of reform had empowered women, enabling them to contest and refine outstanding discriminatory legislation. While it may not have achieved all of its objectives, the first phase of reform had generated a new climate for the second round of debate by creating enabling conditions for new networks of women to emerge.

The 2004 Morocco family law reform followed 2 decades of relentless campaigning by women's groups. In 1997, the 1957 version of Mudawana (family code) was partially modified regarding polygamy and guardianship. However, discriminatory provisions remained. Key to the ultimate success of the campaign was the political support given by King Mohammed VI and his predecessors and senior political leaders, and the endorsement of religious leaders who provided theological backing for the reforms.

Sources: Bordat and Kouzzi 2004; Charrad 2007; Ennaji 2009; Moghadam and Roudi-Fahimi 2005.

---

apply for a passport, but a married woman of any age requires her husband's permission. These laws make work and travel more difficult for women than for men, and thereby constitute a major barrier to women's full participation in political and economic life. The laws also limit women's access to capital for business purposes.

The majority of the MENA economies (10 of 14) included by the World Bank Women Business and the Law database have constitutions or laws that mandate equal pay for equal work (World Bank 2012b). Nevertheless, even though countries such as Algeria and Egypt have legislation against discrimination in the workplace, in practice, the enforcement of antidiscrimination laws is uneven. Moreover, equal pay provisions are undermined by inequalities in nonwage benefits, such as child and family allowances, which usually are paid to the husband (Kelly and Breslin 2010). A minority (5 of 14) of the MENA countries covered by the Women Business and the Law database have legislation that outlaws discrimination in hiring practices (World Bank 2012b). All countries in the Region mandate some form of maternity leave, and some countries have provisions for childcare to enable married women to re-enter the workplace after maternity. Paradoxically, laws that require firms to pay for maternity leave and child care facilities also can function as disincentives to hiring women. Meanwhile, pension laws that mandate a retirement age earlier for women than for men effectively reduce the amount of pension that a woman receives, and can disincentivize women by limiting their expected career progression.

Globally, labor laws also can limit women's opportunities. In some MENA countries, they do. MENA women are banned from working in certain industries that are deemed dangerous, hazardous, or morally harmful to their reputation. Women also often are barred from working at night, in some cases from as early as 7 p.m. Such provisions originally were designed to protect women and are rooted in articles of International Labour Organization conventions. However, in keeping with social norms regarding segregation, some MENA countries have made these provisions more stringent.[10] The ultimate effect of such provisions is to limit women's participation in numerous sectors of the economy and to limit the flexibility of women's work arrangements.

Economic Incentives Dampen Participation in the Workforce

In addition to social norms and legal restrictions, women's labor force participation is influenced directly by the social contract, based on which MENA governments have provided public employment, generous benefits, and subsidies to citizens.[11] Over time, governments repeatedly have extended these policies to deal with economic shocks and social unrest. In the nonoil countries, the heavy involvement of the state via the social contract has led to economic distortions and increasing levels of public debt. Recognizing these outcomes, over the past 2 decades, some countries (especially in North Africa) have made efforts to rein in government spending and subsidies. However, in the wake of the earlier (2011) Arab Spring protests, many governments responded by increasing spending on subsidies and public sector wages.

The social contract has boosted public sector employment and compensation at the expense of private sector job creation. On average, the public sector in MENA accounts for 45 percent of total employment. Public employees are offered higher pay, subsidies, pensions, and relatively more generous working conditions than similarly qualified workers

FIGURE O.7

Public Sector Wage Gap: Difference in Average Hourly Earnings for Salaried Workers in the Public and Private Sectors

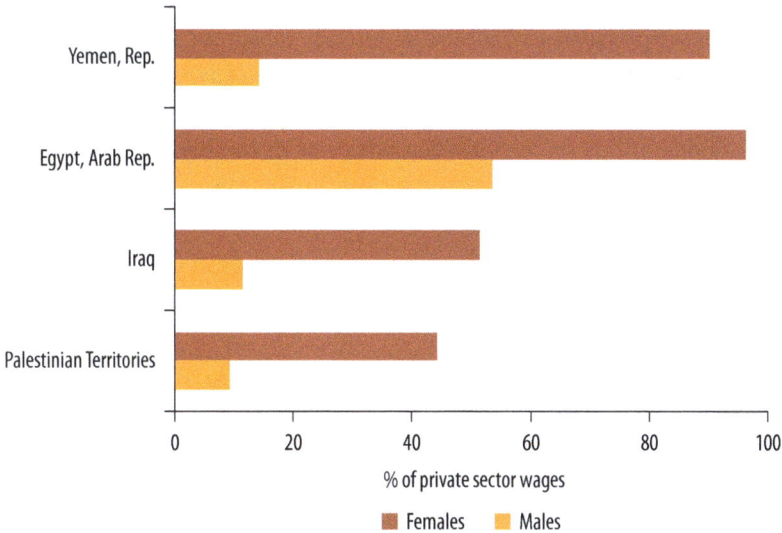

Source: Selected household surveys (appendixes A and C).

in the private sector (figure O.7). Despite the considerable investments that governments have made in education, private sector employers complain that the education system does not equip young graduates with the skills that companies need. As a result, returns to education are higher in the public sector. These factors have made it more costly for private sector firms to hire skilled workers, reducing the number of jobs that firms can offer. Together with the recent trend of declining public sector jobs in the resource-poor countries, the impediments to private sector hiring have contributed to the Region's extremely high rates of unemployment among educated youth.

Women's employment outcomes have been affected by the social contract in three main ways:

- Women tend to study certain subjects rather than others, partly reflecting traditional gender ideals and partly hoping to get public sector jobs in "female-friendly" fields such as teaching and administration.

- The public–private pay gap is greater for women than for men, in part because the women working in the public sector have higher average levels of education than do the men.

- Finally, families are offered a plethora of subsidies and benefits, which increase household income levels and thereby decrease the financial incentive for women to work.

In an environment in which public sector employment encompasses many aspects of what is perceived as a "good job" in the Region, many women see private sector jobs as an inferior substitute. From their point of view, private sector employers are hesitant to hire women, who are perceived to be less productive and more costly. Discouraged by the lack of suitable public sector jobs, the difficulty of finding private employment, and its relative unattractiveness, many women decide not to enter the workforce after graduation. This decision has serious consequences for the economy as a whole, because potential productivity gains and economic growth are sacrificed by discouraging a large part of the educated labor force from working.

Seizing the Window of Opportunity for Reform

The ongoing popular protests and calls for change across the Region reflect a shift in aspirations. Young people, including women, are calling for a greater role in society and access to better economic opportunities (box O.6). Moreover, an unstoppable demographic transition is underway, in which people under 30 comprise 60.5 percent of the population (figure O.8). The high unemployment rates among this generation despite the increasing levels of education surely contribute to the current instability and unrest. Finally, the social contract is no longer fiscally sustainable, especially in the labor-abundant, oil-poor economies of the Region. Given the growing number of jobseekers and worsening fiscal conditions, governments that once sought to respond to discontent by creating public sector jobs cannot continue to do so.

The profound demographic trends in MENA have been influenced by, and in turn influence, women's education and employment decisions. Women are staying in school longer, delaying marriage, and bearing fewer children. Education opens doors to work opportunities for women, the potential to contribute to their households' welfare, and economic empowerment. Along with the strong increase in years of schooling among women, fertility rates in the Region have been declining consistently since the late 1980s. While the choice to work depends on individual and household preferences and social norms, trends observed in countries around the world suggest that, with fewer children and higher levels of education, in coming years, more and more MENA women will choose to work outside the home. This trend is depicted in figure O.9,

---

BOX O.6

Women's Voices on the Arab Spring

Our demands are somehow similar to men['s], starting with freedom, equal citizenship, and giving women a greater role in society . . . Women smell freedom at Change Square, where they feel more welcomed than ever before. Their fellow [male] freedom fighters are showing unconventional acceptance [of] their participation and they are actually for the first time letting women be, and say what they really want.

—Faizah Sulimiani, 29-year-old female protest leader, Yemen[1]

I grew up in a world where we believed we could not do anything. Generations believed we could do nothing, and now, in a matter of weeks, we know that we can.

—Mariam Abu Adas, 32, online activist who helped create a company to train young people to use social media, Jordan[2]

We want women from today to begin exercising their rights. Today on the roads is just the opening in a long campaign. We will not go back.

—Wajeha al-Huwaidar, female activist speaking out on a campaign to secure women's rights to drive, Saudi Arabia[3]

Prior to the revolution, we knew nothing about politics. We were ignorant. So how would we participate in something we knew nothing about?

—Employed female, urban Qena, Egypt[4]

Sources: (1) Rice and others 2011; (2) Slackman 2011; (3) Murphy 2011; (4) World Bank 2011d.

---

which projects the working-age and employed populations of women and men through the end of this century. If all those in the working age population look for work, the Region will need to create almost 200 million more jobs by 2050 to fulfill these aspirations, 75 percent of them for women.

As noted above, the traditional response of several MENA governments has been to absorb growth in the labor force by creating new public sector jobs. Given the massive growth of the workforce projected over the next 50 years, this no longer is a plausible policy option. Many nonoil MENA countries run persistent fiscal deficits so are in no position to pay for or subsidize large increases in public employment. Even in the oil-rich MENA countries, which are enjoying a revenue boost from higher oil prices, government spending and nonoil deficits have risen persistently (figure O.10). In Saudi Arabia, the oil price per barrel

FIGURE O.8

Demographic Transition: MENA's Male and Female Age Structure, 2010 and 2050

population in millions

a. MENA male and female population by age, 2010

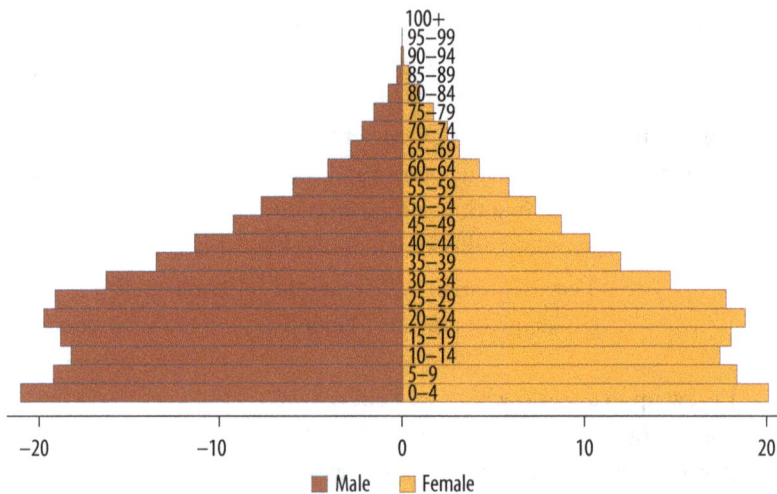

b. MENA male and female population by age, 2050

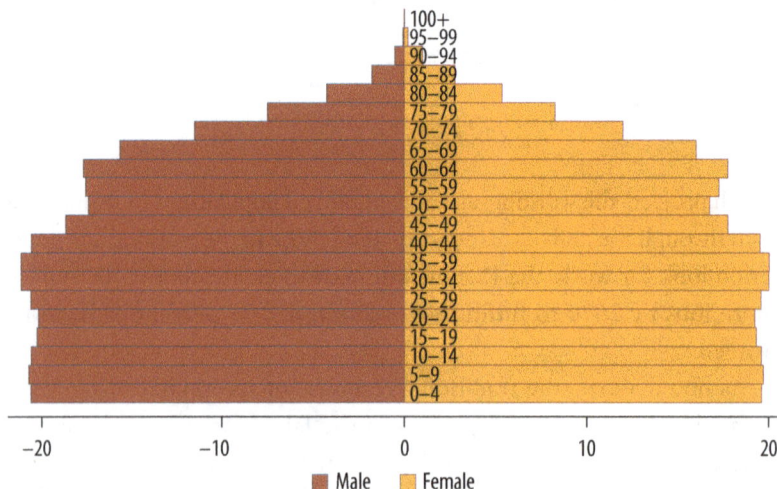

Source: UN DESA 2010.

required to finance government spending rose from $30 in 2005 to $80 in 2011, illustrating how increases in revenues from higher oil prices are not necessarily easing the fiscal situation. Thus, the new jobs required will need to come from the private sector, highlighting the importance

FIGURE O.9

Necessity to Create Jobs for Women and Men, 1950–2100
population in millions

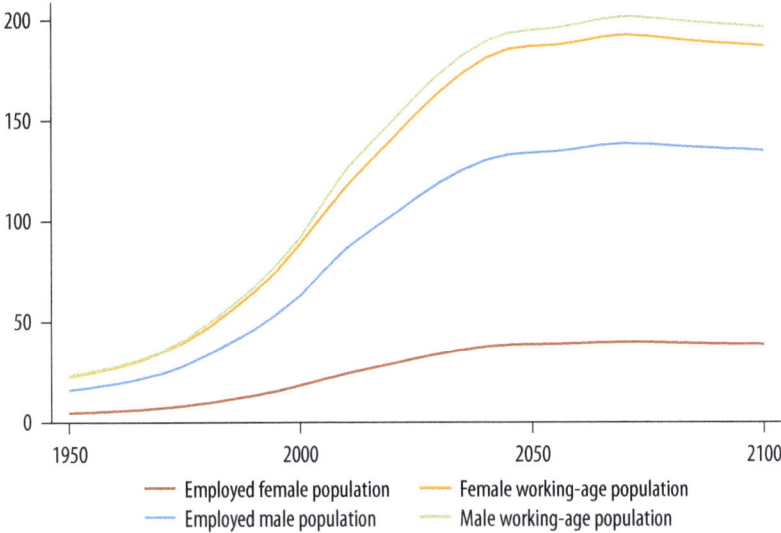

Sources: UN DESA 2010; WDI 2011 (World Bank multiple years).

FIGURE O.10

GCC Primary Nonoil Balance, 2000–11
percent of nonoil GDP

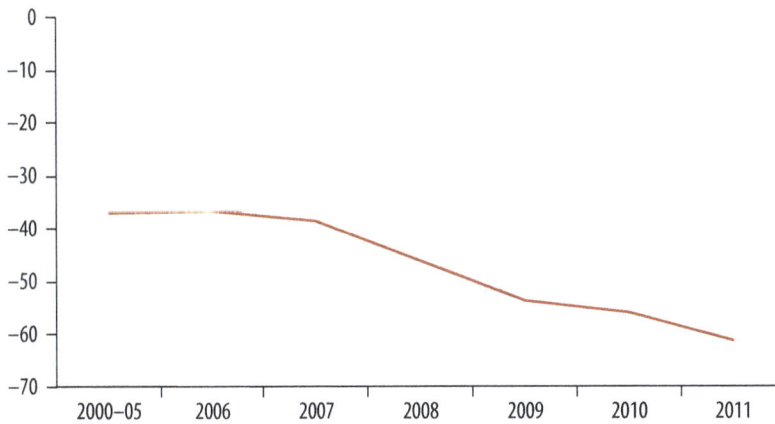

Sources: IMF 2011.

of encouraging private sector investment and growth. However, job creation alone will not guarantee women an equal place in society and economic life. New jobs will need to be complemented by reforms to expand women's access to opportunities.

Opening Doors to Women: Concerted Action Is Needed on Multiple Fronts

The analysis in this report points to four broad policy priorities. Depending on the country context and reform priorities, countries in the Region may need to make complementary and coordinated efforts on multiple fronts to:

- Bridge the remaining gender gaps in health and education and improve the quality of service delivery.

- Foster women's economic opportunities by removing constraints to participation in the formal labor market and nurturing entrepreneurship.

- Give women greater voice and legal agency.

- Promote evidence-based policymaking. To this end, pilot programs need to be rigorously evaluated. National statistical data also should be made publicly available.

The majority of countries in the Region already have made marked progress on human development issues: closing gaps in access to health care, decreasing mortality rates, and increasing educational attainment. Nevertheless, these issues remain challenges for the lower income countries in MENA, primarily Djibouti and the Republic of Yemen, as well as in poorer areas of other MENA countries.

Across the Region, reforms are necessary to create more jobs and make women more employable. Given the lack of scope for significant increases in public spending, it is critical that governments focus on reforms that support economic diversification and private sector investment and growth, and boost the employability of the growing class of educated young women and men (World Bank 2009). Reforms are needed to remove bureaucratic bottlenecks that over-regulate labor markets and limit support for entrepreneurship. Finally, reforms to the education system are essential to provide young people with the skills demanded by employers. Having access to the skills wanted by employers is a particular problem for tertiary-educated young women, who face some of the highest unemployment rates.

Making it easier for women to create and grow their own businesses is another important avenue to boost innovation, growth, and employment in the Region. Given the challenges that they face in obtaining formal private sector wage employment, facilitation of self-owned businesses is especially important for women. Nevertheless, despite MENA's having one of the largest informal sectors in the world, women entrepreneurs face significant difficulties relative to men. Foremost among these is access to credit, especially since personal laws limit women's ownership of family assets. However, access to credit is not enough.[12] Many countries are experimenting with "microcredit-plus" models. These models combine credit with training in business skills and measures to facilitate access to local and broader markets.

Efforts also are needed to encourage women's participation in the labor market, and to increase their employability. Strategies to increase women's attractiveness to employers should go hand in hand with policies to encourage women to work. For example, evidence from the US Earned Income Tax Credit (EITC) program suggests that tax and benefits systems can be reformed so that they do not penalize women for choosing to work, or penalize firms for employing them. Such reforms have been shown to promote women's labor force participation.[13] In addition, policies such as internships and scholarships can change employers' attitudes toward women workers through practical experience while giving women the skills and experience that they require to succeed in the modern workplace. In Jordan, a recent pilot, Jordan NOW (New Work Opportunities for Women), provides employability skills training and a short-term incentive for firms who employ young women. While early results suggested that the incentives for firms increased short-term employment and valuable labor market experience, the pilot also revealed that labor market regulations limited the sustainability of these results.

Surveys in MENA countries identify the lack of safe, reliable transportation as a significant constraint on women's ability to work. Addressing this deficiency is relatively inexpensive and could greatly increase the work opportunities available to women. In India and Mexico, public buses and trains designate spaces reserved for women to safely travel to and from work. The private sector also can directly ease mobility constraints for women. For example, some Indian firms provide corporate buses to take women from their homes directly and safely to the workplace.

More also needs to be done to reform laws and improve implementation to give women greater freedom of mobility, ensure their safety in the workplace, relax restrictive regulations on their employment, and encourage entrepreneurial activity. Without such reforms, the impact of economic reforms on women's employment will be limited. While some MENA countries, including Algeria, the Islamic Republic of Iran, Morocco, and Tunisia, generally have advanced women's agency and made reforms to legal systems, the rest of the Region has not yet done so. Effective enforcement of the law also is essential. Without enforcement, such reforms have little effect in practice.

A number of steps can be taken to promote women's participation in the legal and political spheres. First, women's agency can be fostered at the grassroots level. Where women have been and are encouraged to participate in local community development councils, evidence shows that local service delivery improves and perceptions about women as leaders change.

At the national level, there is a need to boost women's confidence in the legal system and their understanding of it. Accomplishment of these two objectives could take a top-down form of increased representation of women in judiciaries, a bottom-up approach of providing legal aid clinics and mobile courts, or both.

In addition, the power of social and traditional media to convey messages about women cannot be overstated. Initiatives in other countries have shown how perceptions of women's roles and capacities can be changed rapidly through dramatizations, social campaigns, and examples set by prominent female figures.

Finally, policies are most effective when predicated on evidence. Region-wide, there is a paucity of relevant data on gender issues and evidence on the effectiveness of policies to address them. With the exceptions of Djibouti, Iraq, Palestinian Territories, and the Republic of Yemen, data access is a major issue. As a result, two additional challenges are to identify country-specific gender gaps and to formulate nuanced policy interventions. Countries can prioritize investing in learning what works within their own social and economic contexts. Rigorously evaluated policy pilots can provide invaluable lessons. Apart from recent studies in Egypt, Jordan, Morocco, and Tunisia, the MENA Region has a vast knowledge gap in this area. Such pilots are essential to ensure that larger scale policies are designed and implemented appropriately based on learning from rigorous evaluation. Providing public access to data and rigorously evaluating projects have become global best practice. The MENA Region has much to gain from being part of this process.

Notes

1. The "natural resource curse" argument, as it often is called, is not new. For a review of the current knowledge on the issue, see Frankel 2010. Whether and the extent to which "the curse" is relevant for MENA are still subject to debate. See, for example, Groh and Rothschild 2011.
2. As part of the Jordan NOW (New Work Opportunities for Women) pilot.
3. In the absence of any codified legislation, Article 1 of the Algerian Civil Code allows a judge to apply religious and customary law.
4. The Protocol to the African Charter on Human and Peoples' Rights and the Rights of Women in Africa (2003) as well as the Arab Charter on Human Rights (2004) are examples of Regional treaties.

5. Bahrain: 15; the Islamic Republic of Iran: 13; Kuwait: 15; Lebanon: 17 for Sunni Muslim and Druze, 14 for Armenian and Syrian Orthodox Churches, 14 for Catholic; Qatar: 16; West Bank: 15; and Gaza: 17 (UNSTAT Legal Age of Marriage) (UNSTAT 2012; UN OHCHR 2008a).

6. OECD 2012; Yemen Country Profile http://genderindex.org/country/ yemen; JICA 2009; Equality Now 2012. There is some ambiguity because UNSTAT 2012 gives the minimum age of marriage in the Republic of Yemen as 15 for both boys and girls based on the age of majority.

7. Prior to reunification in 1990, South Yemen had a minimum marriage age of 16, and North Yemen had a minimum marriage age of 15. After reunification, the legal minimum age of marriage was set at 15 until a 1999 amendment to the Civil Law abolished the minimum age completely.

8. *Mahr* is the amount to be paid by the groom to the bride at the time of marriage (*nikah);* or the marriage may be delayed, according to what is agreed by the spouses. The mahr is a gift to the bride to spend as she wishes. In some contexts, it does provide some financial security, especially when there is a risk of bankruptcy proceedings against the husband. However, this risk does not apply to all marriages; and in many cases, the mahr agreed by the parties to the marriage is unlikely to be financially equivalent to 50 percent of the joint marital assets.

9. The Islamic Republic of Iran, Oman (married women), Saudi Arabia, and the Republic of Yemen require male permission for women to apply for a passport. The Islamic Republic of Iran and Saudi Arabia also require male permission to travel outside the country.

10. Night work restrictions are based primarily on ILO's Night Work (Women) Convention (C89), rev. 1948.

11. In this report, "social contract" follows the definition in Yousef 2004: "The social contract refers generally to an agreement [among] the members of a society, or between the governed and the government, defining and limiting the rights and duties of each. . . . In MENA countries, the social contract encompasses a wider array of factors. . . . Conceptualized not solely as an institutionalized bargain among collective actors, it encompasses norms and shared expectations for the overall organization of a polity. Accordingly, these norms and expectations have significant institutional consequences. They define the boundaries of acceptable policy choice, and they affect the organization of interests in society, helping to determine who wins and who loses in a given political economy."

12. In Sri Lanka, grants had no effect on women's incomes, even though women did not invest less in their businesses than did men (De Mel and others 2008).

13. Several rigorous studies have found the EITC to have had a large positive effect on the labor supply of women. For example, Meyer and Rosenbaum 2000 found that the employment of single mothers in 1996 was 7 percent higher because of the EITC.

References

ACHPR (African Commission on Human and People's Rights). 2003. *Protocol to the African Charter on Human Rights and the Rights of Women in Africa*. Banjul, the Gambia. http://www.achpr.org/instruments/women-protocol/.

Assaud, Ragi, and Ghada Barsoum. 2007. "Youth Exclusion in Egypt: In Search of 'Second Chances.'" Middle East Youth Initiative Working Paper No. 2, Wolfensohn Center for Development/Brookings Institution and Dubai School of Government. Washington, DC.

Bordat, Stephanie W., and Saida Kouzzi. 2004. "The Challenge of Implementing Morocco's New Personal Status Laws." *Arab Reform Bulletin* 2 (8). http://www.ceip.org/arabreform; http://www.globalrights.org/site/DocServer?docID=663.

Charrad, Mounira. 2007. "Tunisia at the Forefront of the Arab World: Two Waves of Gender Legislation." *Washington and Lee Law Review* 64 (4):1513–27.

De Mel, Suresh, David J. McKenzie, and Christopher Woodruff. 2008. "Returns to Capital in Microenterprises: Evidence from a Field Experiment." *Quarterly Journal of Economics* 123 (4): 1329–72.

Ennaji, Moha. 2009. "The New Muslim Personal Law in Morocco: Context Proponents, Adversaries, and Arguments." http://www.yale.edu/macmillan/africadissent/moha.pdf.

Equality Now. 2012. Action 34.3: "Yemen: End Child Marriages by Enacting and Enforcing a Minimum Age of Marriage Law." May 21. http://www.equalitynow.org/take_action/adolescent_girls_action343.

Frankel, Jeffrey 2010. "The Natural Resource Curse: A Survey." Harvard Kennedy School (HKS) Faculty Research Working Paper RWP10-005, Harvard University, Cambridge, MA. web.hks.harvard.edu/publications/workingpapers/.

Fryer, Roland, and Steven Levitt. 2009. "An Empirical Analysis of the Gender Gap in Mathematics." Working Paper 15430, NBER (The National Bureau of Economic Research), Cambridge, MA.

Groh, Matthew, and Casey Rothschild. 2012. "Oil, Islam, Women, and Geography: A Comment on Ross (2008)." *Quarterly Journal of Political Science* 7 (1): 69–87.

Hallward-Driemeier, Mary, and Tazeen Hasan. 2012. *Empowering Women: Legal Rights and Economic Opportunities in Africa.* Africa Development Forum Series. Washington, DC: World Bank.

Hijab, Nadia. 2002. *Women Are Citizens, Too: The Laws of the State, the Lives of Women.* UNDP (United Nations Development Programme), New York.

Household Surveys. Appendixes A and C.

IMF (International Monetary Fund). 2011. "Economic Transformation in MENA: Delivering on the Promise of Shared Prosperity." Note prepared by the Staff of the IMF prepared for the May 27, 2011 summit of the Group of Eight in Deauville, France.

IPU (International Parliamentary Union). 2011. Geneva. http://www.ipu.org/wmn-e/classif.htm.

JICA (Japan International Cooperation Agency). 2009. *Yemen: Country Gender Profile.* Public Policy Department, Sana'a.

Kelly, Sanja, and Julia Breslin. 2010. *Women's Rights in the Middle East and North Africa: Progress amid Resistance.* New York, NY: Freedom House; Lanham, MD: Rowman & Littlefield.

Meyer, Bruce D., and Dan T. Rosebaum. 2000. "Making Single Mothers Work: Recent Tax and Welfare Policy and Its Effects." Working Paper 7491, NBER (The National Bureau of Economic Research), Cambridge, MA.

Miles, Rebecca. 2002. "Employment and Unemployment in Jordan: The Importance of the Gender System." *World Development* 30 (3): 413–27.

Moghadam, Valentine. 2004b. "Women's Economic Participation in the Middle
East: What Difference Has the Neoliberal Policy Turn Made?" *Journal of
Middle East Women's Studies* 1 (1): 110–46.

Moghadam, Valentine M., and Farzaneh Roudi-Fahimi. 2005 *Empowering
Women, Developing Society: Female Education in the Middle East and North Africa.*
Population Reference Bureau, Washington, DC.

Muñoz Boudet, A. M., P. Petesch, and C. Turk with A. Thumala. Forthcoming.
*On Norms and Agency: Conversations about Gender Equality with Women and Men
in 20 Countries.* Directions in Development. Washington, DC: World Bank.

Murphy, Brian. 2011. "Saudi Women Tap Road Rage against Driving Ban." *AP
News*, May 24.

OECD (Organisation of Economic Co-operation and Development). 2012.
Social Institutions and Gender Index 2012. Yemen Country Profile. http://
genderindex.org/country/yemen

Offenhauer, Priscilla, 2005. *Women in Islamic Societies: A Selected Review of Social
Scientific Literature.* Library of Congress, Washington, DC.

Rice, Xan, Katherine Marsh, Tom Finn, Harriet Sherwood, Angelique Chrisafis,
and Robert Booth. 2011. "Women Have Emerged As Key Players in the Arab
Spring." *The Guardian*, April 22. http://www.guardian.co.uk/world/2011/
apr/22/women-arab-spring.

Ross, Michael. 2008. "Oil, Islam and Women." *American Political Science Review*
102 (1): 107–23.

Slackman, Michael, 2011. "Bullets Stall Youthful Push for Arab Spring." *The New
York Times*, March 18. http://www.nytimes.com/2011/03/18/world/
middleeast/18youth.html?pagewanted=all.

UN DESA (Department of Economic and Social Affairs). 2010. *Population
Division, Population Estimates and Projections Section.* http://www.un.org/esa/
population/; http://www.unpopulation.org.

UN OHCHR (United Nations Office of the High Commissioner for Human
Rights). 2008a. *CEDAW (Convention on the Elimination of All Forms of Discrimination against Women) Committee. Consideration of reports submitted by States
Parties under Article 18 of the Convention on the Elimination of All Forms of Discrimination against Women.* Third periodic report of States Parties Lebanon
(July 2006) CEDAW/C/LBN/3. UN OHCHR (Office of the High Commissioner for Human Rights), Geneva. http://www.un.org/womenwatch/daw/
cedaw/; http://www2.ohchr.org/english/bodies/cedaw/.

UNSTAT (United Nations Statistics Division). 2012. New York. http://data.
un.org/DocumentData.aspx?q=minimum+age+of+marriage&id=294.

UN Women (United Nations Entity for Gender Equality and the Empowerment
of Women). 2011. *Progress of the World's Women: In Pursuit of Justice.* New
York. http://www.unwomen.org/publications/progress-of-the-worlds-
women-in-pursuit-of-justice/.

World Bank. 2009. *From Privilege to Competition: Unlocking Private-Led Growth in
the Middle East and North Africa.* MENA Development Report, Washington,
DC

_____. 2010. *Bridging the Gap: Improving Capabilities and Expanding Opportunities
for Women in the Middle East and North Africa Region.* Office of the Chief
Economist and MNSED, MENA Region, Washington, DC.

_____. 2011a. *Reclaiming Their Voice: New Perspectives from Young Women and Men in Upper Egypt*. Washington, DC.

_____. 2011b. "Defining Gender in the 21st Century: Talking with Women and Men around the World: A Multi-Country Qualitative Study of Gender and Economic Choice." Dataset Collected for *World Development Report 2012: Gender Equality and Development*. World Bank, Washington, DC.

_____. 2012a. *Aspirations on Hold: Young Lives in the West Bank and Gaza*. Washington, DC.

_____. 2012b. *World Development Report 2012: Gender Equality and Development*. Washington, DC.

_____. 2012c. Women, Business and the Law database. http://wbl.worldbank. org/.

_____. Forthcoming. "Yemen Gender Policy Note." Washington, DC.

_____. Multiple years. *WDI (World Development Indicators)*. Washington, DC. data.worldbank.org/data-catalog/world-development-indicators.

WVS (World Values Survey Association). 2005. *World Values Survey*. www .worldvaluessurvey.org.

Yousef, Tarik M. 2004. *Employment, Development and the Social Contract in the Middle East and North Africa*. World Bank, Washington, DC.

CHAPTER 1

Gender Equality in MENA: The Facts and the Puzzle

Impressive Achievements in Human Development

Since 1970, countries in the MENA Region have recorded the world's fastest progress in human development (UNDP 2010). Over these 40 years, 5 MENA countries (Algeria, Morocco, Oman, Saudi Arabia, and Tunisia) have been among the top 10 fastest movers. Over that time, the growth rates of key indicators such as female literacy rate, infant mortality, and life expectancy on average exceeded those of most other developing regions (figures 1.1 and 1.2). Between 1985 and 2010, the Region also did well in closing the gender gap in education, as evidenced by the high rate of growth in the ratio of female-to-male primary enrollment.

As a result of these advances, the health and education status of women in the Region now compares favorably with that of other developing countries. MENA's maternal mortality rate is less than half the low- and middle-income countries' (LMI) average, and female life expectancy is nearly four years longer than the LMI average. Primary school enrollment rates for MENA girls are well above the LMI average and close to the world average, reflecting the substantial investments over recent decades by MENA governments, communities, and families in their children's health and education.

Little Discrimination between Girls and Boys within the Household

Large and persistent gender inequalities at the household level characterize many societies worldwide and often have been particularly resilient to policy interventions. Yet, it is striking that, in the MENA Region, health and education investments at the household level reflect largely equal treatment of daughters and sons. This equality is in stark contrast to the conditions in East and South Asia and Sub-Saharan Africa, in which unborn and newborn girls face lower survival probabilities than elsewhere in the world, and women typically obtain much lower levels of education.

FIGURE 1.1

MENA's Progress in Women's Literacy, 1985–2010

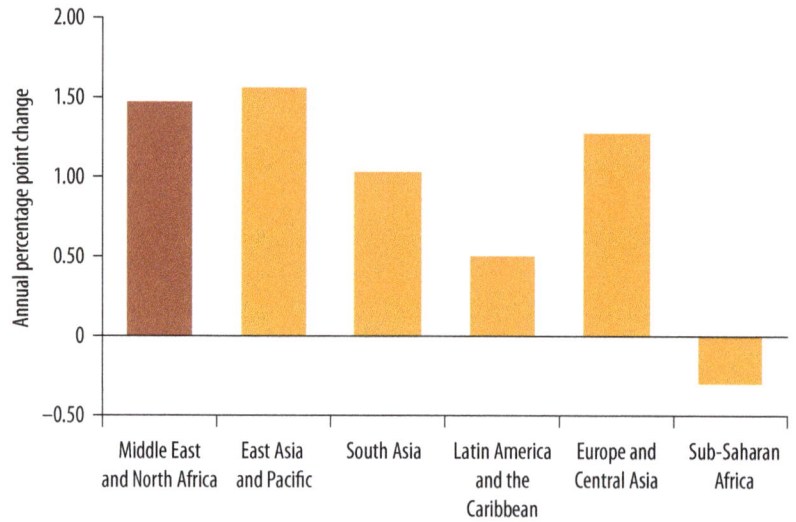

Source: Staff calculations based on WDI 2011 (World Bank multiple years).

FIGURE 1.2

MENA's Progress in Women's Health and Education,
1985–2010 (Average Annual Growth Rates in Key Indicators)

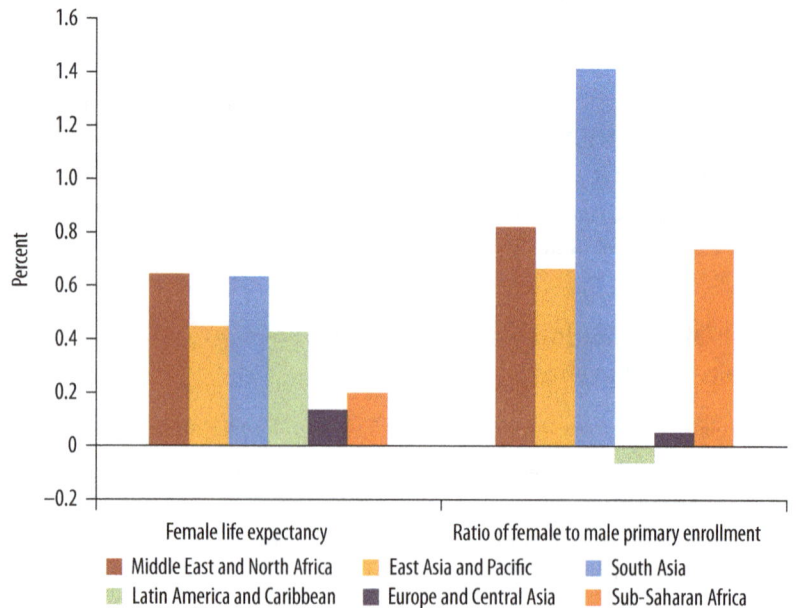

Source: Staff calculations based on WDI 2011 (World Bank multiple years).

FIGURE 1.3

Skewed Sex Ratios at Birth and Excess Female Mortality in MENA and the Rest of the World, 1990 and 2008

(Girls Missing at Birth and Excess Female Deaths after Birth, 000s)

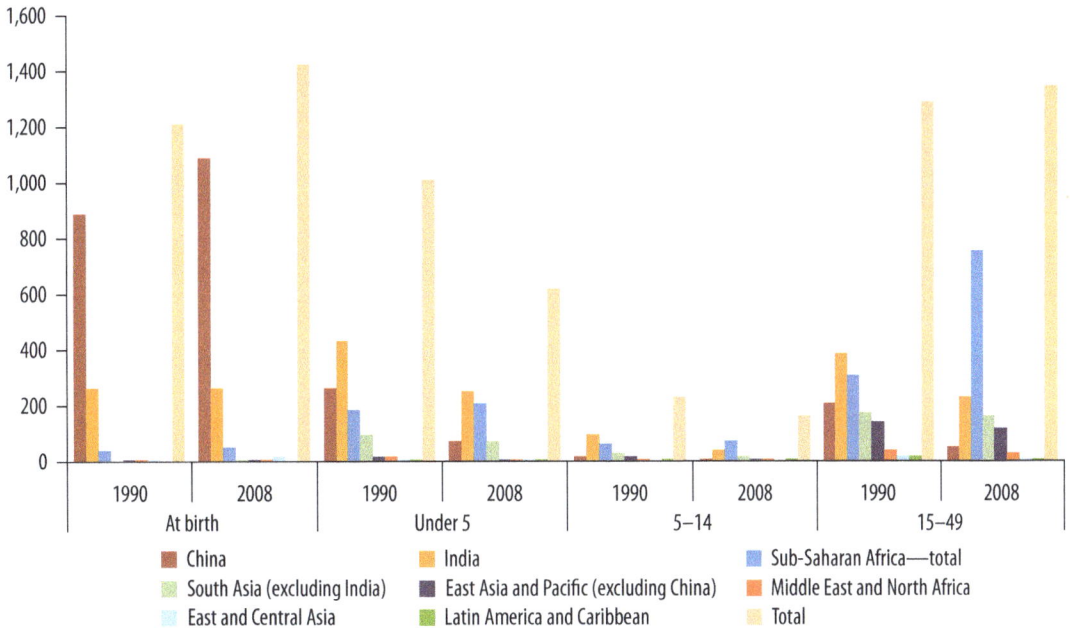

Source: Staff calculations based on data from WHO and others 2010 and UN DESA 2009.

Note: Israel and Malta are included in the MENA numbers.

One of the Lowest Rates of Excess Female Mortality in the World

Excess female mortality (a measure of how many fewer women would have died each year had they been living in a high-income country) is lower in the MENA Region than in other developing Regions, and has declined over the last 20 years.[1,2] Djibouti and the Republic of Yemen have MENA's highest rates of excess female mortality. MENA's low rates are in stark contrast to those of China, India, and Sub-Saharan Africa (figure 1.3). Moreover, the number of girls missing at birth and excess female deaths in MENA declined from 80,000 in 1990 to 52,000 in 2008.

Rapid Declines in Maternal Mortality

Between 1990 and 2008, maternal mortality rates in MENA fell by 59 percent, the largest rate of decline in the world (World Bank 2012). This trend reflects the increased investments over those 2 decades in reproductive health services such as prenatal care, births attended by skilled health staff, and contraceptive use. Moreover, within 2 decades, fertility rates in MENA almost halved from 5.4 children per woman in 1990 to 2.8 children per woman in 2010. The Islamic Republic of Iran and Morocco took just 10 and 20 years, respectively, to achieve similar results (World Bank 2012). It is no surprise, then, that average female life expectancy at birth in MENA has risen dramatically from 55 years in 1975 to 73 years in 2010.

More Girls in School Than in Much of the World

MENA's gender gap in literacy has been declining steadily since 1975, and more women in the Region are literate than ever before. This progress is striking, since in some countries, such as Saudi Arabia, girls were granted the right to education only in the 1960s. In fact, girls in MENA spend more years in school today than 3 decades ago, and more than girls in most other Regions. Between 1980 and 2010, the average years of schooling for females aged 15–19 in MENA more than doubled from 3.5 to 8.1 years—among the fastest increases in the world. Worldwide, it took an average of 3 decades for the share of 6- to 12-year-old girls in school to increase from 75 to 88 percent. MENA achieved the same increase in 2 decades: from 1990 to 2010.

Virtually No Gender Gaps in Enrollment, and Reverse Gender Gaps in University and Mathematics Performance

These increases in the level of schooling are reflected clearly in MENA's female-to-male enrollment ratios, which are close to or above 100 in many countries in the Region (figure 1.4). The obvious exceptions to this achievement are Djibouti and the Republic of Yemen, in which girls continue to be disadvantaged. It is striking that, as MENA's education levels increase, the gender balance in education shifts from favoring boys to favoring girls. From 1975, the ratio of females to males enrolled in tertiary education in the Region tripled to 112 percent in 2010. In fact, eight MENA countries have a "reverse gender gap" in education at the tertiary level (figure 1.5). Reverse gender gaps also show up in primary education. Contrary to global patterns, girls in the Region outperform boys in mathematics in grade 4, and this trend continues in some MENA countries through grade 8 (Fryer and Levitt 2009).

MENA's Positive Human Development Performance Explained Largely by Economic Development and Wealth

How much of the successful performance of MENA countries in achieving gender parity in education and health care can be explained as a natu-

FIGURE 1.4

Female-to-Male Enrollment Ratios: MENA Countries, 1975–2010

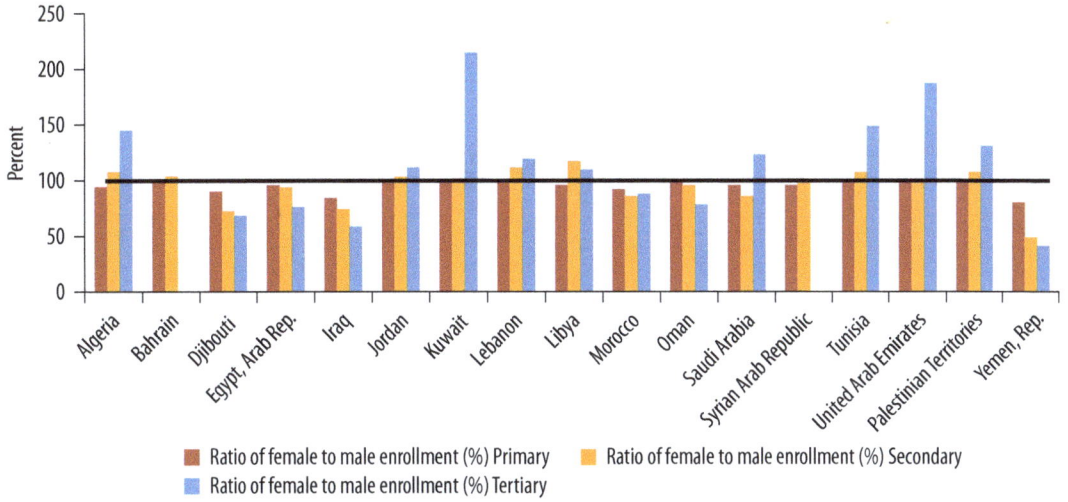

Source: WDI 2011 (World Bank multiple years).

FIGURE 1.5

More Women Than Men Attend University in Many MENA Countries, 2011

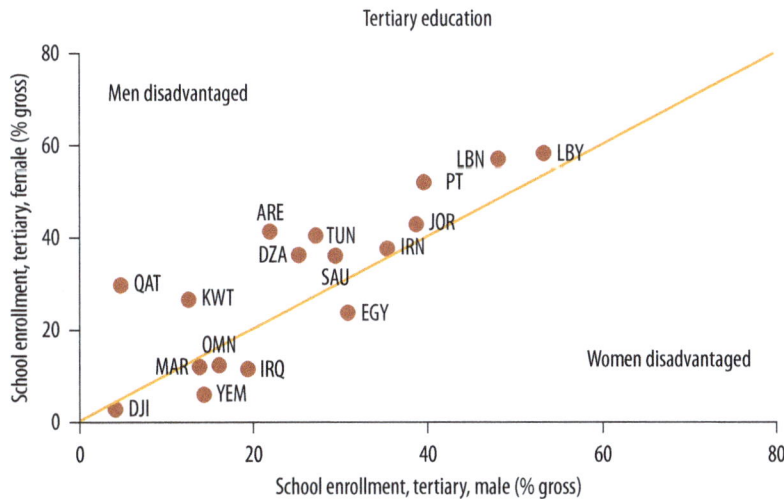

Source: Staff calculations based on WDI 2011 (World Bank multiple years).

Note: The 45 degree line shows gender parity in enrollments. Any point above the 45 degree line implies that more women are enrolled than men.

FIGURE 1.6

Per Capita Wealth Is Positively Related to Female Health Outcomes

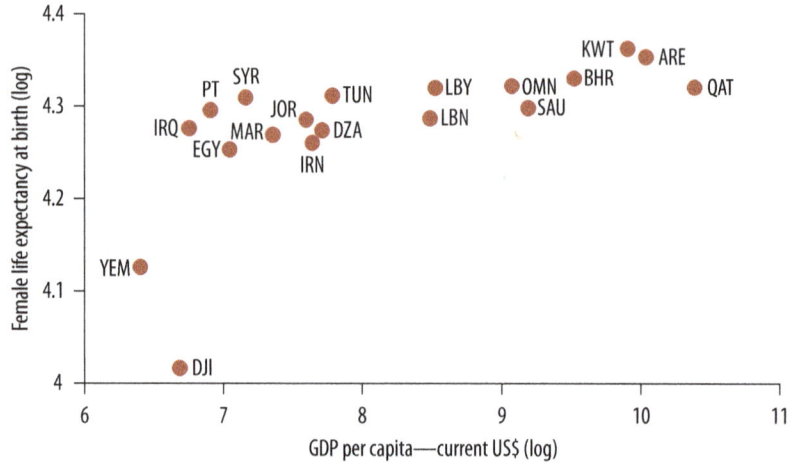

Source: WDI 2005–09 (World Bank multiple years).

ral consequence of MENA's economic development and wealth creation? All countries in the Region are either middle- or high-income countries. Figure 1.6 confirms the positive correlation between a country's wealth (measured by its per capita gross domestic product in current US$) and female life expectancy at birth.

The dominant influence of wealth in explaining human development outcomes also is confirmed in regression analysis that controls for the influence of common Regional characteristics. Wealth's dominance is true irrespective of the indicator of interest used: female adult literacy; gender parity in enrollment in primary, secondary, and tertiary education; female life expectancy at birth; female child and adult mortality; and maternal mortality (appendix B, table B.1, panels A and B).

These results support the assertion that MENA's better performance in human development compared to other countries is driven almost entirely by differences in wealth. As an illustration, consider female life expectancy at birth. MENA countries have an average female life expectancy at birth that is 9.1 percent higher than other non-OECD countries. The regression results suggest that this difference is driven entirely by the fact that, on average, MENA countries are richer. Overall, a 10 percent increase in real gross national income (GNI) per capita is associated with a 0.82 percent increase in female life expectancy at birth (appendix B, table B.1, panel B, columns (1) and (2)]. The relationship between human development outcomes and per capita incomes is evident even within MENA. Djibouti and the Republic of Yemen, whose per capita incomes are lower than those of the rest of the Region, have commensurately lower human development outcomes.

Remaining Challenges

While the Region as a whole has made impressive strides in human development outcomes for both girls and boys, the countries vary widely in outcomes. For example, Djibouti and the Republic of Yemen lag in many respects so they need to continue to invest in human development. In several countries, female primary and secondary school completion rates remain unusually low relative to enrollment rates.[3] Moreover, the higher the level of education, generally the larger is the gender gap in completion rates. In the Arab Republic of Egypt, the Islamic Republic of Iran, Jordan, Morocco, the Syrian Arab Republic, Tunisia, and the United Arab Emirates, the gender gap in completion is highest for tertiary education (WDI 2011 [World Bank multiple years]). For the Region as a whole, the overall primary school dropout rate is the second lowest in the world. However, this ranking masks wide variation across countries. Girls drop out more than boys do, especially in Iraq and the Gulf Cooperation Council (GCC) countries (which include most of the Region's oil-producing states).

There also are lagging regions within some MENA countries. In Egypt as a whole, youth illiteracy is 11 percent, whereas, in Upper Egypt, the corresponding rate is 17 percent. Young women in Upper Egypt have illiteracy rates of 24 percent, twice the rate of their male counterparts, and 10 percentage points higher than the national average for young women. Among those who are not enrolled in school in Upper Egypt, 45 percent of women have no education, compared to 20 percent of men (World Bank 2011a).

There is evidence in MENA that, once girls reach puberty, social norms regarding their roles and status in society sharply limit their access to educational opportunities. Survey data from Iraq (2006–07) illustrates that girls cite different reasons from boys for having to drop out of school: "it was time to end their education," "social reasons," and because the "family was no longer interested" in sending them to school (figure 1.7). Boys face pressures, too: the inability of the family to "afford their education" or because "traveling to school is difficult or unsafe."[4] Qualitative research in the Palestinian Territories and the Republic of Yemen (box 1.1) reveals the importance of gendered social norms in explaining dropout behavior for girls. Nevertheless, both girls and boys indicated that economic difficulties remain a significant impediment to staying in school.

The quality of education remains a broad challenge across the Region. In focus group discussions undertaken as part of a larger study in Upper

FIGURE 1.7

Boys and Girls Drop Out of School for Different Reasons: Evidence from Iraq, Ages 11–24

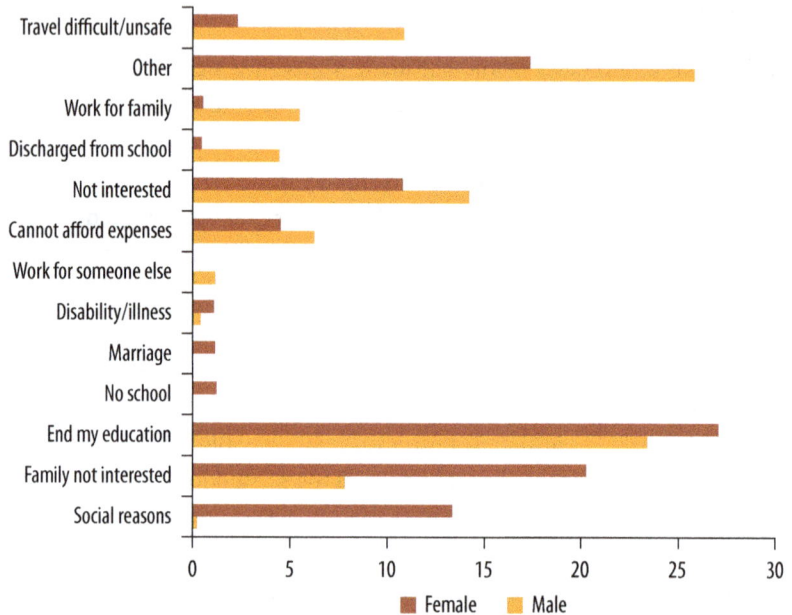

Source: Iraq Household Socio-Economic Survey 2006–07 (IHSES 2007).

Egypt, young people frequently cited the poor quality of teachers, over-crowded schools, and lack of basic supplies in schools (World Bank 2011a). Poor school facilities, inadequate teacher training, and a lack of female teachers may have a disproportionate effect on girls' completion rates. Similarly, the availability of safe and reliable transportation to school is an especially important prerequisite for girls' school attendance in MENA countries.

Another important concern related to women's education is the possible mismatch between what is learned in school and what is demanded by employers. This problem is common to both young women and men but possibly is more severe among women. For example, women tend to cluster in certain subjects that are considered more "gender appropriate" but may be less sought after in the job market. This clustering, in turn, could diminish women's returns from education and discourage them from pursuing further study.

Women's Participation outside the Home Is Limited

In contrast with investments in access to basic education and health care, which have come to be viewed as universal rights, outcomes in the labor

BOX 1.1

Education Cut Short

A large majority of the youth who participated in the qualitative assessment in the Palestinian Territories and the Republic of Yemen aspired to attend college.[a] Nevertheless, many of the school-aged children in the focus groups no longer were attending school. Nearly all who had ended their schooling felt that they had had little choice in the matter. A young woman from a village in the Republic of Yemen explained that, once her older sister had married, "There was no one else to do the housework." "It is difficult," stated a young man from the same village about his decision to leave school, "but what can I do? My father suffers from diabetes and he is not able to work, so I work instead of him." Both male and female youths mentioned their family's difficult economic circumstances as an important reason for stopping their education.

However, large gender differences in the reasons for ending education also emerged. Female study participants were more likely to mention being pulled out of school by diverse factors related to gendered social norms. "It was really hard for me to drop my education, but after I had my first child, my main concern was only my children," shared a young woman residing in a Gaza refugee camp. Similarly, adolescent girls from an urban Yemeni community stated that most of their peers will not make it to university: "The majority finish secondary school and get married."

Although less common, in villages visited in the Republic of Yemen and Palestinian Territories, young women spoke of being unable to attend secondary school because there was not a nearby school for girls. When asked if free transport to the nearest girls school would have made it easier for them attend, many girls said yes but that their fathers still would have had to be convinced to let them go.

Sources: WDR 2012 Global Qualitative Assessments, Palestinian Territories and Yemen (World Bank 2012a, forthcoming).
a. As part of the global qualitative assessment for the 2012 WDR.

market and in political life remain very much the result of individual preference and choice—and of opportunities to participate in economic and political life.

Across the world, on average, only one in five legislative representatives is a woman. Only one in two women in the working age population is either employed or actively seeking work. Underlying this worldwide average of 50 percent female labor force participation is a wide variation across Regions from 25 percent in MENA to 65 percent in low-income countries (LICs) (figure 1.8). In LICs, the high rates of female participation in the workforce are partially explained by the compulsion of having to work to make ends meet. In the high-income (OECD) countries, the development of a sophisticated system of incentives—social security systems, flexible work options, and maternity and paternity benefits—have

FIGURE 1.8

Female Labor Force Participation across Regions, 1980–2009

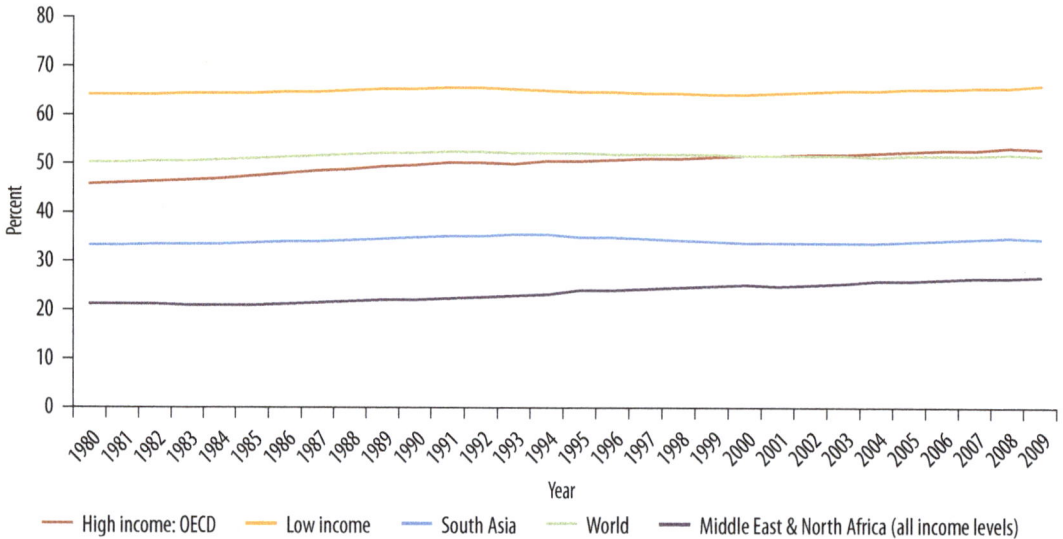

Source: WDI 2011 (World Bank multiple years).

enabled women to enter the workforce in larger numbers. At the same time, this incentive system has helped women balance their dual roles of work and family life.

It is striking how slowly these rates of participation changed over the 30 years from 1980 to 2009. One possible reason could be that gender norms about the role of women in the workplace are difficult to change. In the 1930s in the United States, only 10 percent of married women participated in the labor force. Moreover, an overwhelming majority of husbands disapproved of their wives working if the husbands could support their families. Accompanied by changes in the economic structure that created more and flexible work opportunities for women, and changes in laws and formal and informal rules about whether and where women could work, gender norms also shifted gradually over the course of the century. Today, more than 80 percent of husbands in the US approve of their wives working, and the married female labor force participation is upwards of 70 percent.

There also are examples of countries in which the participation of women in the labor force has expanded considerably within a relatively short period. Figure 1.9 shows the female labor force participation rates for a select group of countries that all started out at levels well below the world average. During the 1980s, many of these countries saw little change in women's participation. Since then, Greece, Ireland, and Spain have seen rapid increases in female participation fueled by integration in

FIGURE 1.9

Female Labor Force Participation Rate, 1980–2009

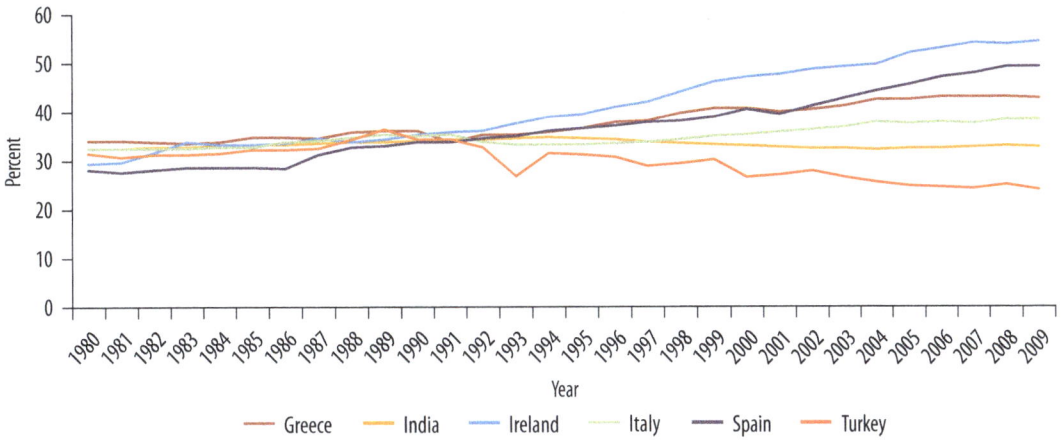

Source: WDI 2011 (World Bank multiple years).

the euro-zone and the accompanying economic boom. In contrast, despite high rates of economic growth following liberalization in the 1990s, India saw almost no change in officially reported statistics. This lack of movement arose in part from rapid urbanization and the accompanying loss of agricultural and rural employment for women. From 1994 to 2009, Turkey's female labor force participation also trended downward. As the country was caught in a transition of rapid urbanization, the observed decline in women working was due perhaps to relatively low educational attainment for women and falling agricultural employment.

In the instances in which economic growth created new opportunities for women, the increase in female participation in the workforce was supported by accompanying changes in the legal and institutional framework, including flexible work options and the creation of a conducive work environment for women (box 1.2).

Women in the Workforce

In recent decades, expanding economic opportunities have pulled large shares of women into the formal economy worldwide. In MENA, however, considerable investments in women's human capital have not been matched by increases in economic participation. In Sub-Saharan Africa, East Asia and Pacific, Europe and Central Asia, and Latin America and Caribbean, more than 50 percent of the female population aged 15 and above participates in the labor market. In MENA, the corresponding figure is only 25.2 percent.

BOX 1.2

Transition in Irish Female Labor Force Participation

Over the last 40 years, Ireland has undergone a pronounced transition in female labor force participation. This shift can be divided into two distinct phases.

First, between the early 1970s and early 1990s, the total female participation rate grew slowly but steadily from the mid-20 percent range to the mid-40 percent range (depending on year and measure used). Although this advance still left participation well below EU averages, it showed a sharp reorientation of the labor market toward female employment. Over those 4 decades, the number of women participating grew by 50 percent; the number of women employed grew by 38 percent; and the number of men employed fell by 4 percent.

In the second phase, Ireland experienced a dramatic surge in female participation from levels well below 1991 EU averages to approximately 67 percent today, on par with the larger EU economies, although still below Scandinavia. The increase was particularly pronounced during 1998–2007, when 300,000 women in Ireland (approximately 8 percent of the population) joined the labor force.

The two phases share some common elements. Most notably, participation has grown the most among married women, older women, and women with older children. By contrast, participation has been sluggish for younger women and single women (with and without children), and married women with young children.

In other respects, the two phases have quite different explanatory factors. From the 1970s to the early 1990s, the key forces were related to Ireland's overall economic transition away from a peripheral and relatively rural economy. The first factor was that agriculture was rapidly shrinking as an employment source. This decline explains the lack of overall growth in male employment noted above. Second, changing social mores toward birth control (which occurred prior to the legalization of contraception) were associated with a steep decline in fertility, which in turn was linked to increased participation of married women.

The third factor was the expanded access to secondary education in the mid-1960s, which reduced the entry of young women and men in the labor force. In the 1970s and 1980s, this reduction was complemented by a similar dynamic in tertiary-level education. As a result, there were strong cohort effects with younger, less educated groups leaving the labor market, and older educated groups entering later—an effect that tended to favor women. Finally, reforms to unemployment benefits reduced discrimination against married women and increased their incentive to be in the labor force.

An element that cut across these four change factors was the weakening of the "male breadwinner" model. As traditional sectors for male employment shrank, attitudes toward female employment changed, while emigration had become a less viable response to the lack of opportunity at home.

As the strong growth associated with the Celtic Tiger accelerated from the mid-

(continued on next page)

1990s, female participation responded to the pull of job opportunities. Between 1998 and 2008, female employment grew by 55 percent. In addition to economic growth, key factors included a demographic bulge in important cohorts for participation (especially ages 25–34), rising educational attainment, and reforms to the tax and benefit system to reduce disincentives to the participation of married women.

An important aspect of the highly elastic response of female participation to Ireland's economic boom seems to be the pent-up supply created by the earlier structural changes whose impact initially had

been repressed by the difficult economic circumstances of the 1980s. Thus, the combination of education, attitudes, demography, and incentives wrought their full effect only when opportunities expanded. Nonetheless, Ireland still displays significant gender disparities in the labor market, especially regarding occupational segregation and nonemployment linked to lack of access to childcare. Sixty-three percent of women are in only five occupational categories, while having a pre-school child reduces the likelihood of participation by nearly 20 percent.

Sources: Russell and others 2009; Walsh 1993, 369–400.

Rates of female labor force participation are low throughout the Region. Almost all MENA countries have participation rates below the LMI average of 51 percent (figure 1.10). Not surprisingly, the lowest participation rates are in fragile or conflict-affected states such as Iraq, Palestinian Territories, and the Republic of Yemen. Within MENA, the women's workforce participation varies widely as well: from 5 percent in the Republic of Yemen to 48 percent in the United Arab Emirates. However, for the Region as a whole, women's participation has increased by only 0.17 percentage points annually over the last 30 years. This stagnation has occurred despite the healthy rates of growth of some economies, such as Egypt (box 1.3).

Even over the last decade, as MENA women have become increasingly better educated, labor force participation rates have increased only modestly. Below the surface, however, the story is more complex. Table 1.1 illustrates this complexity for Egypt and Tunisia, two countries for which detailed survey data are publicly available. In Tunisia, the share of women with primary education or lower who are active in the labor force has fallen over the last decade. Meanwhile, tertiary-educated Tunisian women have become more involved in the labor force. The increasing number of women in school may be holding down Tunisia's participation rate, since women in school are counted as inactive. As these women leave school,

BOX 1.3

Is Growth the Silver Bullet to Expand Women's Participation in the Workforce? Evidence from Egypt, 1998–2006

From 2000 to 2010, the Egyptian economy expanded at an annual rate of nearly 5 percent. Cross-country evidence suggests that, in a middle-income developing country such as Egypt, this level of growth should be accompanied by a marked increase in female labor force participation rates. However, in Egypt during this decade, participation rates did not rise commensurately.

Why? One possible explanation could be that that female employment was concentrated in relatively low-growth sectors. The distribution of the female share in employment ("female intensity") across industrial sectors in Egypt is very uneven. Almost half of all industries have minimal (below 10 percent) female presence. Very few industries (including education, health, social work, agriculture, and textiles) have above-average female employment intensity. Moreover, the pattern of female employment intensity by industry remained largely unchanged during 1998–2006, the years covered by the Egypt Labor Market Panel Survey (ELMPS).

In Egypt, during 1998–2006, overall, industry-level gross domestic product and employment growth figures show that there was no systematic relationship between industry growth (as measured by total employment or output) and female employment intensity. Thus, the decade was a period of high growth that was in no way biased against sectors that employ women.

The fact that female participation rates did not rise despite such economic growth in Egypt strongly suggests that growth alone is unlikely to be the solution for Egypt. The reason is that, in part, many female-intensive sectors are small in terms in total employment. Another explanation could be that women are locked in low-productivity sectors, with low returns to work, causing nonparticipation to appear more attractive. However, again, comparing growth across low and high female-intensive industries shows that, during 1998–2006, there was no systematic relationship between sectoral labor productivity and female intensity. Furthermore, growth in labor productivity was not systematically different across high and low female-intensive industries. This finding suggests that if women do face lower returns in the labor market, it is not simply because they are locked into a few low-productivity sectors. Conversely, female participation did not expand in industries that were growing rapidly. In fact, during this period, most industries saw no change in female labor force participation rates.

Combined, these findings highlight the importance of moving beyond an approach that relies on growth or on sectors or industries that are seen as being inherently more amenable to female employment. Instead, what need to be investigated are the fundamental constraints that obstruct women from finding employment in private firms, irrespective of the industry.

Source: World Bank 2010c. Egypt Gender Assessment Update. Washington, DC. https://openknowledge.worldbank.org/handle/10986/2192.

FIGURE 1.10

Female and Male Labor Force Participation across MENA

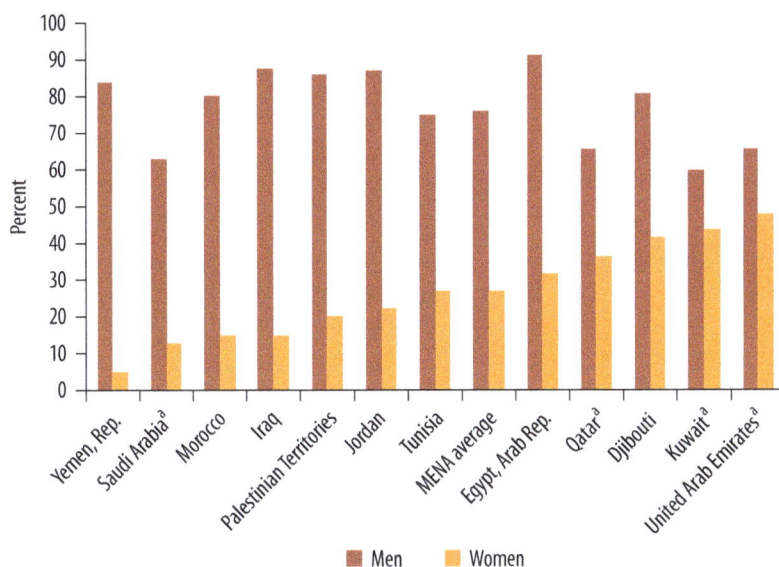

Source: Household surveys (appendixes A and C).

a. Official estimates for national nonimmigrant population.

they likely will increase the participation rates of educated women. In contrast, in Egypt, less educated women have increased their participation, whereas the more educated have decreased theirs. A recent gender assessment by the World Bank (2010c) found that the fall in participation of more educated women in Egypt may be related to cutbacks in public sector employment.

As is the case worldwide, labor force participation estimates also tend to underestimate participation in that they do not fully account for informal employment. In the Region as a whole, women and men are equally

TABLE 1.1

Female Labor Force Participation Rates by Education
percent

	Tunisia (all women aged 15+)		Egypt, Arab Rep. (all women aged 15+)	
	2000	2010	1998	2006
Overall	23.8	24.9	25.6	28.2
By education				
None	14.0	12.5	16.4	22.6
Primary	24.0	21.2	8.4	10.7
Secondary	33.6	25.9	35.8	31.1
Tertiary	54.6	60.1	64.3	59.2

Sources: ELMPS 1998, 2006; Tunisia Labor Force Surveys 2000, 2010.

likely to hold informal jobs in the private sector. Within the labor force as a whole, the relative shares of women and men in informal work vary according to the structure of the economy. For example, in countries in which agricultural employment constitutes an important share of overall employment, as in the Republic of Yemen, women often are employed in unpaid, subsistence agriculture. In these countries, women are present in the informal sector in high numbers. On the other hand, in countries in which the public sector constitutes a large share of employment, women—especially educated women—are well represented in the public sector. In Egypt, Iraq, and Syria, for example, women's participation in the informal sector is lower relative to men (World Bank 2011a).

Unemployment rates are extremely high in MENA countries. Compared to the averages for LMI countries and the world, MENA has far higher unemployment rates, especially for youth and women (figure 1.11). Young MENA women face unemployment rates of nearly 40 percent. In the Islamic Republic of Iran, for example, young people account for approximately 70 percent of the unemployed population (box 1.4). Furthermore, over the last 25 years, MENA's already wide unemployment gap between women and men doubled from 5.5 percent in 1985 to more than 10 percent in 2010.

While it may be argued that preferences for domestic life explain the low rates of female labor force participation in MENA, an equally plausible explanation is that women who otherwise want to work find it more

FIGURE 1.11

Unemployment in MENA and Rest of the World

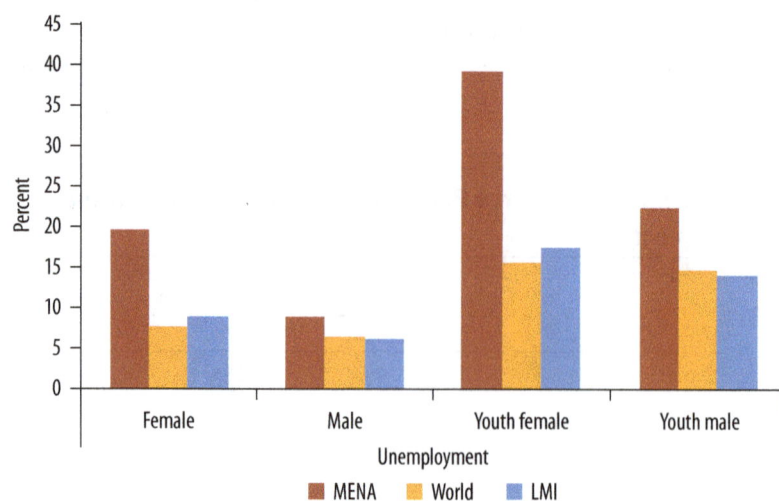

Source: Staff calculations based on WDI 2011 (World Bank multiple years).
Note: LMI = Low and middle income.

BOX 1.4

Being Young and Female in the Islamic Republic of Iran's Economy

Young women and men are playing an increasingly important role in Iran's politics. Nevertheless, they have fewer opportunities to participate in economic life than their older cohorts. As a result of a baby boom in the early years of the Islamic Revolution (roughly 1979–84), the Iranian youth cohorts are the largest in the country's history. While this demographic change can be a positive force for economic growth in many countries, in the Islamic Republic of Iran, this change may be a potential source of social and political instability. The country's economy is unable to absorb this record-high number of young workers. Iranian youth, especially women, wait a long time to find their first jobs after graduation: the average unemployment duration is 1.25 years for men and 3 years for women.

Since the 1980s, Iran's female labor force participation rate has increased in parallel with the growing size of the entering cohorts. At the same time, women's employment prospects have deteriorated. Between 1984 and 2007, unemployment rates among young women more than doubled, from 16.6 to 37.9 percent, respectively. In 2008, this figure jumped up to 46.3 percent, twice as high as unemployment for young men. Young and educated women are the worst-off, with college graduates facing an unemployment rate of a striking 52.6 percent.

Source: Salehi-Isfahani 2011.

---

difficult than men to find jobs. In the face of high rates of unemployment, women are discouraged and may even drop out of the labor force. A look at Tunisia's 2010 Labor Force Survey data supports this hypothesis.[5] Figure 1.12 plots participation and unemployment rates for each of Tunisia's 24 governorates in its 7 regions. Participation and unemployment rates vary widely across regions but not as much within regions. Furthermore, in governorates in which unemployment rates are high, participation rates tend to be low. Discouragement thus may understate the severity of the disparity in job creation across the country.

The overall figures also mask significant differences among women of different education levels. Figure 1.13 plots the same data as does figure 1.12 but broken down by education level as well as governorate. Women with less than primary education face relatively lower unemployment rates. Participation rates in this group tend to be low but vary significantly across governorates. Although the relationship is not robust, governorates with higher rates of unemployment have very low rates of participation among this group of women.

FIGURE 1.12

Tunisia: Unemployment and Participation Rates by Governorate for Women Ages 15–64

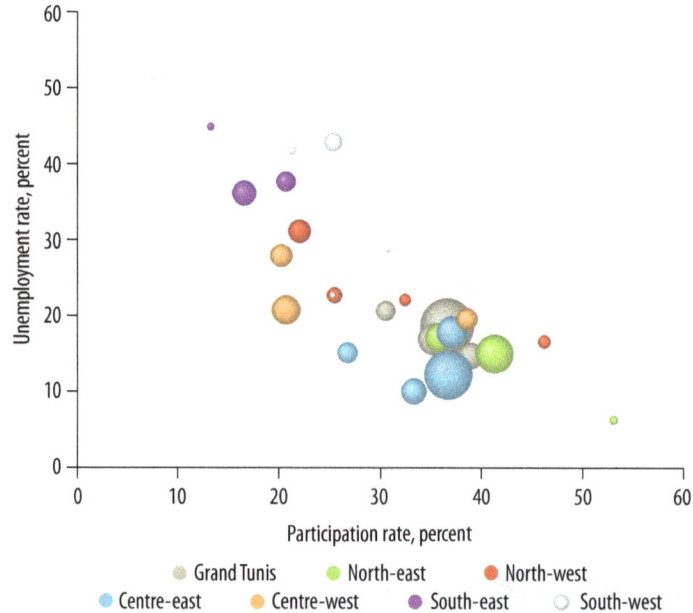

Source: Staff calculations based on 2010 Tunisia Labor Force Survey.

Note: Size of each bubble indicates relative size of its population; color of each bubble indicates region.

As education levels rise, so does participation. The variation in unemployment rates across governorates is higher for primary- and secondary-educated women. Nevertheless, the inverse relationship between unemployment and participation remains.

Among women with tertiary education, the situation is profoundly different. Notwithstanding the painfully high unemployment rates that Tunisian women face in some areas, participation rates are uniformly high across the country. Indeed, participation rates for tertiary-educated women are almost identical to those for tertiary-educated men. However, the unemployment rate is twice as high for these women. This trend is true for many other MENA countries, perhaps because, despite limited job opportunities, highly educated women are willing to search longer for jobs in the hope of eventually realizing a return on their educational investments.

Women in Business

Although female entrepreneurs are a minority everywhere, their share in MENA is far lower than in the other middle-income Regions. Of the

FIGURE 1.13

Tunisia: Unemployment and Participation Rates by Governorate and Education Level, Women Ages 15–64

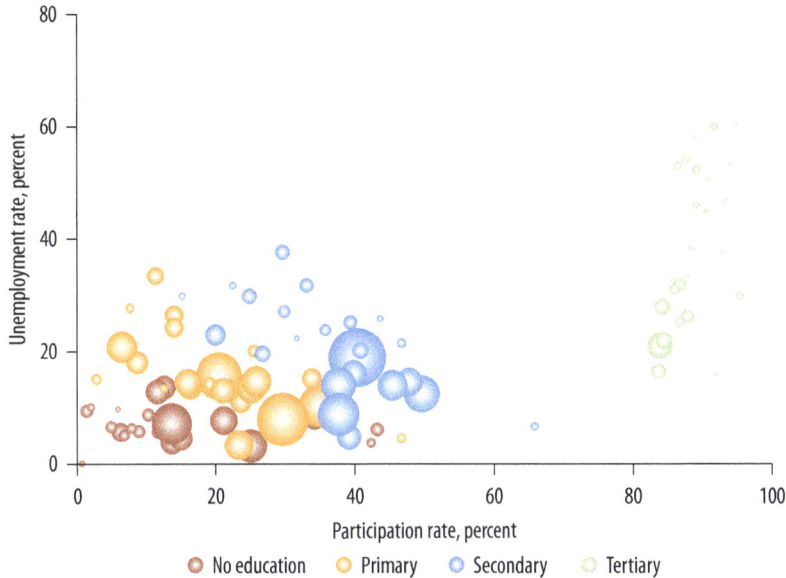

Source: Staff calculations based on 2010 Tunisia Labor Force Survey.

5,887 firms in 10 MENA countries surveyed by the World Bank between 2003 and 2010, only 15 percent were female owned. Although few in number, female-owned firms defy commonly held views. The widely held perception is that female entrepreneurs in MENA are mainly in the informal or formal microsector (employing fewer than 10 workers) and are producing less sophisticated goods and services. In fact, of the female-owned firms surveyed, only 18 percent had fewer than 10 workers (figure 1.14). More than 35 percent were medium-to-large firms employing more than 50 workers. Moreover, the female-owned firms surveyed were as well established as the male-owned firms. On average, female-owned firms were 21 years old, whereas male-owned firms were 20 years old. Furthermore, women were not owners in name only. In Algeria, Lebanon, and Syria, at least 50 percent of female-owned firms were managed by their owners.

Notably, there are only small differences in labor productivity and sales between male- and female-owned firms (Chamlou and others 2008). An important difference is that female-owned firms hire more women (figure 1.15). Women make up approximately 25 percent of the workforce in female-owned firms, compared with 21 percent in male-owned firms. This difference may not seem large, but female-owned

FIGURE 1.14

Distribution of Female-Owned Firms by Firm Size

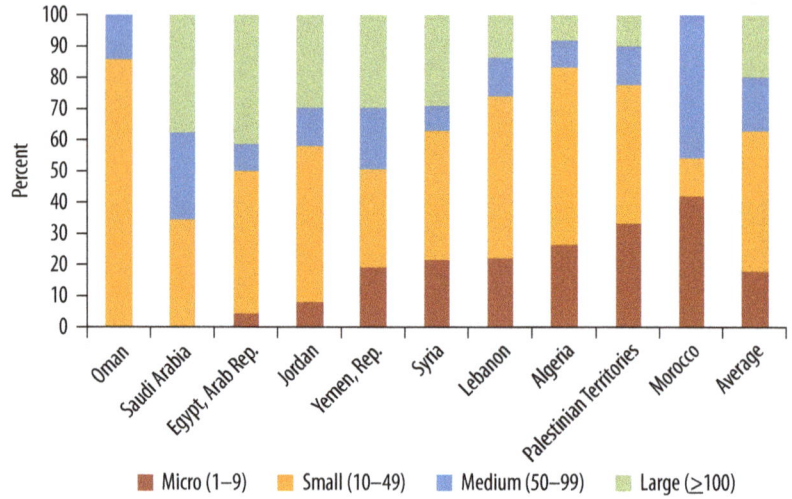

Source: Business Enterprise Surveys (appendixes A and C).

FIGURE 1.15

Share of Female Workers by Gender of Owner

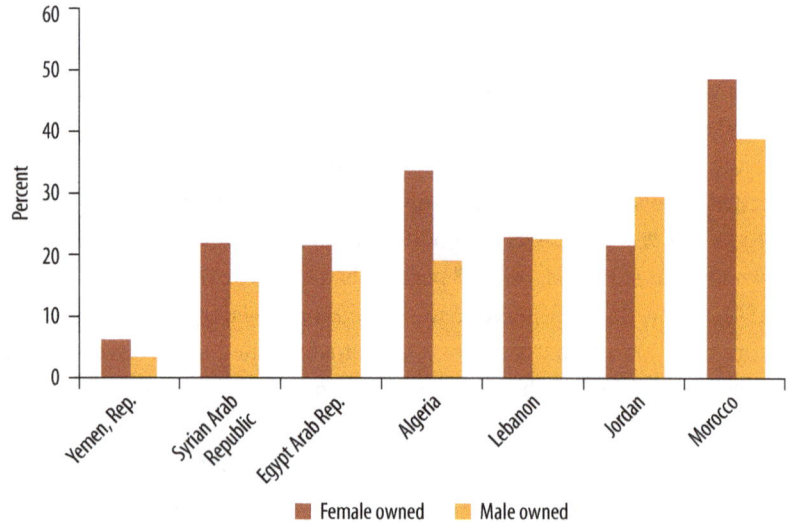

Source: Business Enterprise Surveys (appendixes A and C).

firms also employ a larger share of female workers at professional and managerial levels. These facts point to these firms' potentially strong role in absorbing the growing female labor force, particularly tertiary-educated women.

BOX 1.5

Saudi Women Granted Right to Vote and Run for Office

In September 2011, King Abdullah used the occasion of the new term of the Shura Council (an appointed consultative body) to announce that, beginning with the council's next term, women could be appointed to it. Although the councils have little formal power, they have an important say over the portion of the central budget allocated for municipal projects. At the same time, the King announced that women could be candidates in the municipal council elections scheduled for 2015 and vote in them.

These announcements were made after the preparations for the all-male 2011 municipal elections had been completed. The announcements left open the possibility that women still may need their guardians' permission to run or vote in the 2015 municipal elections. However, subsequent interpretation has confirmed the generally understood meaning of the announcement as giving women autonomy in their decision to participate in the elections.

Women in Politics

Finally, throughout the last half-century, the rest of the world witnessed an expansion in female participation in civil society and politics. This trend has not yet emerged in MENA. Although this figure has increased slowly over time, MENA women remain underrepresented in politics, holding on average only 7 percent of seats in parliaments.

During the last decade, however, progress was made in extending the rights of women to vote and run for political office. Saudi Arabia, until recently the only exception, has granted women the right to vote and run for office, beginning with the next round of municipal elections scheduled for 2015 (box 1.5). In 2005, women in Kuwait were granted the same political rights as men. In other GCC countries, including Bahrain, Oman, and the United Arab Emirates, women are being appointed or elected to political office (Kelly and Breslin 2010). Iraq and Jordan have introduced electoral quotas for women in parliamentary and municipal elections (figure 1.16).

What Explains the MENA Puzzle?

Despite the great strides in human development, the low levels of participation of women in the workplace and in political life across the MENA Region are a puzzle. What common features, if any, could explain it?

FIGURE 1.16

Women in Legislatures (Lower or Single Houses)

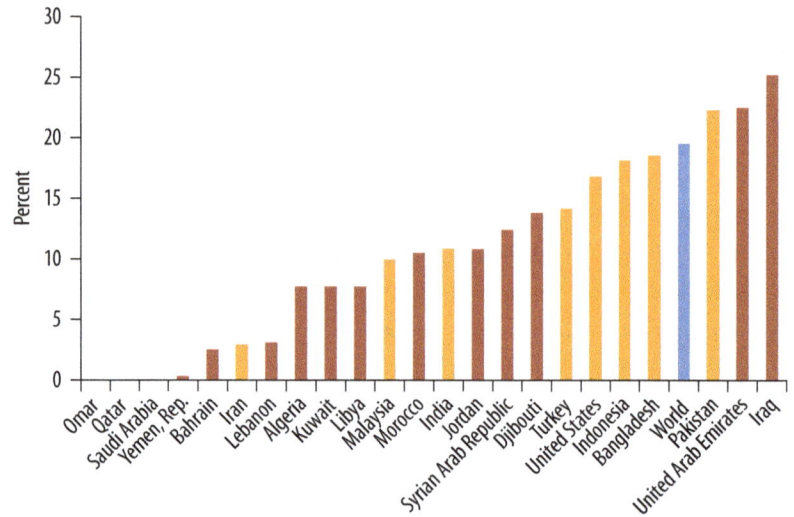

Source: IPU 2011.

Aside from their ancient, rich common cultural heritage and shared history, MENA countries as a group are distinct from the rest of the developing world in numerous ways. MENA countries have relatively higher per capita incomes, relatively traditional gender norms, common religious identity for the bulk of the population, legal frameworks that share many common features, economic structures that are characterized and influenced by dominant public sectors, and the majority share of the world's oil reserves. All of these features—the nature of gender norms, the legal framework, and the structure of the economy—powerfully influence the incentives, preferences, opportunities, and ability of women to participate in work and politics, not in MENA only but across the world. This report argues that it is this complicated nexus that lies at the heart of the MENA puzzle of low rates of female workforce participation.

Notes

1. Following the approach of the World Development Report 2012 (WDR 2012), these estimates of excess female mortality characterize female disadvantage in health. This methodology was pioneered by Anderson and Ray (2010) to construct estimates for (a) girls missing at birth and (b) excess female mortality. For a detailed description of the methodology, refer to chapter 3 of WDR 2012 (World Bank 2012).

2. Girls missing at birth are estimated by comparing the sex ratios at birth in countries around the world to those in comparable populations in which there

is relatively no discrimination. Excess female mortality is computed by comparing the mortality risks of women relative to men in every country and at every age with those seen in developed economies today (WDR 2012, chapter 3). Based on life tables from the UN and demographic data from United Nations Development Programme (UNDP), the WDR 2012 measure computes the annual number of excess female deaths in countries in MENA and other Regions at three points in time: 1990, 2000, and 2008.

3. Note that the completion rate is defined as a % of those who are of school completion age. For example, the female secondary completion rate is the % of females of secondary school completion age who have completed secondary school. Thus, the completion rate depends on both the enrollment rate and the rate at which those who were enrolled finished school.

4. This response was consistent with the security situation in Iraq at the time of the survey.

5. Staff calculations based on 2010 Tunisia Labor Force Survey (Tunisia 2010; appendixes A and C).

References

Anderson, Siwan, and Debraj Ray. 2010. "Missing Women: Age and Disease." *Review of Economic Studies* 77: 1262–300. http://www.econ.nyu.edu/user/debraj/Papers/AndersonRay.pdf.

Business Enterprise Surveys (appendixes A and C).

Central Statistical Organization. 2007. *Iraq Household Socio-Economic Survey 2006–07 (IHSES 2007)*. Baghdad.

Chamlou, Nadereh, Leora Klapper, and Silvia Muzi. 2008. "The Environment for Women's Entrepreneurship in Middle East and North Africa." World Bank, Washington, DC. http://elibrary.worldbank.org/content/book/9780821374955.

ELMPS (Egypt Labor Market Panel Survey). 1998 and 2006. Economic Research Forum, Cairo.

Fryer, Roland, and Steven Levitt. 2009. "An Empirical Analysis of the Gender Gap in Mathematics." Working Paper 15430, NBER (The National Bureau of Economic Research), Cambridge, MA.

Household Surveys (appendixes A and C).

Institut National de la Statistique. 2000 and 2010. *Tunisia Labor Force Survey*. Tunis.

Kelly, Sanja, and Julia Breslin. 2010. *Women's Rights in the Middle East and North Africa: Progress amid Resistance*. New York, NY: Freedom House; Lanham, MD: Rowman & Littlefield.

Nasr, Sarah. 2010. *Egyptian Women Workers and Entrepreneurs: Maximizing Opportunities in the Economic Sphere*. Washington, DC: The World Bank.

Russell, Helen, Frances McGinnity, Tim Callan, and Claire Keane. 2009. *A Woman's Place: Female Participation in the Irish Labour Market*. Equality Research Series. The Equality Authority and the Economic and Social Research Institute, Dublin.

Salehi-Isfahani, Djavad. 2011. "Iranian Youth in Times of Economic Crisis." Iranian Studies 44 (6): 789–806.

UNDP (United Nations Development Programme). 2010. *The Real Wealth of Nations: Pathways to Human Development*. 20th Anniversary Ed. Human Development Report 2010, New York.

UN DESA (Department of Economic and Social Affairs). 2009. *Population Division, Population Estimates and Projections Section*. http://www.un.org/esa/population/; http://www.unpopulation.org.

Walsh, Brendan. 1993. "Labour Force Participation and the Growth of Women's Employment, Ireland 1971–1991." *The Economic and Social Review* 24 (4). 369–400. www.esr.ie/.

WHO (World Health Organization), UNICEF (United Nations Children's Fund), UNFPA (United Nations Population Fund), and World Bank. 2010. *Trends in Maternal Mortality: 1990 to 2008*. Geneva.

World Bank. 2011a. *Reclaiming Their Voice: New Perspectives from Young Women and Men in Upper Egypt*. Washington, DC: World Bank.

_____. 2012a. "Aspirations on Hold: Young Lives in the West Bank and Gaza. Washington, DC: World Bank.

_____. 2012b. *World Development Report 2012:* Gender Equality and Development. Washington, DC: World Bank.

_____. 2012c. Forthcoming. "Yemen Gender Policy Note." Washington, DC: World Bank.

_____. Multiple years. *WDI (World Development Indicators)*. Washington, DC. data.worldbank.org/data-catalog/world-development-indicators.

CHAPTER 2

Traditional Gender Norms and the Legal Framework Limit Women's Agency

Agency, broadly defined, is the capacity and authority to act, and underpins an individual's ability to shape her own life: freedom of choice, expression, and decision making. In the absence of equality in agency, gender parity in some dimensions, such as human development, may not necessarily translate into equality of opportunity in others. This chapter considers some of the Region's norms about gender and the role of women. It then examines the relevant legal frameworks and their roles in circumscribing women's capacities to exercise agency within the household and participate in the economic and political spheres.

A country's legal framework outlines the formal space, granting women and men rights and defining the rules of the game and the environment within which individuals can exercise agency. Norms about the roles of women can shape the legislative framework and dampen the enforcement of laws. In turn, by formalizing unequal rights for women and men, the legal framework can reinforce restrictive gender norms. On the other hand, when the community as a whole sanctions those who deviate from gender norms and those who do not enforce them, gender norms can be resilient even in the face of legal reform because the costs of deviating from the norms are high.

Norms about the roles of girls and women within and outside the household are influenced by multiple factors:

- History and customs

- Prevailing cultural and social norms and the influence of religious beliefs

- Legal framework, which delineates the rights of women and men

- Structure of the economy, which is influenced by the country's resource endowment and geography and, in turn, shapes the incentives and opportunities for women to participate.

Expressions of Agency

The 2012 World Development Report focuses on four important expressions of women's lack of agency. They are women's ability to earn and control income and own and use resources and assets; their ability to make decisions about their movements and to move outside their homes; their ability to make decisions about family formation (when and whom to marry, how many children to have and when, and when to leave a marriage; and freedom from the risk of violence including domestic violence); and their ability to influence society and policy through participation in politics and civic associations.

There is a burgeoning and dynamic academic literature on the role of these factors in explaining the relatively low rates of female labor force participation in Middle East and North Africa (MENA).

One strand of this literature argues that the economic structure, social norms, and institutions characteristic of oil-rich economies discourage women from formal sector work (Moghadam 2004). With more than half the world's proven oil reserves concentrated in only five countries in the Region (the Islamic Republic of Iran, Iraq, Kuwait, Saudi Arabia, and the United Arab Emirates) , MENA's low female labor force participation often is attributed to oil (Moghadam 2003, 2004). Ross (2008), for instance, argues that oil production "reduces the number of women in the labor force, which in turn reduces their political influence."[1]

Indeed, oil-rich countries tend to have undiversified private sectors, in which employment is male dominated, and large public sectors (box 2.2). Consequently, employment opportunities for women often are highly concentrated in the public sector. Data does support the view that oil systematically affects countries' economic structures by dampening growth in the demand for female labor. On average globally, an increase in oil reserves is associated with lower rates of female labor force participation.

Counter-examples do exist. Oil producers and exporters such as Norway and the Russian Federation have significantly higher rates of female labor force participation at 56 and 62 percent, respectively. Conversely, the lack of oil does not necessarily mean higher rates of female labor force participation. Oil-importing countries within MENA have rates of female labor force participation on par with their oil-exporting neighbors. In fact, MENA countries clearly are outliers. Their labor force participation rates are well below what would be predicted by their oil reserves or their potential demand for female labor.

BOX 2.2

Oil Endowments and the Demand for Female Labor

In all MENA oil-rich countries (except the Republic of Yemen), the "manufacturing of refined petroleum products" comprises the lion's share of total exports (appendix B, table B.2), leaving other sectors with a total share of less than 5 percent of exports. Worldwide, the fact that employment in oil-related industries tends to be male dominated carries significant implications for female labor force participation. In MENA countries as well, oil-related industries are among the most male-biased: 87 percent of employees in the "manufacturing of refined petroleum products" are male. The garment and textile industries appear to be much more female friendly: 71 percent of

employment in sectors such as "wearing apparel, except fur apparel" is female. In other words, oil-rich countries in MENA generate less demand for female labor in the private sector. Following Do and others (2011), a country-level measure of the potential demand for female labor can be constructed by calculating the average of female employment shares across industries, weighted by the export share of each industry in a given country.[a] Figure B2.2a relates the extent of oil reserves per capita in a country and the estimated potential demand for female labor from exporting firms in the manufacturing sector for each country. The heterogeneity within MENA as a

FIGURE B2.2a

Oil and Export-Driven Demand for Female Labor

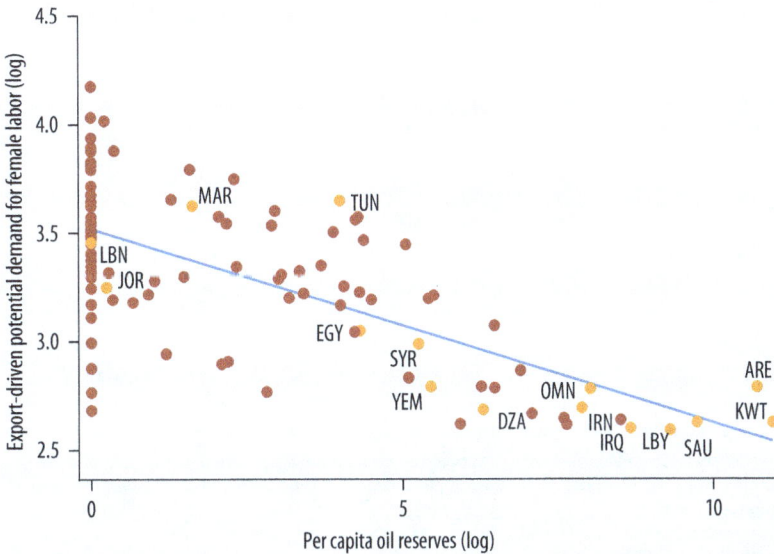

Sources: UN COMTRADE 2007; UNIDO 2009; US CIA 2009; WDI 2011 (World Bank multiple years).

(continued on next page)

BOX 2.2   *Continued*

whole is striking. Oil-rich MENA countries with high per capita oil reserves have relatively low, export-driven supplies of female-friendly jobs. On the other hand, oil-poor MENA countries are generating a relatively high female-friendly demand for labor (figure B2.2b).

Such heterogeneity also matters to a country's longer term potential to absorb female labor. On average across the world, an increase of 10 percent in the potential demand for female labor leads to an increase in female labor force participation by at least 3 percent (Do and others 2011,

table 7.28). Figure B2.2b plots the increasing potential demand for female labor in various Regions over time, driven by the growth of export industries. From 1980 to 2000, the global trend of strong growth in the export industry increased the potential for female employment. Variations within MENA were dramatic on this score as well. In the oil-rich MENA countries, these female-friendly industrial sectors barely have grown at all, whereas, in the nonoil-exporting MENA countries, the export-driven potential demand for female labor has increased by more than 50 percent.

FIGURE B2.2b

Export-Driven Demand for Female Labor in Various Regions over Time, 1980–2000

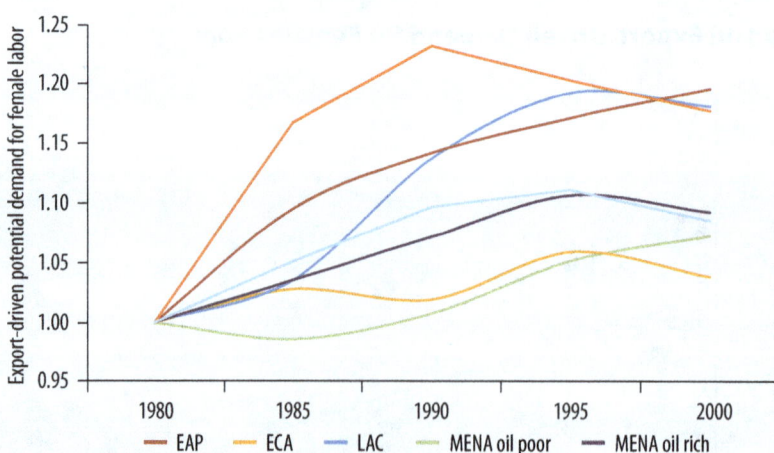

Sources: UN COMTRADE 2007; UNIDO 2009; WDI 2011 (World Bank multiple years).

Note: Female employment shares were computed by taking the average ratio of female to total employment in a given industry observed in the sample of developed and developing countries. The sample comprised Austria, Azerbaijan, Chile, Cyprus, the Arab Republic of Egypt, India, Indonesia, Ireland, Italy, Japan, Jordan, the Republic of Korea, Lithuania, Malaysia, Malta, Morocco, New Zealand, the Philippines, the Slovak Republic, Thailand, Turkey, and the United Kingdom. Due to data constraints, analysis was restricted to manufacturing industries.

a. Values in 1980 normalized to 1.

These findings suggest that other important factors explain MENA's low female labor force participation rates. A recent strand of the literature points to the importance of historical patriarchal kinship networks, which well preceded the discovery of oil in the Region. It is argued that these kinship networks, and the cultural norms associated with them, were particularly strong in the Arabian Peninsula. These networks and norms are stubbornly persistent and are associated with low present-day female labor force participation (Charrad 2009). Thus, some argue that the underlying cause is the deep cultural history rather than the recently discovered oil, the latter being purely a geographic coincidence.

Another argument that emphasizes the role of history was put forward by Alesina and others (2011). They argue that agricultural heritage, as measured by the historical use of the indigenous plough, generated entrenched gendered work norms, and therefore explain a significant amount of present-day cross-country variation in female labor force participation rates.

Landes and Landes (2001) and Inglehart and Norris (2003a, 2003b) posit yet another, but related, explanation: Islamic beliefs play a central role in lagging female empowerment in the Middle East. Although this hypothesis can be tested with data, the most commonly used proxies for Islamic beliefs—including percent of Muslims in the population and Muslim-majority country—clearly cannot account fully for the wide and "important variations among Muslim societies" (Norris 2009).

Religion unquestionably has played a significant role in the evolution of MENA's customs, social norms, and laws. However, just as in the rest of the world, within the Muslim world, there is a great diversity of outcomes for women. This diversity can be attributed in part to the local interpretation of religious law and its interaction with local cultures and legal history, factors that vary considerably across Muslim countries. Indeed, as reported in an extensive review undertaken by Offenhauer (2005), most current scholarship highlights the wide variation in Muslim women's status. The literature typically attributes greater causal importance to variations in economic structures and policies among countries, or differences in preexisting cultural values within a given country. These conclusions also echo the findings of Rauch and Kostyshak (2009). They argue that differences between the Arab world and the rest of the world in female economic participation are not due to Islam.

These findings do not mean that religion has not influenced important aspects of economic and social life in the Region. Religious norms undoubtedly have influenced the legal frameworks of MENA countries. However, the interpretations of religious laws across the Region vary significantly. These interpretations manifest in the differing regulations and norms regarding women's rights and opportunities. For instance, a woman's ability to inherit land and to directly contract a marriage without a male guardian depends on the theological school of thought prevailing in the country.[2] Even within particular schools of thought, interpretations evolve over time. Reforms that have enhanced women's participation have been crafted to suit the existing legal framework and have taken into account local customs and norms. For instance, all of the 2004 Moroccan family law reforms were achieved in consultation with, and with the endorsement of, the religious institutions.

The lack of consensus in the literature on any one causal factor of the low labor force participation of MENA women reflects the multiplicity of issues at work, their complicated interplay, and the inability of any of these factors to independently explain the MENA puzzle. The complex interactions of these factors also are evident in the analysis (figure 2.1). It measures the roles of Region-specific factors to explain female labor force participation across Regions relative to the OECD. The analysis attempts to quantify the role of oil, and religion, two of the primary explanations for MENA women's low participation put forward in the academic literature.

This section explores some of the findings. After accounting for the average influence of oil reserves and being a Muslim majority nation, the East Asia and Pacific Region is statistically indistinguishable from the OECD country average female labor force participation rate of almost 50

FIGURE 2.1

Change in Female Labor Force Participation (Relative to OECD Average)
(percent)

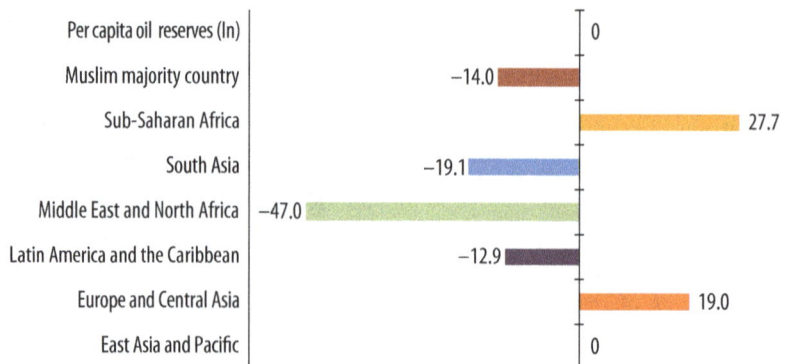

Source: Staff calculations based on WDI 2011 (World Bank multiple years).
Note: S. Asia is statistically significant at the 11 percent level.

percent. Sub-Saharan Africa has 28 percent higher female labor force participation than the OECD average. Per capita oil reserves do not have, on average, any significant impact. In contrast, belonging to a Muslim-majority country lowers female labor force participation by 14 percent relative to the OECD. Most important, there is a large unexplained effect associated with the MENA Region. Just being in MENA lowers female labor force participation relative to the OECD by 47 percent, or almost half.

MENA's singularity also is evident in the following illustrative comparison between Egypt and Indonesia. The two countries are strikingly similar in oil reserves, degree of export diversification, and potential for employing female labor (box 2.3). However, Egypt's female labor force participation rate is only half that of Indonesia. Clearly, in these two countries, norms and attitudes surrounding women and work differ in important ways. Accordingly, there may be specific gender norms, influenced in turn by historical, cultural, social, and economic factors that directly affect women's agency and potentially are far more important in explaining the Region's gender outcomes.

BOX 2.3

Egypt and Indonesia: So Near, Yet So Far

	Egypt, Arab Rep.	Indonesia
Oil reserves (BBL)	4.30	4.05
Largest export sector	Manufacture of refined petroleum products (53.25%)	Manufacture of refined petroleum products (58.18%)
Second largest export sector	Spinning, weaving, and finishing textiles (16.94%)	Production, processing, and preservation of meat, fish, fruit, vegetables, oils, and fats (7.47%)
Third largest export sector	Manufacture of wearing apparel except fur (3.34%)	Manufacture of products of wood, cork, straw, and plaiting materials (4.20%)
HH index of export concentration	0.317	0.351
Female labor need of exports	21.05%	24.50%
GDP per capita PPP (2010)	2,591	3,039

Egypt and Indonesia both are Muslim-majority countries and look very similar in their economic structures. Both countries have similar levels of oil reserves, and their largest manufacturing export sector is refined petroleum products. Both countries have strikingly similar indices of export concentration and are almost equally likely to hire women in exporting firms.

(continued on next page)

BOX 2.3 *Continued*

FIGURE B2.3a

When Jobs Are Scarce, Men Should Have More Right to a Job Than Women

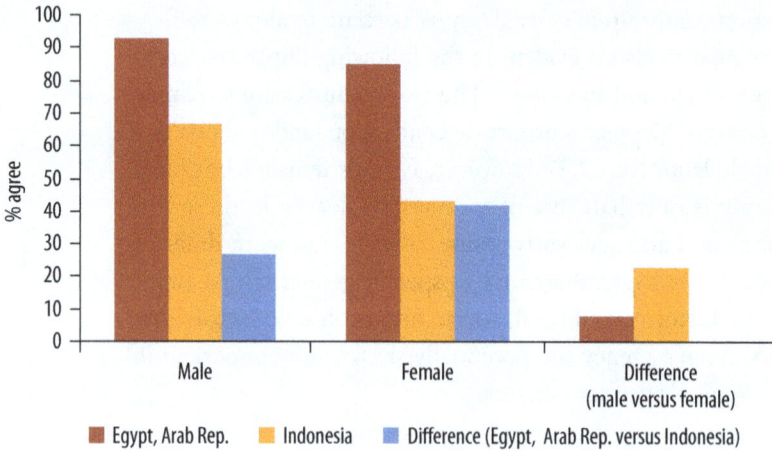

FIGURE B2.3b

Consider Work Rather or Very Important

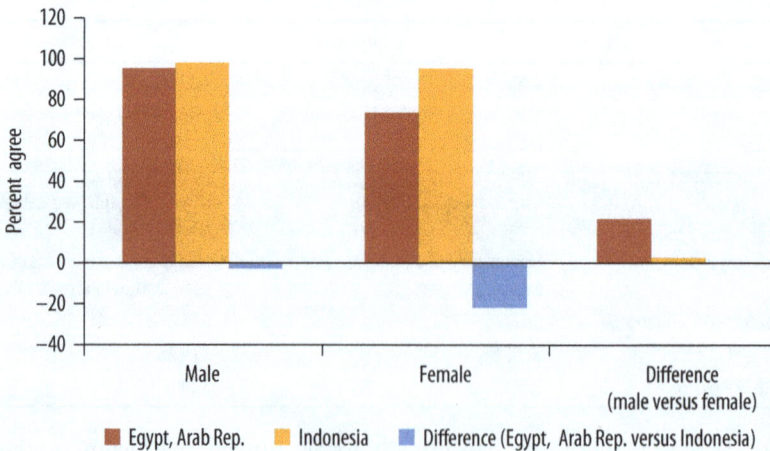

On the other hand, Egypt and Indonesia are very different in other respects. Egypt's female labor force participation is half that of Indonesia. One of the reasons that Egypt and Indonesia are so different in female labor force participation may be differences in norms relating to women and work. Evidence from the 2005 World Values Survey (WVS 2005) suggests that norms related to women's roles differ significantly among the countries.

Gender Norms Constrain Women's Roles outside the Home

A woman's main mission is to raise the kids in the best way possible. If she can balance work and home she can work. But the priority is always for her home.

—Young woman, Rafah neighborhood, Gaza Strip,
World Bank 2012, 2011

Social and cultural norms dictate the "do's and don'ts of individual every-day conduct" (Portes 2006). In the MENA Region, these norms generally place high value on women's role within the home and family and her investments in family life. These norms reflect elements of a patriarchal society in which women and men are partners in a marriage but with separate roles. Women's primary sphere of influence is perceived to be within the home (Moghadam 2004), whereas men are supposed to be the breadwinners and decision makers in the public sphere (Offenhauer 2005). These elements are not unique to MENA society but are perhaps more pronounced there than in other Regions. However, these elements are changing, as education increases and the demographic balance shifts.

The value placed on women's roles within the household is evident from data from the 2005 World Values Surveys. Based on surveys from five countries (Egypt, the Islamic Republic of Iran, Iraq, Jordan, and Morocco), perceptions of women's roles in the home, education, employment, and politics are distinctly more traditional than the global average. Nevertheless, women in these countries are more likely than men to disagree with statements such as, "When jobs are scarce, priority should be given to men." Respondents who were more educated and younger also tended to be more supportive of women's involvement in the public sphere (figure 2.2). However, while women and men in the Region generally hold very similar views, younger and more educated cohorts are less supportive of the housewife stereotype.

Survey evidence from Iraq and Morocco shows that, irrespective of marital status, women spend vastly more time on household chores and child care than do men (figure 2.3). Furthermore, married women spend almost twice as much time on these duties as unmarried women. These trends are broadly true in the rest of the world but not to such an acute degree (World Bank 2012b).

Compared with the rest of world, MENA citizens also hold less favorable views about women in leadership positions as business executives or as politicians. In MENA, only 25 percent of women and 12 percent of men between the ages of 36 and 45 disagreed that men made better business executives. The corresponding figures for women and men in the rest of

FIGURE 2.2

Respondents from MENA and around the World Who Disagree with the Following Statements about Women, Work, Education and Politics

a. Being a housewife is as fulfilling as working for pay

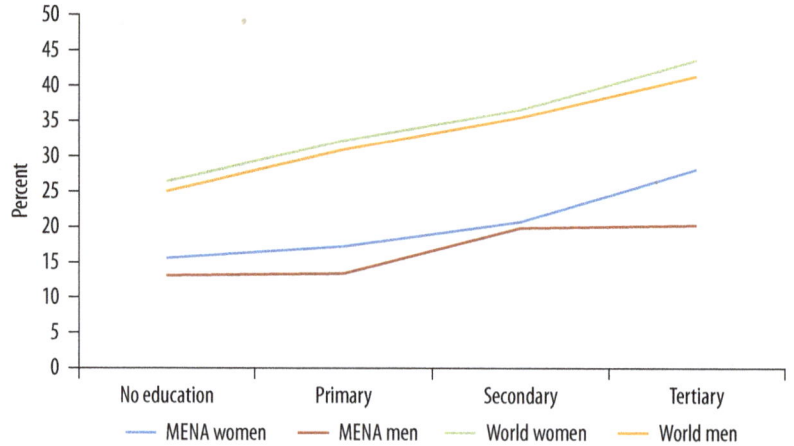

b. A university education is more important for a boy than for a girl

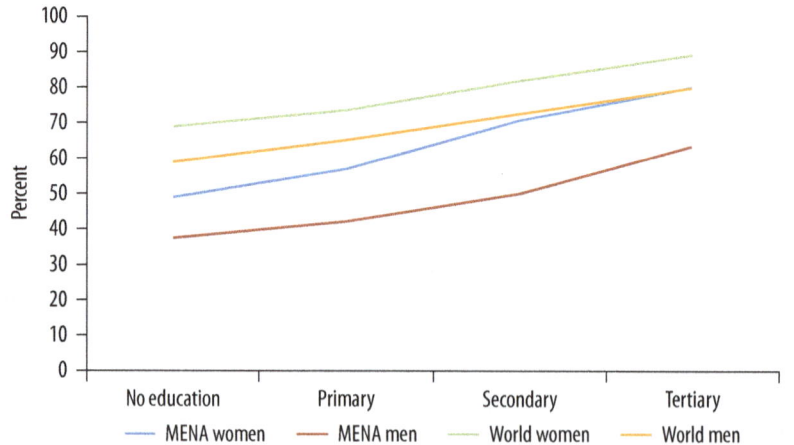

the world are 64 and 53 percent, respectively. The results are equally stark for perceptions about women as political leaders (figure 2.2). However, women and men in MENA share similar views on politics, policy priorities, and attitudes toward governance. The latter finding suggests that the gender gap in political participation does not stem from gender differences in political preferences but from deep-rooted cultural norms about the roles and capacities of women. These norms also are changing: younger and better-educated women in MENA seem to express greater confidence in women's ability to contribute in the public sphere.

FIGURE 2.2 *Continued*

c. When jobs are scarce, priority should be given to men over women

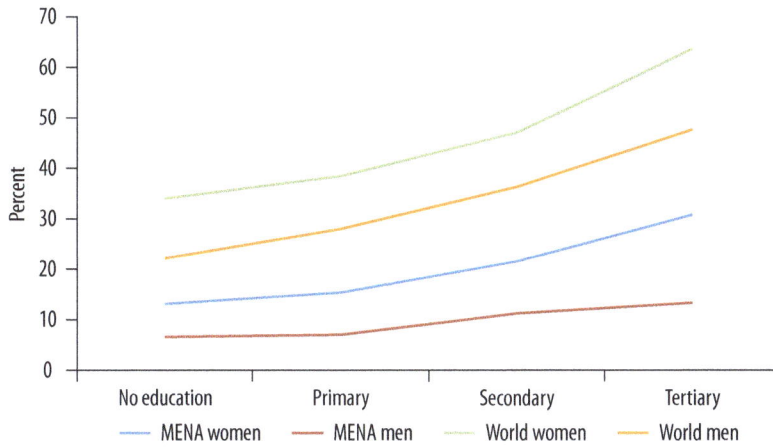

d. Men make better political leaders than women do

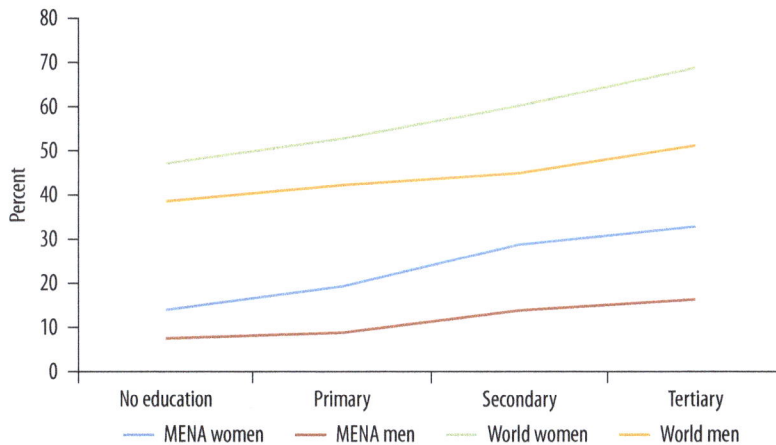

Source: WVS 2005.

Qualitative literature on gender in the Region highlights the diverse social and cultural norms that disadvantage women in many dimensions of their lives (box 2.4). Analysis of focus group discussions by Miles (2002) reveals how gender norms surrounding women's restricted mobility, household care burdens, occupational segregation, and son preference constrain women's economic participation in communities in and around Amman, Jordan. Miles reports, for example, how families more often reserve their scarce wasta (special connections) to help their educated sons, as opposed to their educated daughters, to secure good jobs. Assaud and Barsoum (2007), in their report on the major challenges related to youth employment in Egypt, demonstrate the increased occupational segrega-

FIGURE 2.3

In Iraq and Morocco, Women Spend Far More Time Than Men on Household Chores and Child Care

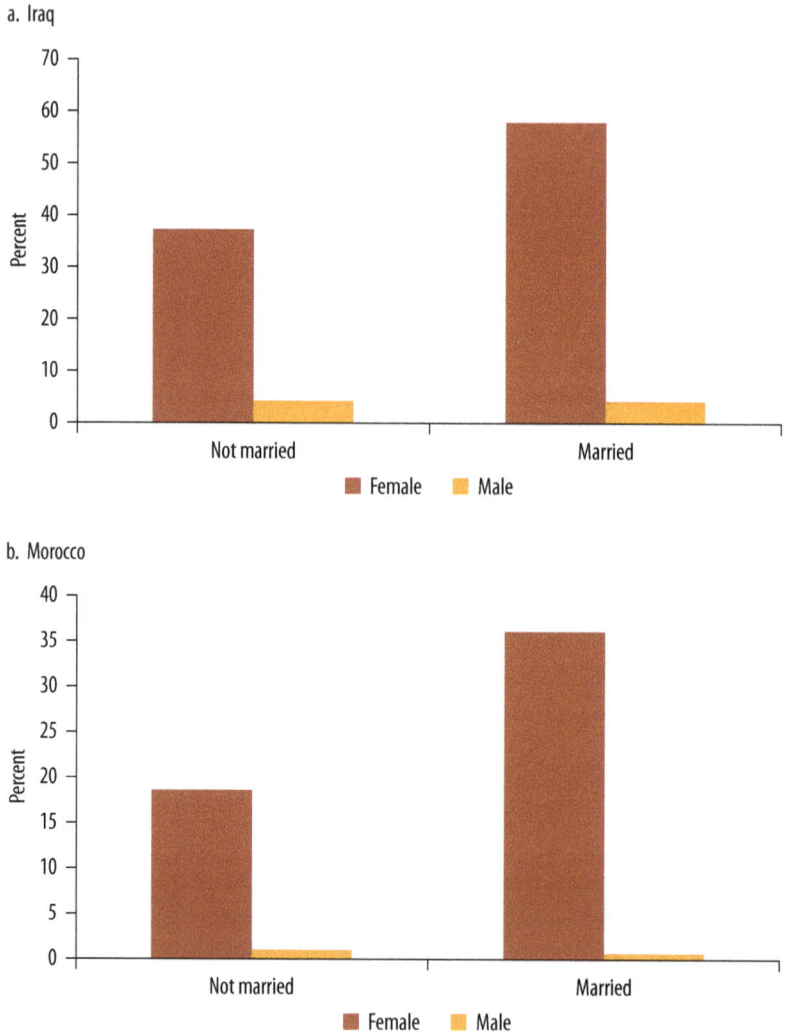

a. Iraq

b. Morocco

Source: Iraq and Morocco Household Surveys (appendixes A and C).

tion along gender lines since the oil boom (and the dampening effects this has had on female wages), and how fears of workplace harassment, especially in smaller workplaces, discourage many women from working in less traditional jobs.

Evolving Norms and Marriage

Despite restrictive gender norms, women do aspire to employment. In a 2010 World Bank survey of Jordanian female community college gradu-

BOX 2.4

BOX 2.4

Little Mercy for Working Women: Palestinian Territories

It was widely agreed by women and men in focus group discussions in the Palestinian Territories that it would be quite unlikely for a woman to take any kind of work that required a distant commute. Travel would interfere with women's household duties and expose them to risks of harassment unless chaperoned. Yet, in the men's focus group in an urban community of the West Bank, a 39-year-old trader confided how other important pressures having to do with men maintaining a dominant status and the low priority accorded to women's economic roles also may be keeping women from entering the labor force:

> A man can go anywhere to work and . . . gets jealous of his sister if she goes to a nearby place to work. So how do you think it will happen that she can go to a faraway place? . . . But the

man's responsibilities are different. He has to work; otherwise he will never build his home or get married. But for the girl it is different . . .

Similarly, a man from another urban neighborhood of the West Bank argued that the lack of public safety for women is a troubling consequence of the transition underway in gender norms: "Women have just started entering society, so the man is still trying to maintain his control." The young men's group from this same neighborhood similarly posited that a woman encounters ongoing harassment and low wages because she is "not able to speak up and defend herself because she is weak." "And as you know," added a 21-year-old university student, "our customs and traditions don't have mercy."

Source: Palestinian Territories Qualitative Assessment for 2012 WDR (World Bank 2012b, 44, forthcoming).

ates, 92 percent said they planned to work after graduation, and 76 percent said they expected to work full-time.[3]

These statements are consistent with attitudes reflected in the 2005 World Values Surveys in which 80 percent of women in Egypt and Jordan disagreed with the statements, "A woman with a full-time job cannot be a good mother" or "Having a full-time job interferes with a woman's ability to have a good life with her husband." These views do not change for married women (figure 2.4).

A 2011 follow-up survey of the Jordan NOW graduates found surprising results. Although there was no change by marital status in their desire to work, employment outcomes were strikingly different. Compared with 21 percent of single women and 14 percent of engaged women, only 7 percent of married women reported being employed. These results are consistent with labor force participation rates across the Region (figure 2.5).

FIGURE 2.4

Number Who Agree That "Being a Housewife Is Just as Fulfilling as Working for Pay"

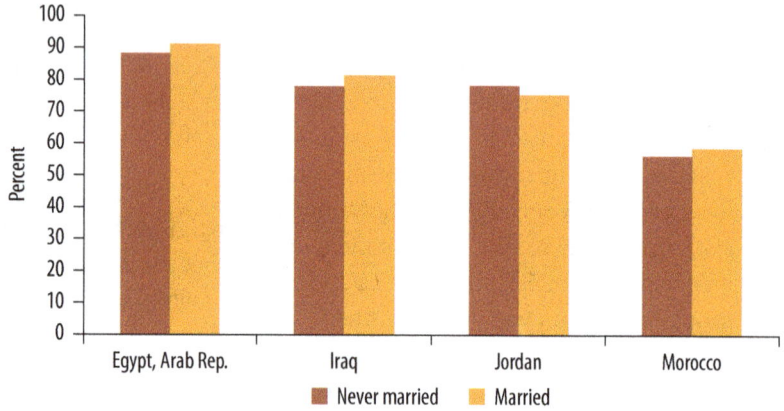

Source: WVS 2005.

FIGURE 2.5

Labor Force Participation of Women by Marital Status
(Ages 15–64)

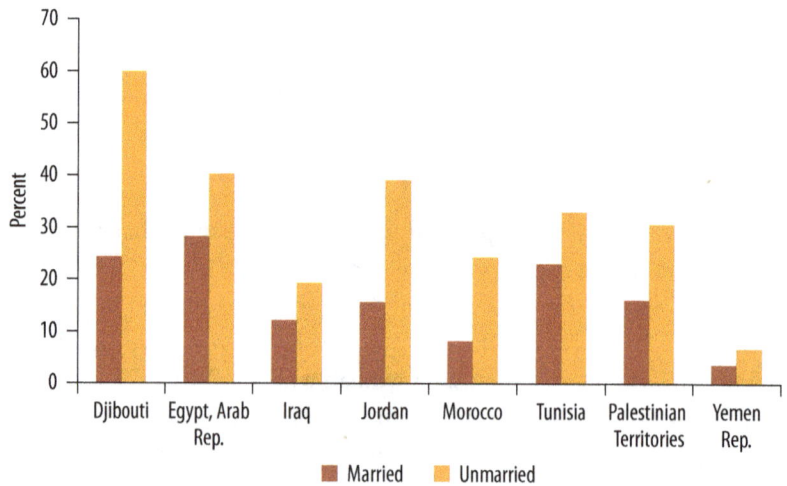

Source: Household surveys (appendixes A and C).

The "marital-status gap" in labor force participation (relative difference in labor force participation between married and never-married women) ranges from 30 percent in Egypt to 70 percent in Morocco. This same statistic is a mere 9 percent in the United States and 14 percent in France. Thus, even for women who wish to participate in the

---

BOX 2.5

Community Sanctions and Social Norms: Evidence from the Republic of Yemen and the Palestinian Territories

Focus groups conducted in the Republic of Yemen and Palestinian Territories for the 2012 WDR brought to life how community sanctions play a strong role in maintaining social norms. According to a young man from a small village in the Republic of Yemen, "If the woman's father or husband is alive, it is shameful for her to work, and the community would see her in a bad way, even if she was hundred years old."

Women and men across generations also expressed deep concerns about women being exposed to verbal and physical abuse while traveling in public or while working in mixed-sex workplaces (box 2.3). The consequences of such attacks were harmful not only for the victim but also for her fam-

ily's reputation. "We are afraid for our sister," replied a 14-year-old boy from the West Bank when asked about the likelihood that a woman could take a job outside their urban neighborhood. "Our sister is our honor." Similarly, young women from an urban community confided that ". . . a boy's reputation can be fixed; a girl's can't," to explain why they must confer closely with their family about any employment decision. These young women added, "Most girls would behave immorally if they find someone to encourage them." Explanations such as this shed light on how deeply internalized social norms can be and how they may be enforced even by those who are disadvantaged by them.

Sources: World Bank 2012a, forthcoming.

---

economic sphere and manage both family duties and a job, marital status seems to alter their opportunities. One possible explanation for the marital-status gap may be that, after a woman's marriage, social norms concerning her role outside the home are enforced more strongly by her family and society. Community sanctions can play a strong role in enforcing norms (box 2.5).

There is evidence that, in the absence of strong community sanctions, women are better able to pursue their employment ambitions and aspirations. Figure 2.6 reveals that not only are labor force participation rates among female immigrants from MENA to the United States much higher but also the marital gap is much narrower.

Furthermore, an earlier exposure to an immigrant's destination country's culture is strongly correlated with a narrowing of the marital gap (figures 2.7 and 2.8). In both France and the United States, there is a significant difference between the marital gap for women who immigrated during their adulthood and second-generation female immigrants.

FIGURE 2.6

Labor Force Participation of MENA Female Immigrants to the United States

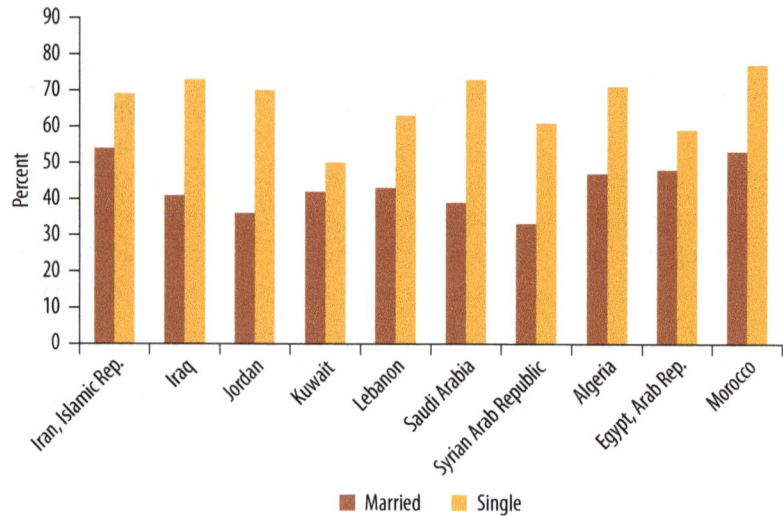

Sources: Staff calculations based on 5% US Census in 2000; ACS surveys 2001–09 (US Census Bureau).

In both France and the US, the marital gap for these two group's decreased by more than half.

It may be argued that the changing employment outcomes reflect a simple selection bias: women who move away from the MENA Region are the same women who would have worked had they stayed in MENA. However, it is unlikely that selection bias, which would be systematically evident in different immigrant characteristics, explains much of the story. The female labor force participation rates for MENA emigrants do not differ dramatically from those of other immigrants to France and the United States. Moreover in these two countries, the changing trend across generations toward a narrower gap does not differ significantly between emigrants from MENA and elsewhere (figures 2.7 and 2.8).

In addition, marital rates for emigrants closely mirror marital rates in MENA. Female emigrants from MENA who live in the United States are as highly educated as their counterparts in the Region, whereas in France they are less educated. Thus, the narrowing trend of the marital gap between immigrants to the United States and France suggests that, in an environment with job opportunities, greater mobility, and limited social sanctions, married women are better able to translate their aspirations into reality. This finding points to the important influence of deep-rooted social and cultural norms. These norms, in turn, can influence and be reinforced by legal constraints to women's mobility and agency.

FIGURE 2.7

Marital Gap in Female Labor Force Participation of Emigrants from MENA

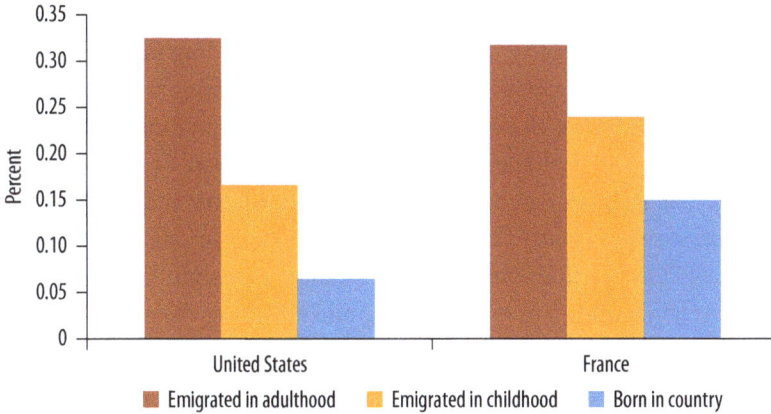

Sources: World Bank staff calculations based on the 5% US Census in 2000 and ACS surveys 2001–09; French Enquête emploi en continu 2009.

FIGURE 2.8

Marital Gap in Female Labor Force Participation of Emigrants from Other Regions

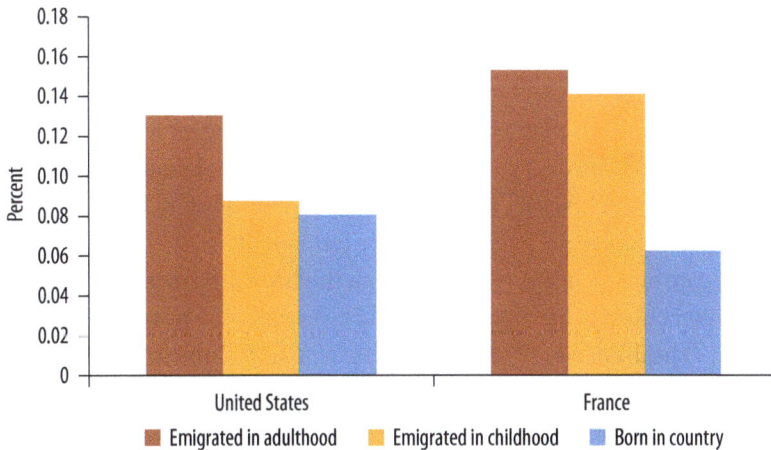

Sources: World Bank staff calculations based on the 5 percent US Census in 2000 and ACS surveys 2001–09; French Enquête emploi en continu 2009.

Equality under the Law and Its Enforcement Are Critical for Women's Agency

The role of the law in institutionalizing social norms cannot be underestimated. When the institutional framework formalizes unequal rights, male authority over the everyday decisions, actions, and movements of the female members of the household becomes state condoned, limiting women's choices and participation in society.

Almost all MENA countries have constitutional clauses setting out the equality of citizens, and many have ratified international conventions affirming gender equality. Nevertheless, laws, including family and personal, often differentiate between the sexes to reinforce traditional gender roles within the household and in the wider community (box 2.6). Family and personal laws not only impact a woman's role within her family but also can determine her access to property and her ability to function independently. Labor and pension laws also can limit women's options. This section outlines some of these constraints and the challenges facing women in implementing and enforcing their legal rights.

Legal Systems Differ Widely and Derive from Multiple Sources

Legal constraints to women's equality are not unique to the MENA Region. For instance, spousal permission for a wife to work continued to be

---

BOX 2.6

UN Convention on the Elimination of All Forms of Discrimination against Women

The Convention on the Elimination of All Forms of Discrimination against Women (CEDAW) is an international convention that was adopted by the UN General Assembly in 1979 and came into force in 1981. States ratifying the convention are required to enshrine gender equality in their domestic legislation, repeal all discriminatory provisions in their laws, and enact new provisions to guard against discrimination against women. Since coming into force, CEDAW has become a benchmark for a country's progress on gender rights that can be used by its policymakers and civil society advocates, and the international community. Ratification demonstrates a member country's positive commitment to prohibit and eliminate discrimination against women and to promote the progressive implementation of the articles of the convention in its domestic legislative framework.

Aside from the Islamic Republic of Iran, all countries in MENA have ratified CEDAW.[1] Libya and Tunisia also have ratified the Optional Protocol. It enables individuals or groups of women to submit claims to the CEDAW Committee about violations of rights protected under CEDAW. The protocol also permits the committee to initiate inquiries into serious recurring violations in member countries.

However, implementation of the laws has been a challenge. In some signatory

BOX 2.6 *Continued*

countries, ratification has achieved limited de facto change. For example, the Republic of Yemen ratified CEDAW in 1984 but, since then, has made little progress in reforming its family and citizenship laws to conform to the convention. Married women in the Republic of Yemen still need their spouses' permission to work, and Yemeni men can legally restrict their wives' and daughters' movements. Until recently, most of the MENA signatories also had reservations about key articles covering women's equality within the household, such as nationality, freedom of mobility, choice of residence, and equality in marriage and family life.

Due in large part to international pressure and campaigns by women's groups, some countries have made progress in implementing CEDAW and on lifting reservations. In May 2009, the Government of Jordan declared that it was lifting its reservations relating to freedom of mobility and choice of residence.[2] In 2008, both Algeria and Egypt officially removed their reservations to the CEDAW articles on nationality laws, which enable mothers married to non-nationals to pass on their citizenship to their children.[3] In addition, in 2008, after a 14-year campaign by Morocco's civil so-

ciety organizations (CSOs), Morocco announced its intention to lift all reservations to CEDAW. In August 2011, Tunisia's transitional government adopted a draft decree lifting all reservations to CEDAW. However, the decree retained a general declaration that Tunisia "shall not take any organizational or legislative decision which would conflict with the provisions of Chapter 1 of the Tunisian Constitution." Meanwhile, the governments of Morocco and Tunisia have yet to lodge any official documentation with the UN related to these changes.

As a number of countries in the Maghreb redraft their constitutions over the coming few years, it remains to be seen whether CEDAW will help secure constitutional changes that protect women's rights. At consultation meetings held in Tunis in September 2011, participants expressed concerns that the present ambiguity about CEDAW's status and the effectiveness of its implementation could impede future reform. In the aftermath of the very recent revolutions, sentiment in the Region about women's rights is unclear since much of the progress made in the last decade (for example, in Egypt and Tunisia) was prominently linked to the former regimes.

Sources: Association Démocratique des Femmes du Maroc 2009; Kelly and Breslin 2010; Khalife 2011; UN OHCHR 2010; World Bank 2004a, 2009b.

Notes:

1. Due to its political status, the Palestinian Territories is not eligible to ratify CEDAW, but the Palestinian Authority's President Mahmoud Abbas symbolically signed CEDAW in 2009.

2. Jordan still has reservations to Article 9.2 relating to nationality; Article 16.1 c relating to financial relief upon divorce; Article 16.1 d relating to equal rights of parents vis-à-vis their children; and Article 16.1 g relating to right to choose family name, profession, and occupation.

3. Egypt established a committee of high-level government delegates to study the withdrawal of its reservations.

FIGURE 2.9

Timeline of Legal Reforms in Selected Countries, 1931–2004

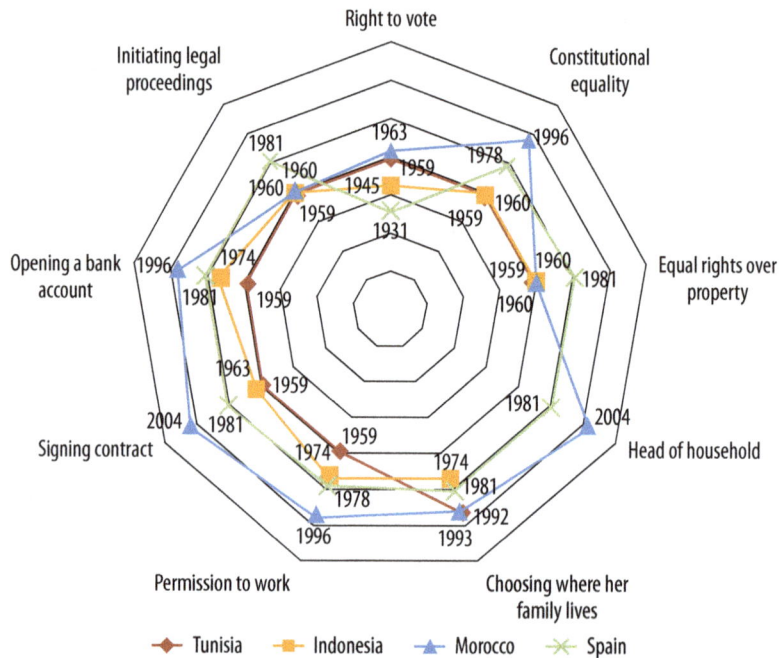

Source: Women's Legal and Economic Opportunities data supported by UK DFID in partnership with Women, Business and the Law.

required in Spain until 1979 and in Switzerland until 1984. In East Asia and Pacific, Indonesia repealed the provision in 1973. In MENA, Tunisia rescinded spousal permission to work as early as 1959 and Morocco as recently as 2004. In South Asia, Bangladesh and Pakistan never had such a legal requirement (figure 2.9).

The legal framework and institutions in the MENA Region have evolved from a plethora of sources (Gautier 2005): religious law and customary law[4]; colonial legislation (French Napoleonic codes and English statutes and common law); constitutional law; international conventions; and regional treaties.[5] For example, the post-independence Jordanian nationality laws were modeled on British laws, whereas the Lebanese nationality laws were based on the French Law Decree of January 15, 1925 (Hijab 2002). This plurality of legal systems is not unique to the MENA Region; practically every legal system in the world is legally pluralistic in some manner.

Interpretations of religious law vary significantly in the Region—and even within countries. Interpretation arises from the theological school of thought that prevails within a particular community. For example, the inheritance of land or the need for a guardian's consent in marriage is determined differently across the Maliki and Ja'fari theological schools. Lebanon has 18 state-recognized religions, including different Muslim and Christian denominations. Each of these communities adheres to its own set of personal laws.

Plurality extends to the implementation and enforcement of laws as well. A range of formal and informal institutions can exist to deal with disputes including formal civil and criminal courts, religious courts, and mediatory bodies such as informal family councils. Understanding legal pluralism is key to bringing about legislative reform in the Region and improving the implementation of such change. In Morocco, a survey of family courts revealed that 68 percent of women who had suffered from domestic violence preferred to resolve matters within the family. The women who did use the formal justice system preferred to access the family courts and ask for divorces rather than to approach the police and bring proceedings in the criminal courts.

Legal reform can take its cue from shifts in social norms or, conversely in some cases, it can aim deliberately to bring about major changes in these social norms. The initial push for legislative change often comes from the urban, educated elite communities and can take time to extend to rural communities. Tunisia was an early reformer in the Region and embedded transformational changes immediately after independence, removing many vestiges of patriarchal power from its personal code in the late 1950s (UN Women 2011). More recently, other countries, such as Morocco, have overhauled their codes supported by broad-based consensus building (box 2.7). Although discriminatory legislation remains, a major challenge for these countries is the implementation and enforcement of the laws.

BOX 2.7

Political Economy of Reform in Tunisia and Morocco: Momentum for Change

Tunisia is hailed throughout the Arab world as an early reformer of its laws and as a legislative model for gender equality. The first phase of reforms came immediately following independence in 1956 and was seen as government driven. The intention was to create a modern sovereign state; the driving force was nationalism. The first phase of reform empowered women and enabled them to contest and refine outstanding discriminatory legislation. The new Personal Code outlawed

(continued on next page)

BOX 2.7   *Continued*

polygamy, prohibited the husband from unilaterally repudiating his wife, and allowed women to file for divorce. Divorce proceedings had to go before a court, and both women and men had equal rights to initiate divorce. The code established the principle of alimony and improved women's rights to custody (although men retained guardianship). A woman could contract her own marriage, and marital rights over the wife were abolished. Married women could travel and work without permission from their husbands.

Top-down reforms may not necessarily achieve all their intended outcomes within all sections of the community, but they can generate a new climate for the next level of debate. They also can create enabling conditions for new networks of women to emerge. Women's groups had emerged in the late 1970s and were firmly established in the 1980s and 1990s. One of the first associations was Club Tahar al Haddad, a forum for women professionals, such as academicians, lawyers, and journalists. Other groups emerged, including female sections of trade unions, political parties, and informal networks such as business associations and religious groups. In Tunisia's second wave of reforms in 1993, women's organizations played an active role. The main focus of the campaign was to reform discriminatory citizenship laws, which prevented a woman married to a non-national from passing her nationality to her children. These laws were successfully reformed.

The Morocco family law reform of 2004 came after 2 decades of relentless campaigning by women's groups. The 1957 version, Mudawana, or Family Code, was modified partially in 1993 in relation to polygamy and guardianship, but discriminatory provisions remained. Women's groups mobilized support by organizing discussion groups and workshops, lobbying parliament, and educating the public on the benefits of the reform. Key to the ultimate success of the campaign was the political support given by King Mohammed VI and his predecessors, senior political leaders, and religious leaders who provided theological backing for the changes.

Under the terms of Morocco's new 2004 Family Code, the husband and wife are jointly responsible for the family; adult women are entitled to self-guardianship; the right to divorce is granted to both women and men and is subject to court supervision; and there can be divorce by mutual consent. The wife can stipulate a ban on polygamy in her marriage contract. Even in the absence of such a clause, polygamy is subject to judicial approval and in effect becomes very difficult. The wife retains custody of her children, even upon remarriage in certain cases. Finally, the reform raised the minimum marriage age for girls from 15 to 18.

Sources: Bordat and Kouzzi 2004; Charrad 2007; Ennaji 2009; Moghadam and Roudi-Fahimi 2005.

Legal Constraints to Women's Agency in MENA

Moderator:
> In many countries, laws have been changing to provide women with more rights. What new laws of this kind are you aware of?

Women's focus group in a village in Yemen:
> We heard of the law limiting marriage.
> We haven't heard of these laws.
> I don't have a radio.

> World Bank, forthcoming

For many countries in the Region, reforms have been more piecemeal, with progress in certain areas and stagnation (or even regression) in others. In determining women's participation in the public sphere, certain aspects of the letter, interpretation, and implementation of the law are particularly salient.

Some of these aspects directly affect and limit women's agency within their households. For example, restricting a woman's mobility and access to capital can profoundly influence her ability to participate outside the home and the range of options available to her. These aspects also can limit opportunities for her family and investments in her children. Women, Business and the Law 2012: Removing Barriers to Economic Inclusion looks at gender differentiations in legal treatment that impact on women's participation in the economy (World Bank 2011b). These differentiations are, in effect, discriminatory laws that constrain women's access to institutions, access to and use of property, ability to get a job, incentives to work, ability to build credit, and access to the court system. All 14 MENA countries covered in the report have one or more legal differential (or discriminatory law) related to women's accessing institutions or accessing property. Married women in particular can be affected by legal constraints that pertain to marriage. Figure 2.10 illustrates the high prevalence of some of these constraints in the MENA Region.

Mobility and choice of work

• *Legal guardianship and head of household status*—A range of countries in the Region still retain many laws limiting female mobility and autonomy within the household. Fathers and husbands are still the legal gatekeepers of women's and girls' activities (box 2.8). Applying for a passport,[6] traveling outside the country,[7] working outside the home, and deciding to marry all can require male permission.[8] The delegation of ultimate authority to a male relative can follow a woman throughout her

FIGURE 2.10

Most Common Restrictions for Married Women in Five Regions

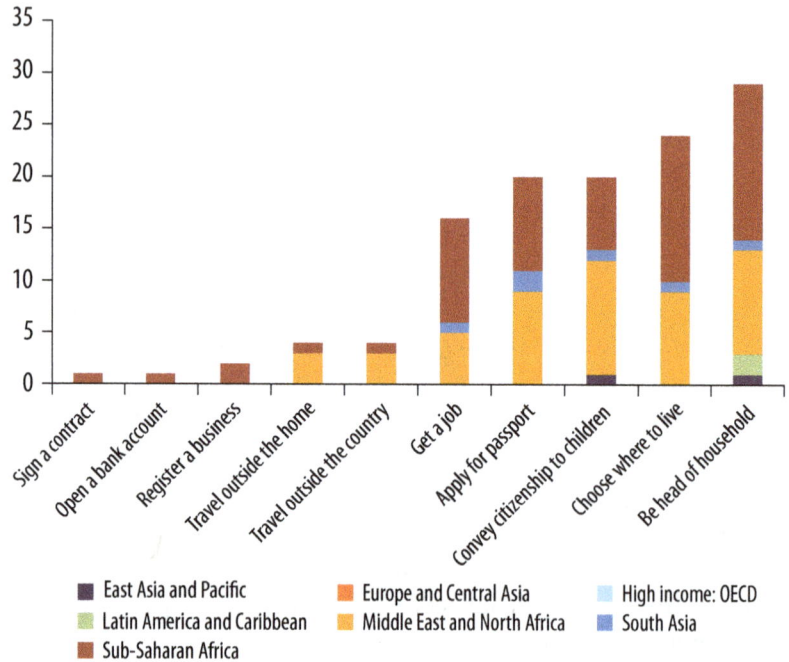

Source: WBL database (World Bank 2012b).

BOX 2.8

The Family Book in Jordan: A Record of Guardianship

In accordance with the Jordanian Civil Status Law 9 (2001), a women's guardianship must be recorded in the family book (daftar al-a'ilah). After marriage, the woman is transferred to her husband's family book. The daftar is needed for nearly all official arrangements, including voting for or running for elected office, the registration of children for schools or universities, obtaining civil service jobs, and access to social services. Only recently has legislation allowed widows and divorcees to start their own daftar books. However, the hold of guardianship remains. Divorcees and widows under the age of 40 still are considered to be dependent on their guardians; and if they refuse that guardianship, they are not entitled to any financial maintenance.

Sources: Euromed Gender Equality Programme 2010a; Moghadam and Roudi-Fahimi 2006.

whole life, and the legal constraints that pertain to marriage can entrench and exacerbate the lack of female autonomy. In the Islamic Republic of Iran and the Syrian Arab Republic, a husband can withdraw financial support if his wife goes out to work without his permission. In both countries, a wife is legally required to obey her husband, in return for which, the husband is legally obliged to maintain her. In Qatar, a wife needs her husband's permission to apply for a driver's license, although she can now apply for a passport on her own. In Jordan, an unmarried woman over the age of 18 does not need the permission of her guardian to apply for a passport, but, under Article 29 of the 1969 Passports Law, a married woman did need the permission of her male guardian or husband. In 2003, there had been an effort to amend the law by the Interim Passports Act. However, the proposed amendment did not go through the proper constitutional channels so it was not passed by parliament. In June 2012, the Jordanian Ministry of Interior declared that a new proposal to amend Article 29 of the 1969 Passports Law would be presented to the government. This proposed legislation is under review (Keilani 2012; Malkawi 2012). If it is approved, married women will be able to apply for passports in the same way as do married men. However, under the Personal Status Law, a husband can still bar his wife from leaving the country with any children of the marriage (Kelly and Breslin 2010).

Over half of the MENA countries require the presence of a wali, or guardian, to conclude the marriage contract of a woman, whereas there is no such requirement for a man (World Bank 2004a). In Algeria, recent changes have rendered the guardian's presence largely symbolic, but it is still a condition. Guardianship can extend to areas beyond marriage, and, in some countries, a woman's ability to be recognized legally as head of the household can be very limited or nonexistent.

Previously, all single women in Kuwait, including widows and divorcees, as well as all women married to non-nationals, were legally ineligible for government loans for housing. Such loans were offered only to Kuwaiti males. In September 2011, the legislation was changed to allow, for the first time, widows, divorcees, women married to non-nationals, and unmarried women over the age of 40 to qualify for housing loans.

In October 2011, the state-owned Kuwaiti Savings and Credit Bank announced that it was accepting public housing loan applications (Kuwait News Agency 2011). The measure will open opportunities for many Kuwaiti women. This group is estimated to comprise 27,500 divorcees, 21,200 widows, 11,000 women married to non-nationals, and 8,600 unmarried women over the age of 40. Married women and single women under the age of 40 will continue to be ineligible for the government loan schemes, because only their husbands or male guardians qualify.

Usually, only heads of households are eligible for government welfare benefits. In Jordan and Kuwait, only widows or divorcees can be defined as female heads of household, excluding, for example, women married to unemployed men and deserted wives.

• *Inequality in the workplace*—The majority of countries in the MENA Region have laws against discrimination in the workplace and legislation mandating equal work for equal pay. In practice, the enforcement of non-discrimination laws is difficult. The equal pay provisions are undermined by inequalities in non-wage benefits (which usually are allocated to the husband). In Algeria and Kuwait, the state supplements family incomes for public sector employees with generous subsidies (box 3.1), but these benefits are paid only to husbands. Women are excluded from these subsidies even if only the wife works in the public sector. In such a case, the family is deprived of this extra income.

Many women are employed in the informal sector (for example, as domestic or agricultural workers) so are not covered by the labor codes. This lack of protection leaves them vulnerable to exploitation and unfair employment practices. Jordan recently amended its labor code to include domestic workers and agricultural workers, thus guaranteeing these groups the monthly payment of salaries and minimum wages, sick leave, and a maximum 10-hour working day (UN Women 2011).

Sexual harassment lawsuits also are difficult to pursue and are rarely an option for women, who are afraid of being stigmatized by their communities. Four countries in the region—Algeria, Iraq, Morocco, and Tunisia— have legislation sanctioning sexual harassment in the workplace by criminalizing such behavior and allowing women to prosecute claims in court (UN Women 2011). As in many countries, implementation and enforcement of these laws are weak.

• *Maternity and child care provisions*—All countries in the MENA Region provide for some form of maternity leave, and some countries have provisions for childcare. These policies can help married women remain in the workplace, or return after pregnancy. On the other hand, mandatory provision of maternity leave and child care facilities can disincentivize employers to hire women. Employers may avoid providing child care by keeping the total number of female employees just below the number that triggers the obligation. Jordan recently reformed its social insurance law by removing the responsibility for financing maternity leave benefits from employers and instead funding these benefits by a payroll tax on all workers, male and female.

• *Restrictions on where and when to work*—Labor laws can limit opportunities for women by not allowing their entry into industries that are deemed dangerous, hazardous, or morally harmful to their reputations. Restrictions on night work also bar women from making their own decisions as to where and when they work. These restrictions can begin as early as 7 p.m. Provisions restricting night work and working in dangerous industries ostensibly were designed to protect women and are rooted in articles of International Labour Organization conventions that have been adopted internationally. However, the heavy impact of these provisions is compounded by social norms relating to segregation. The "morally harmful" clause in these laws gives countries wide discretion to restrict women's entry into certain sectors. Of the 113 countries surveyed by the Economist Intelligence Unit, 11 had restrictions on female employment in jobs that were considered "against women's morals" (UN Women 2011). This clause is particularly prevalent in the MENA Region. Egypt, Kuwait, Morocco, Saudi Arabia, Syria, the United Arab Emirates, and the Republic of Yemen all have labor restrictions on work that may be "morally harmful" or could affect women's social standing. The ultimate effect of all of these types of restrictions can be to prevent women from participating in substantial sectors of the economy.

• *Laws that impact on women's entrepreneurship*—Even gender-neutral business regulations can have differential outcomes on women due to their interplay with discriminatory personal laws. Access to finance often requires collateral, and collateral requirements for loans typically are limited to immovable assets. Requirements for collateral can bar women entrepreneurs, who own less land than men due to cultural norms and face legal constraints on ownership of household property. Women are more likely to own movable assets, such as jewelry. However, these assets rarely are acceptable as collateral for business loans. Furthermore, if their past borrowing has been on a small scale, their lack of credit history may affect female small business owners who wish to expand their businesses. Access to finance is critical to the future growth of a business. Reform in this area should identify and target constraints that specifically affect women (Simavi and others 2010; IFC 2011b).

Agency within the home and financial vulnerability

• *Inadequate minimum age of marriage*—In several MENA countries, the legal minimum age of marriage is lower for girls[9] than for boys. Some countries have no legal minimum age (UNHCR 2008). Delaying marriage potentially can improve a woman's decision-making power within the household by enabling her to satisfy her aspirations for education and choice of work, and be more mature when she chooses her partner (Jensen and Thornton 2003, 9–19).

Some countries have reformed their laws to raise the minimum age of marriage. In Algeria, as a result of 2005 amendments to the Family Code, the minimum age is now 19 for both girls and boys. Jordan raised the minimum age for both sexes to 18. However, the law still allows judges to permit the marriages of girls aged 15–18. Syria differentiates the marriage age for girls and boys as 16 and 18, respectively. However, a judge can authorize the marriage of girls as young as 13 and boys as young as 15, if either the father or grandfather, acting as wali, consents; and the parties appear physically capable; and there is fear for the girl's "morals and reputation." In Syria, an estimated 3.4 percent of women marry before age 15, with even higher figures in some governorates (5.2 percent in Dara'a) (Euromed Gender Equality Programme 2010b). In Bahrain and the Islamic Republic of Iran, legislation set the minimum age of marriage for girls at 15 (2007) and 13 (2002), respectively, with the possibility of girls being married at even earlier age with the court's permission.[10] These laws fall far below the general recommendations of the CEDAW Committee regarding the interpretation of Article 16 of the CEDAW Convention, which relates to setting a minimum age of marriage.[11]

• *Protection against domestic violence*—The ability to leave a marriage or to seek some other form of protection becomes even more important when a woman is being subjected to domestic violence. Egypt, Jordan, and Morocco have made some legislative progress is this area (UN Women 2011). Implementation of these domestic violence laws often is a problem, because in MENA, as in other Regions, women are reluctant to pursue claims. In Jordan, "honor killings" and the light sentences handed out to male perpetrators have been highlighted by recent ongoing reforms. Under the 1960 Jordanian Penal Code, killings carried out in a "fit of rage" attracted a maximum prison sentence of only 2 years. In 2009, to deal with honor crimes, the Jordanian government restructured its legal system to create special courts that could impose longer prison sentences. Recent cases have seen sentences of 10 years being given to some perpetrators (Kelly and Breslin 2010).

• *Citizenship laws*—In multiple countries—including the Islamic Republic of Iran, Jordan, Kuwait, Lebanon, Oman, Saudi Arabia, Syria, and the United Arab Emirates—women cannot pass on citizenship to their children or non-national spouses in the same way as men (World Bank 2011b). These discriminatory citizenship laws prevent women from accessing welfare and educational benefits for their children, alter the inheritance rights of their families, and limit employment opportunities for their husbands. In several countries, NGOs and civil society organizations have lobbied to change these laws. Since 1996, Tunisia has allowed women married to foreign husbands to pass on nationality to their children and, in certain circumstances, to their husbands. This law was further amended in 2010 to give unequivocal rights of citizenship to the child, removing the father's veto power, which had remained under earlier amendments. Similarly, Algeria and Iraq have reformed their laws (Van Wass 2010). Egypt and Morocco have changed their laws to allow such women to pass on their nationality to their children just as men can do, but not to their husbands (World Bank 2011b).

In January 2012, the government of Saudi Arabia announced new measures to deal with anomalies regarding citizenship through naturalization. Stories in the media had highlighted cases of children who were effectively stateless due to the application of the previous Saudi rules combined with other countries' rules about naturalization or dual citizenship. Anomalies were particularly severe in cases of divorce. In general, citizenship is transferred only through a Saudi father. Under the new rules, children of Saudi women who are married to non-nationals can have their children considered for citizenship by the Directorate of Naturalization branch of the Ministry of Civil Affairs under certain conditions, one of which is to have two generations of Saudi citizenship on their father's side (Saudi Gazette 2012). Even though the criteria differ depending on whether the applicant is a son or daughter, the new rules have opened up potential avenues for citizenship for children of such marriages.

• *Limited access to marital property*—The most common form of property ownership within the MENA Region is a separate property regime, in which the each spouse retains control over only the personal assets that s/he owned before, and acquired during the course of, the marriage. This regime limits women's ability to borrow for business purposes, since communal assets cannot be used as collateral for loans. If the wife does not enter the marriage with significant personal assets and does not work during the course of the marriage, her personal wealth may be very limited. This lack of assets leaves her vulnerable in the event of divorce or the death of her husband. Within the separate property regime, this situation can be averted if a wife's nonmonetary contribution (looking after children and the welfare of the family) is recognized in the event of a divorce. In this spirit, in 1992, the Islamic Republic of Iran reformed its Civil Code to provide women with monetary compensation for their past domestic work if their husbands divorce them without cause.[12]

Some countries provide the option of a community of property regime. This regime, which applies only to monogamous marriages,[13] stipulates that all property acquired during the course of a marriage is jointly owned.[14] On divorce or the death of her husband, a woman automatically is entitled to 50 percent of the property or estate. Algeria, Morocco, and Tunisia allow spouses to opt into such a regime. By making it the default option, as is the case in Indonesia and Turkey, more women would have access to this regime without facing the difficult and possibly confrontational task of explicitly demanding it. On the other hand, if a woman is independently wealthy and/or is likely to earn a substantial income during the course of the marriage, she should consider opting for a separate property regime. If her husband is likely to face bankruptcy proceedings, a separate property regime also may be more advantageous to the wife. All polygamous marriages are subject to a separate property regime.

• *Lack of exit options in marriage*—A woman's ability to leave a marriage often is more restricted than her husband's. In general, she must establish that she falls under one or more of a limited set of categories (that can be difficult to prove), whereas a man is free to divorce without any such grounds. Women can stipulate a unilateral right to divorce (*isma*) in their marriage contracts, but, in practice, social pressure means that divorce based on this right is rarely carried out. Reforms in Egypt have opened the doors to unilateral no-fault divorces (*khula*) for women, but on the condition that the wife forfeits all financial entitlements and returns the dowry. Although khula can fast-track notoriously slow divorce proceedings, they place women in precarious financial positions and thus often are considered a rich woman's law. Custody laws also determine the level of maintenance that a divorced woman receives. Major reforms to this effect have been passed in Morocco and Tunisia, where the law now asserts equal rights of divorce and provides for financial relief in the case of unilateral divorce requested by the woman.

Implementation of the Law and Access to Justice

> Moderator: Do you see any changes in recent years because of the gender laws? What has changed?
>
> Yes it has changed because of these laws. If one calls a certain number because of violence, they put the husband in prison and take him to court.
>
> —Woman, village, Gaza Strip

> We are illiterate. We don't know what's going on. We don't know what you are talking about.
>
> —Village woman, Yemen

> Nothing has changed. A woman was and still is ruled by the parents and husband. What's new is that now she gets educated and works.
>
> —Female youth, urban neighborhood, the West Bank

> *Sources:* World Bank 2012a, forthcoming.

Even if beneficial laws exist on the books, in the Region, implementation of the laws can be a major challenge. Lack of capacity and resources in the justice sector, lack of transparency and gender biases within the judicial system, costs of legal services, geographic location of courts and legal services, lack of awareness of rights, and lack of access to legal representation can affect both women and men. However, women can be impacted disproportionately. They may face social stigma and hostility, and have added time constraints in pursuing claims. A lack of awareness of rights exacerbated by literacy issues, particularly for women in low-income rural areas, can compound the difficulties.

Women are stigmatized and afraid to pursue claims against family members, especially in matters of inheritance. A 2005 study in Syria carried out by local institutions in cooperation with United Nations Development Fund for Women (UNIFEM) showed that approximately 20 percent of women in rural areas and 15 percent of women in urban areas did not receive their share of inheritance, even under the law (UNIFEM 2005). The Jordanian government instigated a new strategy to improve enforcement of inheritance rights. Under the provisions of a new provisional Personal Status Law of 2010, the property of the deceased must be registered immediately in the name of the female relative. Moreover, Article 319 mandates a 3-month waiting period, starting from the deceased's date of death, during which a woman cannot waive her inheritance rights. The waiting period temporarily alleviates the social pressure put on women by relatives to waive these rights (Husseini 2010).

Lack of confidence in the legal system also prevails, especially when the judicial system is seen as biased against women. In Egypt, it takes female business owners on average 32 weeks longer than their male counterparts to resolve disputes (Chamlou and others 2008). Enforcement of judgments remains a problem. In the Tangier family courts in Morocco, 20,000 judgments are handed out each year, but there is only one bailiff to help enforce orders. Therefore, few orders are effective (UN Women 2011). As Morocco moves forward after its recent reforms, implementation and enforcement of the law are the next steps. The success of the reforms will depend on capacity building within, and sensitization of, the judiciary, the successful operation of the new family courts; awareness building around the new laws; and broader and greater access to legal services.

Lack of female participation in the judicial process is another issue. Some countries, such as Algeria and Tunisia, were early pioneers in encouraging women to become lawyers and judges. In Algeria, 38 percent of the magistrates are female. Similarly, some countries including Egypt and Jordan initiated strategies to increase their number of female judges. In 2006, Jordan launched an initiative to bring more women into the judiciary. In 2010, the country had 48 women judges, representing 7 percent of all judges—still a relatively low number but an improvement over earlier statistics (Euromed Gender Equality Programme 2010a).

Women work in the higher echelons of the judiciary in several MENA countries. In 2003, the first female lawyer was appointed to the Egyptian High Constitutional Court. In 2004, the first female Constitutional Court Judge was appointed in Bahrain. In 2007, a woman became President of the Military Court in Lebanon. Khadija Abeba sits as the President of the Supreme Court in Djibouti. According to the 2011 UN report, Progress of the World's Women: In Pursuit of Justice, female participation in the Region's judiciary and legal prosecution services is approximately on par with global levels. It is significantly higher than in the South Asia Region and marginally higher than in the East Asia and Pacific Region (UN Women 2011).

Other countries have just started to open up the legal profession to women. The Islamic Republic of Iran and Saudi Arabia legally prohibit women from becoming judges. Although Saudi Arabia's prohibition extends to female lawyers, in 2008 the country's first cohort of women graduated from law school. These women cannot practice law, but the government has allowed them to work as legal assistants to female clients in court (World Bank 2009b). Until recently, Kuwaiti women had been prohibited from becoming judges or public prosecutors, although the legal basis for this prohibition was unclear. In 2010, an administrative court ruled against a female law graduate who had challenged an advertisement offering the post of public prosecutor to male candidates on the basis that the constitution precluded females from holding prosecutorial positions (Human Rights Watch 2011). However, in July 2011, a Supreme Council judge clarified that women could be appointed to the judiciary and be appointed as public prosecutors and that these appointments were in line with the constitution and the law (The Arab Times 2011).

The lack of female participation also extends to other judicial bodies, such as land registries and marriage registries, and to enforcement agencies such as the police (which can be a restricted sector under labor laws). In 2008, Egypt and the United Arab Emirates appointed the first two female marriage registrars in the Region (Al Sherbini 2008). In 2007, Syria's Grand Mufti declared that female graduates of Islamic law colleges were being trained to become muftis to counsel women on religious matters. In 2009, two women were appointed as Shari'a court judges in the West Bank, breaking a long-standing tradition of appointing only male religious court judges in the Region.[15]

The constitutions of the majority of countries in the Region enshrine the principles of gender equality and nondiscrimination. In reality, these constitutional guarantees often are undermined by conflicting and discriminatory laws. Individuals and women's groups around the world have successfully used test cases to challenge the constitutionality of such laws.

A 1994 landmark case in Botswana challenged the country's laws preventing a woman married to a non-national from passing her citizenship on to her children.[16] The Botswana Court of Appeal ruled that the law was discriminatory and therefore unconstitutional. Ongoing pressure from women's groups has led the government to review and reform other discriminatory laws (Hallward-Driemeier and Hasan 2012).

In 2009, women's groups in Kuwait supported a case before the Constitutional Court of a woman who complained that her husband had prevented her from leaving the country. In a landmark ruling, the court overturned the 1962 Passport Law, which required a husband's signature on his wife's passport application. It found the law unconstitutional because it conflicted with provisions guaranteeing freedom and gender equality (Marinero 2009). In another 2009 decision, the Constitutional Court ruled that female members of the Kuwaiti National Assembly did not have to wear headscarves, because this law denied them their constitutional guarantees of personal freedom (McKee 2009).

Notes

1. The "natural resource curse" argument, which highlights the adverse effects that large revenues coming from its resource endowment can have on a country's economic development, is not new. For a review of the current knowledge on the issue, see Frankel 2010. Whether and the extent to which it is relevant for MENA are still subject to debate. See Groh and Rothschild 2012.
2. The MENA Region is home to five major Islamic schools of thought: Hanifi Arab/Middle East, Maliki/North Africa, Shafi/Southern Arabia, Hanbali/Saudi Arabia, and Ja'fari/Iran.
3. The Bank conducted the survey for the Jordan NOW (New Work Opportunities for Women) pilot.
4. In the absence of any codified legislation, Article 1 of the Algerian Civil Code allows a judge to apply religious and customary law (Kelly and Breslin 2010).
5. The Protocol to the African Charter on Human Rights and the Rights of Women in Africa, and the Arab Charter on Human Rights 2004 are examples of regional treaties.
6. Applies to married women in Algeria, Egypt, the Islamic Republic of Iran, Kuwait, Oman, the United Arab Emirates, the Republic of Yemen, and both married and unmarried women in Saudi Arabia (World Bank 2011b). Technically, Jordan still has restrictions for married women. However, an amendment to lift these restrictions has been proposed and is being reviewed by the government.
7. The Islamic Republic of Iran and Saudi Arabia require male permission.
8. In both Syria and the Islamic Republic of Iran, the wife owes the husband a general duty of obedience under the family law in return for spousal financial maintenance.

9. Bahrain 15, the Islamic Republic of Iran 13, Kuwait 15, Lebanon (Sunni Muslim and Druze 17, Armenian and Syrian Orthodox Churches 14, Catholic 14), Qatar 16, West Bank 15, and Gaza 17.

10. In the Islamic Republic of Iran, with parental permission and the approval of the "Righteous Court," girls can be married at the age of 9.

11. Recommendation number 21 of the 13th session of the CEDAW Committee of 1994 recommended a minimum age of marriage of at least 18 for both sexes. Article 1 of the UN Convention on the Rights of the Child defines a child as a person below the age of 18 unless the laws of a particular country set the age for adulthood as older.

12. Additionally, the *mahr*, to which the wife usually is entitled on divorce has been inflation-indexed so that it maintains its real value (COHRE 2006).

13. In polygamous marriages, the only option for each wife is a separate property regime.

14. Apart from gifts or inheritance specifically designated to one spouse, or property clearly intended to be under sole ownership.

15. The only other country to have appointed female judges to the Shari'a courts is Malaysia, in 2010, following a *fatwa* authorizing the appointments in 2005 (Worldwide Religious News 2009).

16. Attorney General of Botswana v. Unity Dow (Appeal Court 1994).

References

Alesina, Alberto, Paola Giuliano, and Nathan Nunn. 2011. "On the Origins of Gender Roles: Women and the Plough." Working Paper 17098, National Bureau of Economic Research, Cambridge, MA.

Al Sherbini, Ramadan. 2008. "First Women Marriage Official to Cut Divorce Rates." *Gulf News*, February 29. http://gulfnews.com/news/region/egypt/first-woman-marriage-official-to-cut-divorce-rates-1.87025.

The Arab Times. 2011. "Appointing Women Judges in Line with Constitution, Law." July 4. http://www.arabtimesonline.com/NewsDetails/tabid/96/smid/414/ArticleID/171092/reftab/36/Default.aspx.

Assaud, Ragi, and Ghada Barsoum. 2007. "Youth Exclusion in Egypt: In Search of 'Second Chances.'" Middle East Youth Initiative Working Paper 2, Wolfensohn Center for Development/Brookings Institution and Dubai School of Government, Washington, DC.

Association Démocratique des Femmes du Maroc. 2009. *Report on the Application of CEDAW in the Arab World.* Rabat.

Attorney General of the Republic of Botswana v. Unity Dow, 6 BCLR 1 (Court of Appeal 1994). http://www.elaw.org/node/2018.

Bordat, Stephanie W., and Saida Kouzzi. 2004. "The Challenge of Implementing Morocco's New Personal Status Laws." *Arab Reform Bulletin* 2 (8). Carnegie Endowment for International Peace, Washington, DC. HYPERLINK "http://www.ceip.org/arabreform" www.ceip.org/arabreform; http://www.globalrights.o9rg/site/DocServer?docID=663.

Central Statistical Organization. 2007. *Iraq Household Socio-Economic Survey 2006–07 (IHSES 2007).* Baghdad.

Chamlou, Nadereh, Leora Klapper, and Silvia Muzi. 2008. "The Environment for Women's Entrepreneurship in Middle East and North Africa." World Bank, Washington, DC. http://elibrary.worldbank.org/content/book/9780821374955.

Charrad, Mounira M. 2007. "Tunisia at the Forefront of the Arab World: Two Waves of Gender Legislation." *Washington and Lee Law Review* 64 (4).

_____. 2009. "Kinship, Islam or Oil: Culprits of Gender Inequality?" *Politics and Gender (A Journal of the American Political Science Association)* 5 (4): 546–53.

COHRE (Centre for Housing Rights and Evictions). 2006. *In Search of Equality: A Survey of Law and Practice Related to Women's Inheritance Rights in the Middle East and North Africa Region.* Geneva. http://www.cohre.org/.

Ennaji, Moha. 2009. *The New Muslim Personal Law in Morocco: Context Proponents, Adversaries, and Arguments.* http://www.yale.edu/macmillan/africadissent/moha.pdf.

Euromed Gender Equality Programme. 2010a. *Enhancing Equality between Men and Women in the Euromed Region 2008–2011: National Situation Analysis Report: Women's Human Rights and Gender Equality: Jordan.* Brussels.

_____. 2010b. *Enhancing Equality between Men and Women in the Euromed Region 2008–2011: National Situation Analysis Report: Human Rights and Gender Equality: Syria.* Brussels.

Frankel, Jeffrey. 2010. "The Natural Resource Curse: A Survey." Harvard Kennedy School (HKS) Faculty Research Working Paper RWP10-005, Harvard University, Cambridge, MA. web.hks.harvard.edu/publications/workingpapers/.

Gautier, Arlette. 2005. "Legal Regulation of Marital Relations: A Historical and Comparative Approach." *International Journal of Law Policy and the Family* 19 (1): 47–72.

Groh, Matthew, and Casey Rothschild. 2012. "Oil, Islam, Women, and Geography: A Comment on Ross (2008)." *Quarterly Journal of Political Science* 7 (1): 69–87.

Hallward-Driemeier, Mary, and Tazeen Hasan. 2012. *Empowering Women: Legal Rights and Economic Opportunities in Africa.* Africa Development Forum Series. Washington, DC: World Bank.

Hijab, Nadia. 2002. *Women Are Citizens, Too: The Laws of the State, the Lives of Women.* UNDP (United Nations Development Programme), New York.

Human Rights Watch. 2011. *World Report 2011: Kuwait.* Washington, DC. http://www.hrw.org/world-report-2011/kuwait.

Husseini, Rana. 2010. "Activists Slam CIJD's Personal Status Draft Law." *The Jordan Times,* April 21. http://www.jordantimes.com/?news=25889.

Inglehart, Ronald, and Pippa Norris. 2003a. "The True Clash of Civilizations." *Foreign Policy* 135: 62–70.

_____. 2003b. *Rising Tide.* New York: Cambridge University Press.

Jensen, Robert, and Rebecca Thornton. 2003. "Early Female Marriage in the Developing World." *Gender and Development* 11 (2): 9–19.

Keilani, Musa. 2012. "Jordan to Scrap Regulation on Passport for Women." *The Gulf Today,* January 17. http://gulftoday.ae/portal/c0602421-8238-49e2-af64-e0408b0014c9.aspx.

Kelly, Sanja, and Julia Breslin. 2010. *Women's Rights in the Middle East and North Africa: Progress amid Resistance.* New York, NY: Freedom House; Lanham, MD: Rowman & Littlefield.

Khalife, Nadya. 2011. "Tunisia on Board with Women's Rights." *The Huffington Post*, September 22. http://www.huffingtonpost.com/nadya-khalife/tunisia-on-board-with-wom_b_981689.html.

Kuwait News Agency. 2011. "Kuwaiti Unmarried Women Set to Receive Housing Loans." September 24. http://www.kuna.net.kw/ArticleDetails.aspx?id=2192355&language=en.

Landes, David S., and Richard A. Landes. 2001. "Girl Power: Do Fundamentalists Fear Our Women?" *The New Republic* 8 (October): 20–23.

Malkawi, Khetam. 2012. "Civil Status Department to Propose New Passports Law Amendments" *The Jordan Times*, June 10. http://jordantimes.com/civil-status-department-to-propose-new-passports-law-amendments.

Marinero, Ximena. 2009. "Kuwait Constitutional Court Rules Women Do Not Need Permission to Get Passport." *Jurist Legal News and Research*, October 22. http://jurist.org/paperchase/2009/10/kuwait-constitutional-court-rules-women.php.

McKee, Megan. 2009. "Kuwait Constitutional Court Rules Women Lawmakers Not Required to Wear Headscarf." *Jurist Legal News and Research*, October 28. http://jurist.org/paperchase/2009/10/kuwait-constitutional-court-rules-women_28.php.

Miles, Rebecca. 2002. "Employment and Unemployment in Jordan: The Importance of the Gender System." *World Development* 30 (3): 413–27.

Moghadam, Valentine. 2003. *Modernizing Women: Gender and Social Change in the Middle East.* 2nd ed. Boulder, CO: Lynne Riener.

_____. 2004. "Women's Economic Participation in the Middle East: What Difference Has the Neoliberal Policy Turn Made?" *Journal of Middle East Women's Studies* 1 (1): 110–46.

Moghadam, Valentine M., and Farzaneh Roudi-Fahimi. 2005. *Empowering Women, Developing Society: Female Education in the Middle East and North Africa.* Washington, DC: Population Reference Bureau.

Norris, P. 2009. "Petroleum and Patriarchy: A Response to Ross." *Politics & Gender* 5 (4): 553–60.

Offenhauer, Priscilla. 2005. *Women in Islamic Societies: A Selected Review of Social Scientific Literature.* Library of Congress, Washington, DC.

Portes, Alejandro. 2006. "Institutions and Development: A Conceptual Reanalysis." *Population and Development Review* 32 (2): 233–62.

Rauch, James, and Scott Kostyshak. 2009. "The Three Arab Worlds." *Journal of Economic Perspectives* 23: 165–88.

Ross, Michael. 2008. "Oil, Islam and Women." *American Political Science Review* 102 (1).

Saudi Gazette. 2012. "Naif Approves Amendments to Citizenship Regulations." January 15. http://www.saudigazette.com.sa/index.cfm?method=home.reg con&contentID=20120115115592.

Simavi, Sevi, Clare Manuel, and Mark Blackden. 2010. *Gender Dimensions of Investment Climate Reform: A Guide for Policy Makers and Practitioners.* Washington, DC: World Bank.

UN COMTRADE. 2007. See appendixes A and C.

UNIFEM (United Nations Development Fund for Women). 2005. *Violence against Women Study Syria 2005.* New York. http://sgdatabase.unwomen.org/uploads/Syria%20-%20key%20findings%20of%20vaw%20study%202005.pdf.

UNIDO (United Nations Industrial Development Organization). 2009. INDSTAT4 (Industrial Statistics database). Vienna. http://www.unido.org/index.php?id=1000309.

UN OHCHR (United Nations Office of the High Commissioner for Human Rights). 2008a. CEDAW (Convention on the Elimination of All Forms of Discrimination against Women) Committee. Consideration of reports submitted by States Parties under Article 18 of the Convention on the Elimination of All Forms of Discrimination against Women. Third period report of States Parties Lebanon (July 2006) CEDAW/C/LBN/3. UN OHCHR (Office of the High Commissioner for Human Rights), Geneva. http://www.un.org/womenwatch/daw/cedaw/; http://www2.ohchr.org/english/bodies/cedaw/.

UN OHCHR (United Nations Office of the High Commissioner for Human Rights). 2010. *Concluding Observations of CEDAW Committee on Tunisia.* UN OHCHR (Office of the High Commissioner for Human Rights), Geneva. http://daccess-dds-ny.un.org/doc/UNDOC/GEN/G10/463/92/PDF/G1046392.pdf?OpenElement.

UN Women (United Nations Entity for Gender Equality and the Empowerment of Women). 2011. *Progress of the World's Women: In Pursuit of Justice.* New York. http://www.unwomen.org/publications/progress-of-the-worlds-women-in-pursuit-of-justice/.

US (United States) Census Bureau. 2001–09 American Community Survey (United States). Washington, DC.

WVS (World Values Survey Association). 2005. World Values Survey. www.worldvaluessurvey.org.

Van Wass, Laura.2010. *The Situation of Stateless Persons in the Middle East and North Africa.* Geneva: United Nations High Commission for Refugees. http://www.unhcr.org/4ce63e079.html; http://www.lauravanwaas.com/publications.html

World Bank. 2004a. *Gender and Development in the Middle East and Africa: Women in the Public Sphere,* Washington, DC.

_____. 2009b. *Status and Progress of Women in the Middle East and North Africa.* MENA Development Report, Washington, DC: World Bank.

_____. 2011b. *Women, Business and the Law 2012: Removing Barriers to Economic Inclusion.* Washington, MENA Development Report, DC: World Bank.

World Bank. 2012a. "Aspirations on Hold: Young Lives in the West Bank and Gaza. Washington, DC: World Bank.

_____. 2012b. *World Development Report 2012: Gender Equality and Development.* Washington, DC: World Bank.

_____. 2012c. Women, Business and the Law Database. http://wbl.worldbank.org/

_____. Forthcoming. "Yemen Gender Policy Note." Washington, DC: World Bank.

_____. Multiple years. *WDI (World Development Indicators).* Washington, DC. data.worldbank.org/data-catalog/world-development-indicators

Worldwide Religious News. 2009. "2 Palestinian Women Become Judges in Islamic Court." February 24. http://wwrn.org/articles/30350/?&place=israel-palestine&section=islam.

CHAPTER 3

Economic Incentives Dampen Participation in the Workforce

In addition to social norms and legal restrictions, women's labor force participation is influenced directly by the social contract to which governments in the MENA Region have adhered since the 1960s. This report uses "social contract" following the definition in the 2004 World Bank report, "Unlocking the Employment Potential in the Middle East and North Africa: Toward a New Social Contract" (World Bank 2004):

> The social contract refers generally to an agreement [among] the members of a society, or between the governed and the government, defining and limiting the rights and duties of each. . . . In MENA countries, the social contract encompasses a wider array of factors. . . . Conceptualized not solely as an institutionalized bargain among collective actors, it encompasses norms and shared expectations for the overall organization of a polity. . . . Accordingly, these norms and expectations have significant institutional consequences. They define the boundaries of acceptable policy choice, and they affect the organization of interests in society, helping to determine who wins and who loses in a given political economy.

In exchange for their support, governments in the Region provided people with employment (in the civil service and state-owned enterprises), and supported family life with generous benefits and subsidies on food, fuel, and consumer goods. Social protection and state ownership were common, and the state was present in all aspects of life. To deal with economic shocks and limit social unrest, governments repeatedly expanded public sector employment and added more benefits and subsidies. This expansion in jobs and benefits was particularly the case in states with large hydrocarbon endowments (Yousef 2004), but the nonoil-producing countries adopted similar policies. These policies resulted in large public sectors; heavily distorted labor, capital, and product markets; and, in the case of nonoil states, high levels of public debt.

In the late 1990s and early 2000s, the social contract became increasingly strained, particularly in the nonoil-producing countries. As world food and fuel prices rose to unprecedented levels, the subsidy bill became fiscally unsustainable. Faced with increasing social and financial pressures, some governments embarked on economic reforms. Morocco and Tunisia began as early as the 1970s, and the Arab Republic of Egypt made significant progress during the last decade. Nevertheless, their reforms have not fully removed distortions in their economies, and private sector growth continues to be hampered by many institutional and regulatory constraints. The public sector still dominates in most MENA economies, and hiring in the public sector is still used to combat unemployment.

Public investment under the social contract substantially improved the level of human development and quality of infrastructure in the Region (Birks and Sinclair 1980). The expansion of the public sector created many jobs, especially for the well educated. Although women have benefited directly from these advances, welfare-state-induced market distortions have impeded women's participation in the public sphere in a number of ways. First, the high level of public sector employment has distorted the labor market by attracting the brightest MENA youth at rates of pay that the private sector cannot match. Second, generous subsidies and family benefits certainly have helped reduce vulnerability and poverty, but also have worked to reinforce a vision of women as homemakers and discouraged them from entering the labor market.

Extensive Public Sector Employment with Generous Compensation

Even today, public sector employment accounts for a significant share of overall employment in MENA countries, and is high relative to other regions of the world. However, important differences exist within the MENA Region (figure 3.1). In the oil-producing (GCC) countries, public sector employment accounts for as much as 80 percent of overall employment of national citizens (Qatar and the United Arab Emirates). In contrast, in the Mediterranean countries, the share of public sector employment is as low as 10 percent (Morocco).

A unique feature of the GCC countries is that they permit large-scale in-migration of foreign labor. Since public sector jobs often are reserved for citizens, the labor markets are almost totally segmented: nationals work in public sector positions, and foreign workers occupy most private sector positions. The high rates of compensation offered to nationals in the public sector are too high for many private sector firms to compete

FIGURE 3.1

Public Employment as a Share of Total Employment

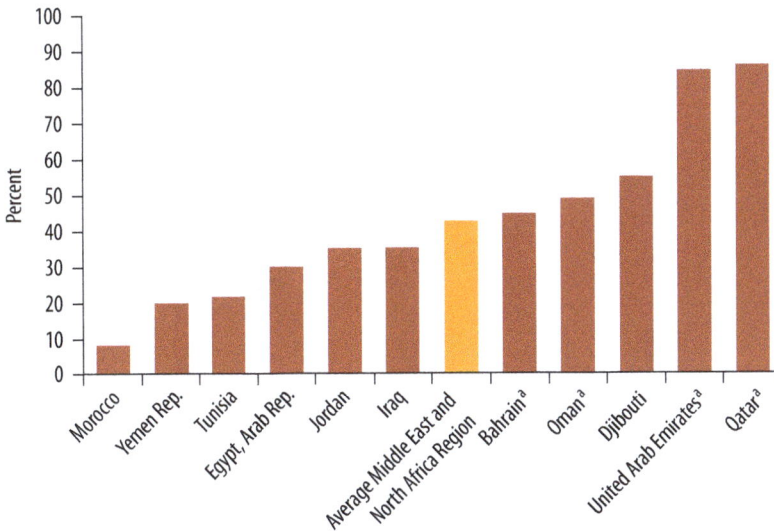

Source: Author estimates based on household surveys and official statistics (appendixes A and C).

a. Official estimates of national populations in GCC countries.

for their labor. Without the public sector option, primarily foreigners are employed in the private sector, usually at lower rates of pay.

The average public sector wage bill relative to GDP and relative to total government spending in MENA is the highest in the developing world (figure 3.2). Here also, countries in the Region vary significantly. For instance, while, in 2008, Jordan's wage bill amounted to nearly 18 percent of GDP, Kuwait's was only 6.5 percent of GDP. Conversely, in the same year, the wage bill made up 47 percent of total spending in Morocco but only 23 percent of total spending in Egypt.

Public sector jobs are substantially better remunerated than private sector jobs. Figure 3.3 shows the public sector wage gap in monetary earnings for four countries in the Region. The differences in pay rates, especially for women, between the public and private sectors are striking. A part of these differences reflect the nature of the jobs in each sector. On average, the public sector requires higher levels of education and employs more workers in urban areas than does the private sector. Nonetheless, even after controlling for differences in education and other characteristics, public sector jobs are more lucrative than those in the private sector. The gaps increase with the level of education. Since women tend to have higher levels of education, their wage gaps are greater than those of men. Partly as a result, in most MENA countries, women are attracted to public sector jobs to a greater extent than are men (figure 3.4).

FIGURE 3.2

Public Sector Wage Bill as a Percent of GDP and Total Expenditure, 2008

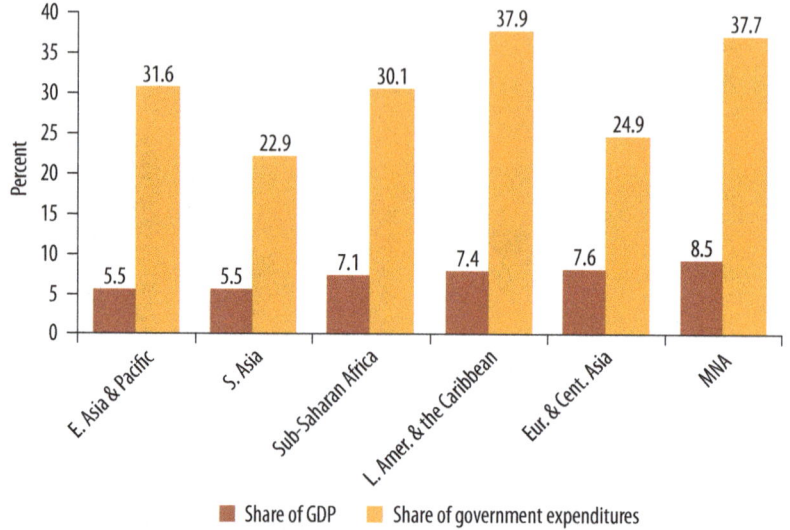

Source: IMF ca. 2008.

Note: Where data are available, they refer to general government spending; otherwise, central government spending is used.

FIGURE 3.3

Public Sector Wage Gap: Difference in Average Hourly Earnings for Salaried Workers in Public and Private Sectors

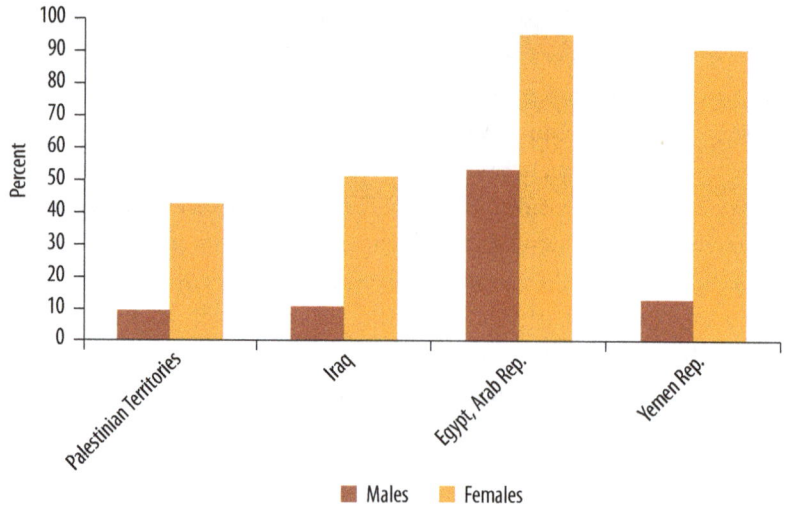

Source: Author estimates based on household surveys (appendixes A and C).

FIGURE 3.4

Public Sector Employment as Share of Total Employment

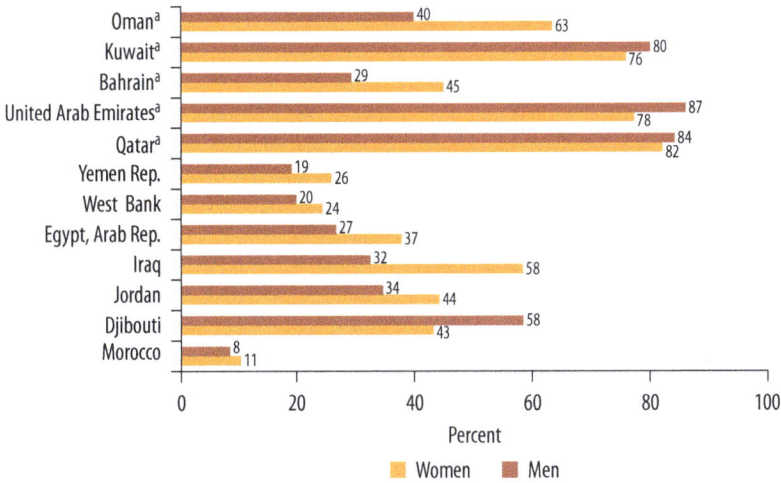

Source: Author estimates based on household surveys and official statistics (appendixes A and C).

a. Excludes non-nationals.

Furthermore, nonmonetary benefits are much higher in the public sector. These benefits include social security, health insurance, greater job security, and paid sick leave (figure 3.5). Once these factors are taken into account, it is no surprise that educated young people, especially women, are attracted to the public sector (figure 3.6). In Jordan, more than 80 percent of women working in salaried public sector jobs have post-secondary education; the corresponding share for salaried private sector jobs is 60 percent. The higher public sector benefits have economy-wide effects on productivity and growth because they distort the market incentives to efficiently allocate skills to their most productive use.

Public sector jobs are distinctly better compensated than equivalent private sector positions, particularly for the highly educated. However, as young people graduate from high school and university, the creation of new positions in the public sector has not kept pace. As a result of the compensation gap, many young people are prepared to remain unemployed in the hope of eventually finding a job in the public sector, leading to a phenomenon called "wait unemployment." This pattern is partly responsible for the extremely high unemployment rates in MENA countries, rates that are most pronounced among youth and more educated individuals, particularly women (figure 3.7).

A recent World Bank study in Upper Egypt highlights the importance of government jobs as the main form of socially acceptable employment, especially for women. Young men and women alike aspire to government

FIGURE 3.5

Incidence of Job Benefits in Public and Private Sectors

a. Social security/pension

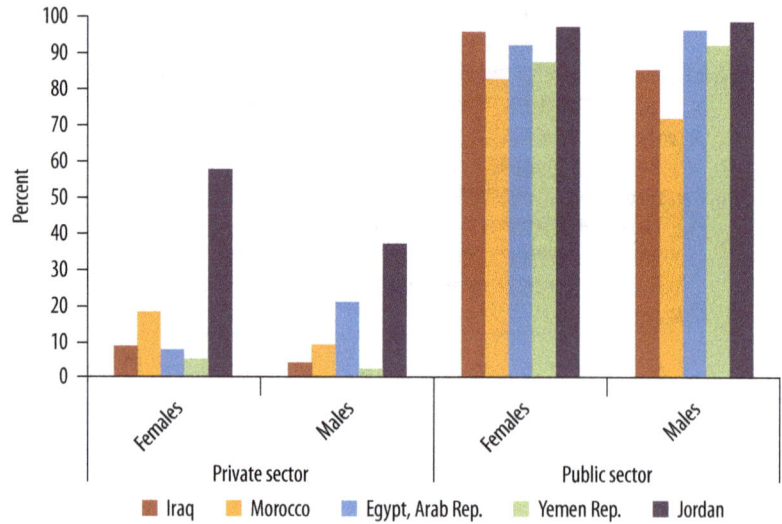

b. Health insurance

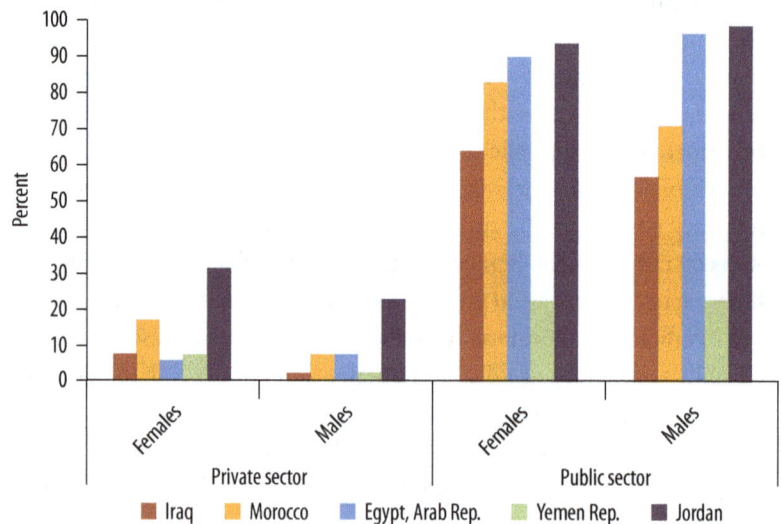

jobs as the ideal. Young women perceive these jobs as being "acceptable," from their own and from society's perspective, because of the compatibility of working hours with housework and the employment security. It is no surprise that 45 percent of employed women in Upper Egypt and 54 percent of employed Egyptian women work in the public sector (World Bank 2011b).

FIGURE 3.5 *Continued*

c. Contracts

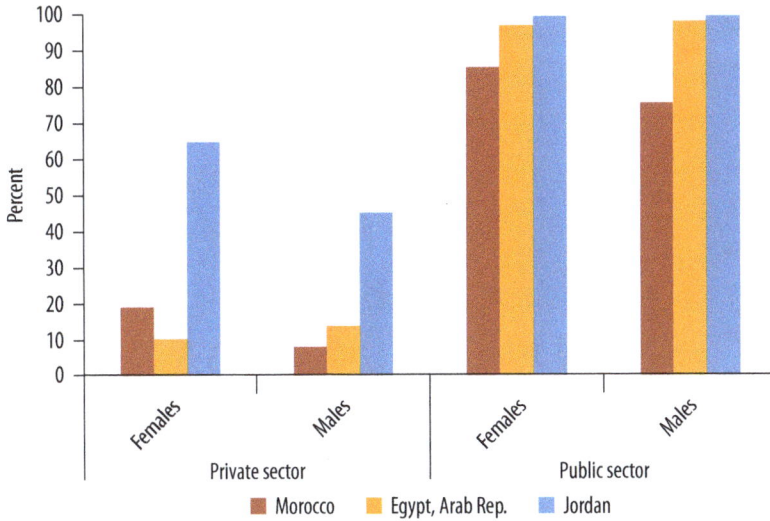

d. Paid sick leave

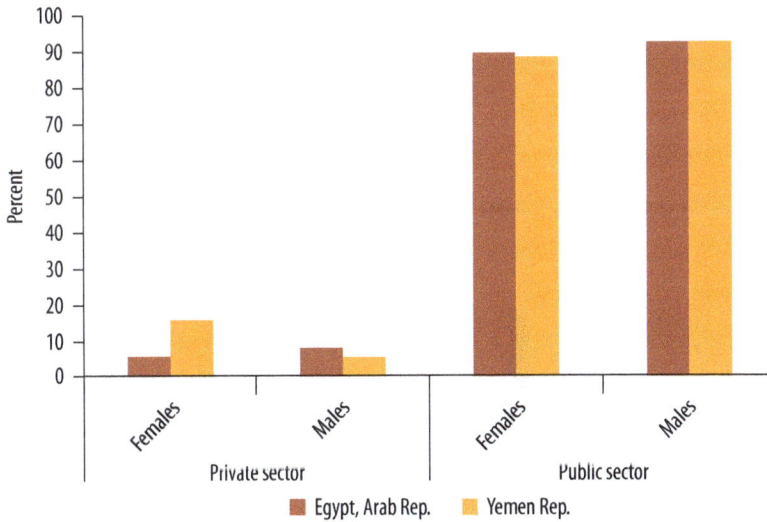

Source: Author estimates based on household surveys and official statistics (appendixes A and C).

Generous Subsidies Encourage Women to Stay at Home

Beyond public sector jobs, an important component of the social contract is the extensive system of direct and indirect subsidies (figure 3.8). These transfers have substantially lowered the cost of living—but at a high fiscal cost. For instance, in Algeria, Egypt, Kuwait, and the Republic of Yemen, consumer subsidies equal more than 5 percent of GDP. In Kuwait, energy

FIGURE 3.6

Share of Workers with Post-Secondary Education

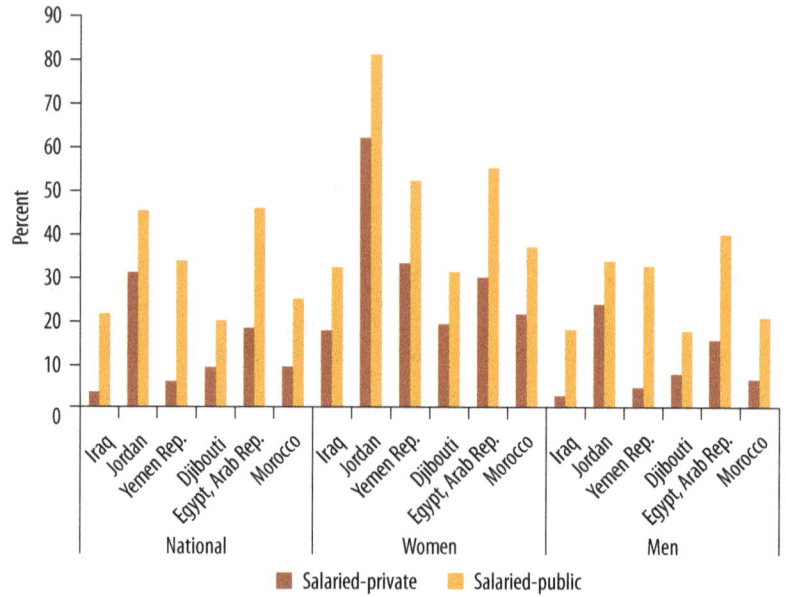

Source: Author estimates based on household surveys (appendixes A and C).

FIGURE 3.7

Female Unemployment Rates by Education Level

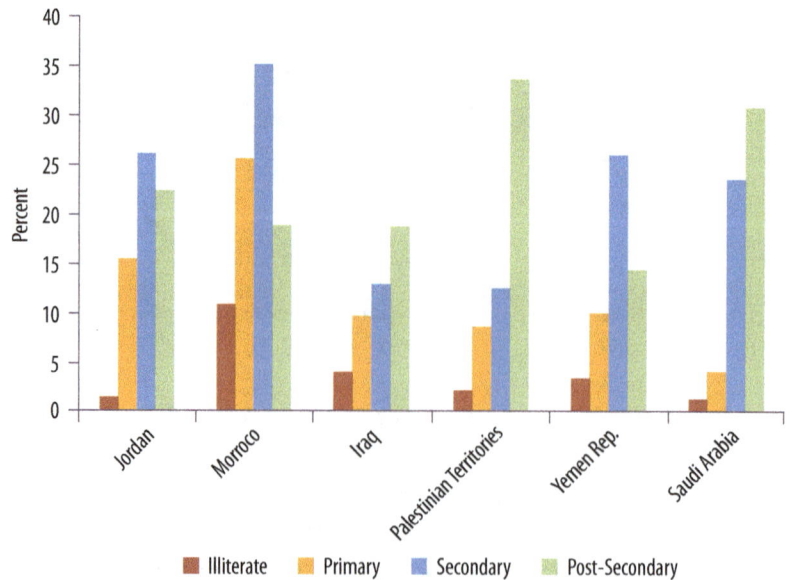

Source: Author estimates based on household surveys (appendixes A and C).

FIGURE 3.8

Subsidies as a Share of GDP, 2009

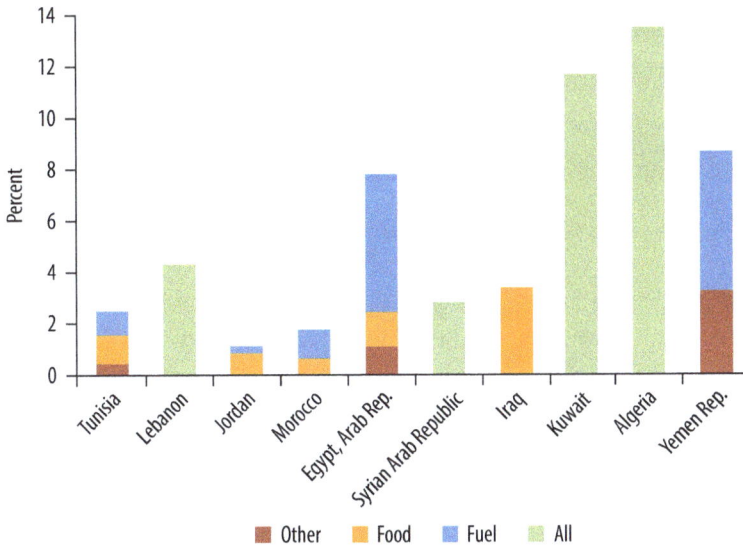

Source: IMF and World Bank Staff calculations 2009.

Note: Lebanon: No food or gas subsidies. Data refer to subsidies of the electricity company, a fraction of which can be considered consumer subsidies. Syria: For 2009, IMF estimates an implicit energy subsidy of 4.9 percent of GDP (6.2 percent compensatory measures − 1.3 percent implicit prices subsidy). Data reported are mostly food subsidies (1.4 percent comes from the Price Stabilization Fund, or PSF, which subsidizes mainly bread and sugar). There also were substantial agricultural producer subsidies administered via domestic prices for wheat, sugar beets, and cotton. Iraq: Direct fuel subsidies were zero. Data reported basically were food subsidies under the Public Distribution System (Source: IMF). IMF estimates 2009 indirect fuel subsidies at approx. 1.5 percent of GDP. Kuwait: Data refer to the explicit subsidy number as calculated by the IMF for 2006–07 and are the last detailed estimate. When many implicit subsidies are counted, Kuwait's total subsidy estimate is 32 percent of GDP. A great part of these subsidies were in social security expenses for that year. Benchmark figure used to add both implicit and explicit subsidies is 20 percent of GDP.

subsidies account for 20 percent of government spending. Similarly, in Saudi Arabia, energy subsidies add approximately 25 percent to on-budget spending.[1]

In the Region as a whole, government spending on subsidies accounts for at least US$50 billion. Even these estimates do not fully capture the complexity and scale of the subsidies. For instance, in the resource-rich countries, high implicit subsidies that do not appear in the budget are incurred by selling domestic oil to consumers at below-market prices. In Iraq, in 2009, indirect fuel subsidies were estimated at 1.5 percent of GDP (US$1 billion).

The generous transfers and subsidies in the MENA Region directly affect the labor force participation decisions of women. By increasing all households' income levels before women take up outside work, subsidies decrease women's incentive to work. Furthermore, in some GCC countries, government family allowances are paid only to men, further widening the gap in compensation between men and women and again discouraging women from working. Kuwait's allowances are extremely generous and exacerbate the pay gap between men and women (box 3.1).

Making Allowances: Civil Service Pay Structure in Kuwait

The differential between public and private sector pay rates in MENA countries is explained partially by the proliferation of additional allowances paid to public employees. A number of factors are involved. They include the implementation of social welfare policies via the public sector pay system and the desire of fiscally strained governments to avoid commitments through pensionable pay as opposed to add-ons and bonuses—even though the latter become de facto commitments in their own right.

These allowances have major effects on the overall pay structure. For example, a study of Egypt found that, in 2008, the lower bound entry salary for a civil servant at basic grade was LE35 per month. However, after adding a series of bonuses and incentives, the entry salary could reach LE289 per month (Abdelhamid and El Baradei 2010). Among the GCC countries, Kuwait's complex civil service pay structure typifies this situation. Over and above base salaries, public sector employees receive numerous allowances, including job allowances and supplements for being married ("social increment") and for having children ("child increment"). Besides the general distortion to incentives, these allowances have a gender impact. Conditional on having a public sector job, these transfers, like subsidies, function as unearned income and tend to reduce household labor force participation, particularly by women. Moreover, these allowances increase with seniority so their fiscal cost is rising rapidly. Between 2005 and 2008, the government's average outlay on public sector salaries and benefits grew 13 percent per annum.

Because of the "reverse gender gap" in tertiary education, women throughout the GCC enter employment later than men and often retire earlier. For example, Kuwait's public retirement system allows women with children to retire on at least at 65 percent of salary after 15 years. Thus, despite the influx of well-educated women into public employment, the overall salary progression in the system favors men, who are in the system long enough to benefit from seniority and skill development, and hold the various family-status-based allowances. Interestingly, the pay gap between women and men may distort the way that higher education is rewarded. Because women's overall pay is lower, the net premium they receive for higher education is more significant as part of their total compensation than that received by men. This relatively higher net premium may explain in part why female enrollment rates in tertiary education are almost double those of males in some GCC countries. If women

(continued on next page)

BOX 3.1 *Continued*

had not completed their tertiary education, the usual gender gap in pay would have deterred them from taking the jobs in the first place. Correspondingly, young men have an incentive to enter the system with secondary or vocational qualifications only and rely on seniority for growth in pay over time. The perverse result for the GCC is that well-educated women leave the system just as their mid-career productivity potential would be deepening, whereas less educated men spend substantial time in low-skilled positions or in catch-up training programs.

In Saudi Arabia, a recently launched unemployment benefit scheme has attracted large numbers of women. Indeed, this benefit has sparked a debate about whether it reflects large latent unemployment or further subsidization of women at home (box 3.2).

BOX 3.2

Why Are Young Women in Saudi Arabia Signing Up for Unemployment Benefits?

The Kingdom of Saudi Arabia has implemented a new unemployment assistance scheme, known as Hafiz (Job Seekers' Bursary), which formally began operations at the beginning of 2012. Policymakers faced the challenge of getting the scheme up and running quickly in a context in which the system of transfers and taxes is basic compared to other high-income countries. Consequently, the identification of beneficiaries was not straightforward. As with all unemployment assistance programs, policymakers needed to trade off the impact of the new benefits on job search efforts with the desire to help the jobless meet basic needs.

The design of the program reflects the fact that it is one of a range of labor market reforms. On its own, it is not intended to be a comprehensive solution to labor market challenges. The program provides a monthly payment of SR2,000 (US$534) to eligible participants. To limit the appeal of the program as a jobs substitute, the duration of payments is one year. The Hafiz is larger than other allowances that are made for low-income households and, in fact, compares favorably with the lower end of the wage range for Saudi nationals. However, according to the Saudi Arabian 2006–07 household income and expenditure survey, the average monthly expenditure of Saudi households, excluding financial services, is approximately SR10,000—substantially higher than the Hafiz payment. Thus, the program is not able—nor is it intended—to provide sufficient support to an unemployed head-of-household who is the main provider.

The Hafiz was announced and refined during 2011, and received 2 million applications. Of these, 700,000 people met the basic eligibility criteria, 70 percent of whom

(continued on next page)

BOX 3.2 *Continued*

were women. However, before payments can begin, participants must supply additional data. Age criteria are set at 20–35 years, and applicants may not have any form of employment (including part-time) or be in receipt of other allowances (such as "social security" programs for low-income households). University graduates must have been out of school for at least 6 months.

Debate about the program in the Saudi media (including social media) has been vigorous. One major topic is whether the high participation of women in the program indicates huge latent unemployment, or reflects a pool of women who were sure of their stay-at-home status but wished to capitalize on the allowance. In addition, the upper age limit has highlighted the problem of the long-term unemployed. The available statistics indicate that the group of unemployed over 35 years old is relatively small. However, among this group are tens of thousands of women with teaching qualifications who have never found full-time jobs. Reacting to the view that a previous batch of such jobs (52,000) had been insufficient to meet the scale of the problem, in 2011, the Ministry of Education announced a large new batch of 28,000 positions for female applicants.

Finally, there has been anecdotal evidence that, despite the time-bound nature of the benefits and their relatively low amount, just the prospect of the program induced would-be participants to quit low-paying and/or part-time jobs. The government introduced a special allowance for private security jobs, which were seen as particularly vulnerable to this phenomenon. More recently, media reports have indicated that some Saudi nationals who had registered as having sponsored migrants or as having small enterprises also sought to enroll in the program. Such perverse effects illustrate the complex role of non-labor income in the Saudi labor market, which in turn is linked to the participation rate of Saudi women.

In tandem with the implementation of the Hafiz, the government heightened the emphasis on creating jobs for Saudi nationals. Regarding jobs for women, new jobs must be created within the parameters of the Saudi social system. In practical terms, the system presents the challenges of transportation for women to and from their jobs, and workplace design to ensure segregation from unrelated men. For the latter reason, jobs in education are a natural option, since the education system itself is segregated. However, female employees in the education system still face the challenge of transport. As a result, such jobs often are restricted to local residents. King Abdullah waived this requirement for the education jobs that were filled during the summer of 2011. However, the general challenge of transport remains significant and imposes an additional expense on households with females in the labor force. For private sector jobs, the government launched a high-profile effort to make retail positions in lingerie shops women-only. Previously, these jobs could be held only by men. This uncomfortable situation had resulted in highly critical comments from female customers and drawn considerable attention from overseas media.

Of course, as more retail sector jobs open to women, they will face the same constraints.

FIGURE 3.9

Labor Force Participation and Marriage: Marginal Effects Relative to Single Women

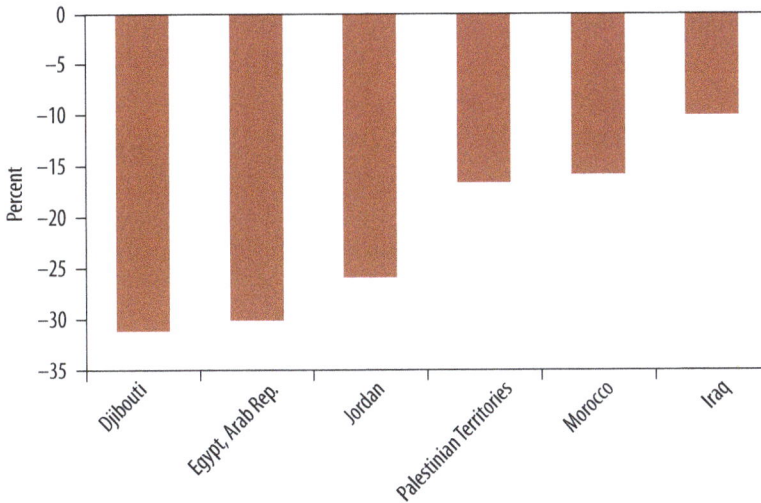

Source: Own calculations based on household surveys (appendixes A and C).

Given the benefits paid to married households and those with children, the nonmonetary costs of labor force participation are even higher for married women, especially mothers. It is no surprise that, after controlling for education and other individual characteristics, the probability that a woman will participate in the labor market is lower if she is married (figure 3.9 and appendix B, table B.4).

State Regulation and Intervention in the Market

Across MENA, the state plays a central role in the market. Recent enterprise surveys conducted by the World Bank in the Region show that the top concerns for businesses relate to the rule of law and how it is applied, including informal and anticompetitive practices, collateral issues, and property rights. In several of these countries, corruption is cited as one of the top five constraints. Regulatory constraints (labor, licensing, tax administration, regulatory policy) also are major issues. To boost private sector growth and encourage job creation, MENA governments will need to address the lack of clear, predictable, and well-enforced "rules of the game" for market activity. To a significant extent, the appropriate policies seem to be there on paper, but the problem arises from their unequal, differential, and preferential application (World Bank 2009).

Most MENA states have reduced the flexibility of the labor market through the regulation of pay and job termination regulations. In the

Islamic Republic of Iran, private sector pay scales are based on schooling and set by the government, and employers bear the burden of proof in laying off low-productivity workers (Salehi-Isfahani 1999, 2000, 2002). Egypt uses a similar system of pay scales linked to education and mandates that employers and employees go through a system of compulsory arbitration (Assaad 1997; Said 2001; Salehi-Isfahani 2005). These relatively strict regulations on firing employees are in place in many MENA countries and extend to notification and approval by a third party before a worker can be dismissed, several weeks of notice period to employees, and a couple of weeks of severance pay (IFC 2011a). Although, on average, these costs to employers are not out of line with the rest of the developing world, they are particularly high in some MENA countries. For example, the Islamic Republic of Iran and the Republic of Yemen require an average of 23 weeks of severance pay, and Egypt an average of 27 weeks. Moreover mandatory paid annual leave in MENA is among the most generous in the world. Djibouti, Egypt, the Syrian Arab Republic, and the Republic of Yemen offer as much as 30 days a year for an employee with 10 years of tenure. Notwithstanding recent reforms to facilitate the ease of doing business, the cost of hiring remains high for private sector firms (IFC 2011a).

Heavy Investment in Education, but Not the Kind That Businesses Want

Finally, a central tenet of the social contract has been heavy state investment in education. The state regulates the education sector and delivers most education services directly to its citizens. Public expenditures on education in MENA are the highest of all developing Regions (figure 3.10) They also constitute a substantial share of total spending in the Region, although there is some variation across countries. For instance, whereas Lebanon spends 8 percent of its total government outlays on education, Morocco spends nearly 26 percent.

Despite the high level of educational attainment in the Region, there is a disconnection between what students learn and what productive jobs require (Figure 3.11). This problem is more pronounced for women. Following gender norms, women are inclined to study education, health and welfare, humanities and arts (figure 3.12). These educational specializations in turn limit the job opportunities available to educated women—predominantly public sector positions in education, health, and administration (figure 3.13). Unfortunately, given fiscal constraints, the number of new positions in these fields has been dwindling.

FIGURE 3.10

Public Expenditure on Education, 2000–10

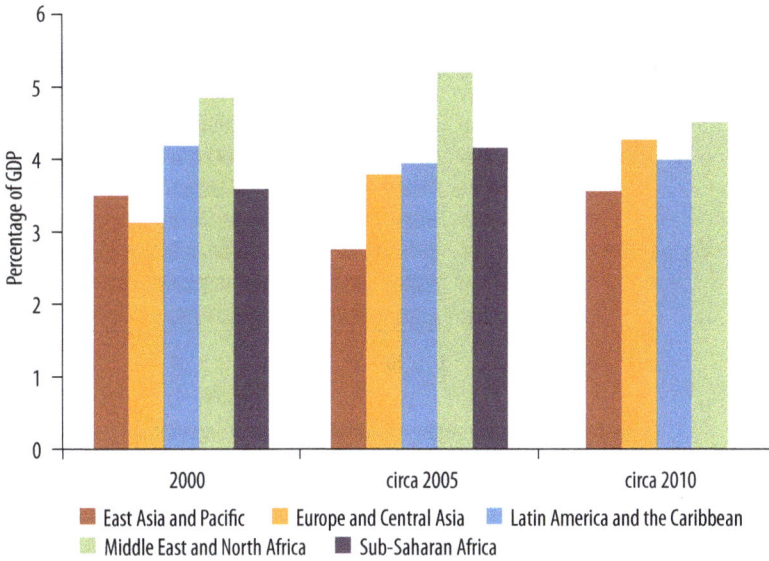

Source: UNESCO 2000–10.

FIGURE 3.11

Firms Identifying Labor Constraints as Biggest Constraint on Doing Business

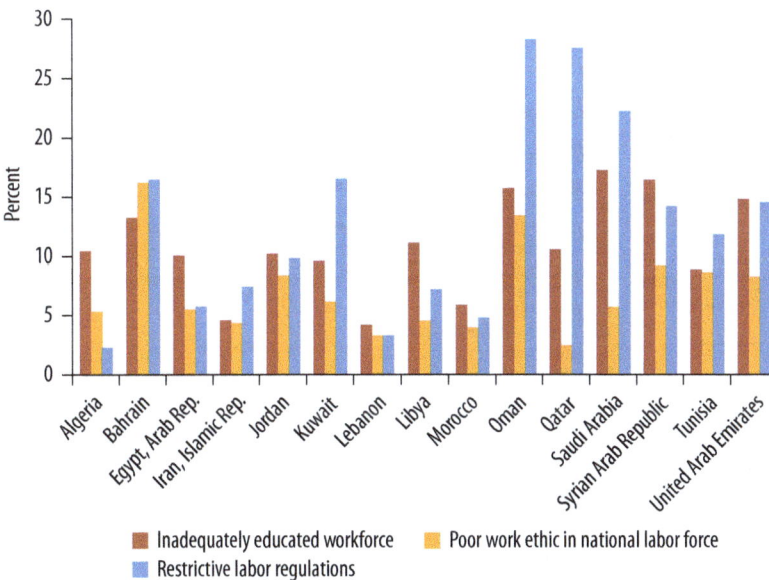

Source: WEF 2010.

Note: From a list of 15 factors, respondents were asked to select the five most problematic for doing business in their country and to rank them from 1 (most problematic) to 5. The vertical bars show the responses weighted according to their rankings.

FIGURE 3.12

Countries in Which Fields of Study Are Male- Female- Dominated

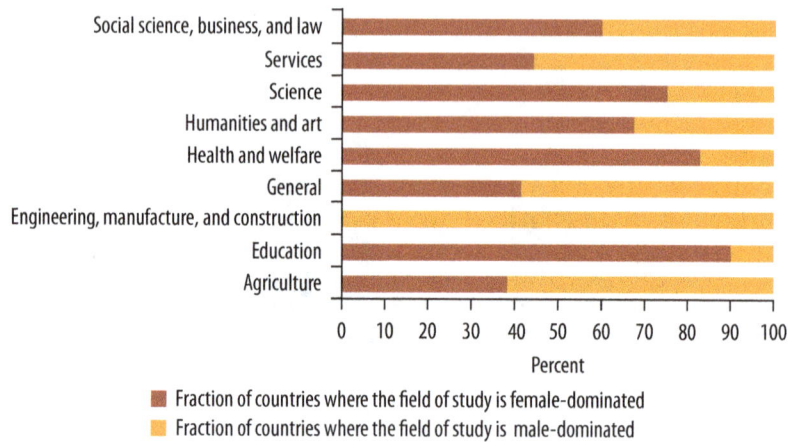

Source: World Bank 2011a.

FIGURE 3.13

Occupational Segregation: Industrial Distribution of Employment by Gender for Three Gulf Countries

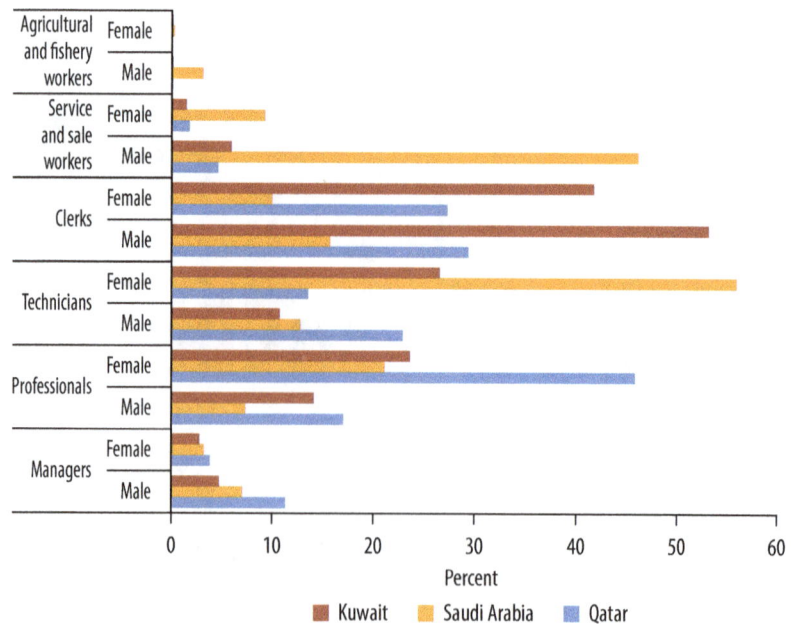

Source: Official statistics for national nonimmigrant populations (appendixes A and C).

FIGURE 3.14

Egypt: Share Acquiring Job-Relevant Skills

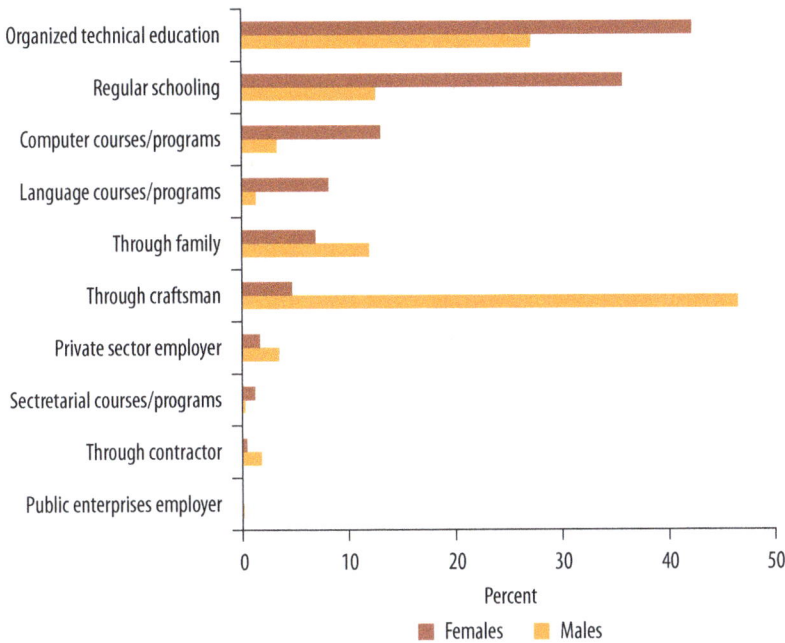

Source: Population Council 2009.

Women also are less likely than men to acquire job-relevant skills outside formal education. For example, in Egypt, only 5 percent of women say that they obtained training from other craftspersons, compared to 46 percent of men (figure 3.14). As a result, women have relatively less diversified and fewer marketable skills than do men. These limitations restrict women's ability to adjust their skills to suit private sector employers. In Upper Egypt, focus group discussions with young adults revealed that many felt that they did not learn job-relevant skills in school, and that even vocational education, when available, was "useless and theoretical." Employers in Egypt share similar views. Less than 30 percent of human resource managers agreed that the university graduates whom they had hired in the previous year possessed the appropriate hard or "soft" skills. Of vocational graduates, managers felt that only 16 percent had relevant hard skills, and only 12 percent had the necessary "soft" skills (IFC 2011b; World Bank 2011b). "Soft" skills encompass job-related technical skills, foreign language and communication, problem-solving, and leadership. Region-wide, the lack of basic employability, or "soft" skills, among young graduates severely inhibits their transition from school to work.

Women in the private sector in MENA more often are unpaid workers or self-employed (figure 3.15). In general, more men than women hold

FIGURE 3.15

Type of Private Sector Work by Gender

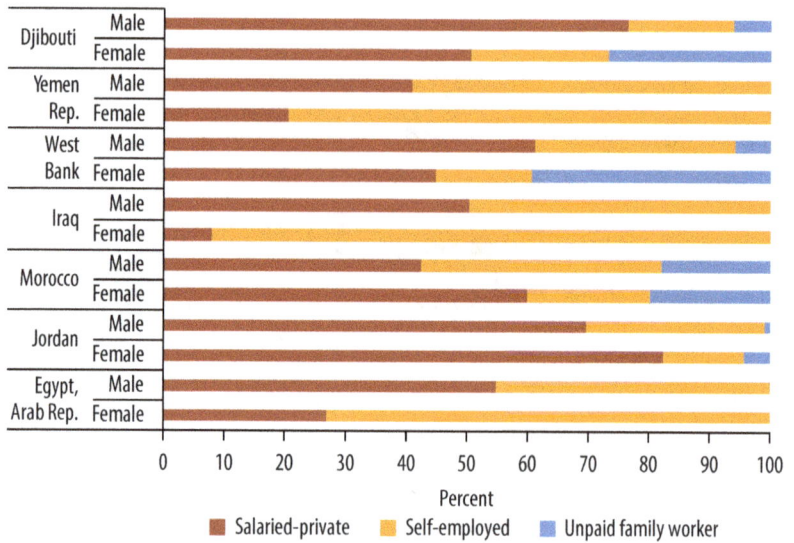

Source: Household surveys (appendixes A and C).

FIGURE 3.16

Informal Workers

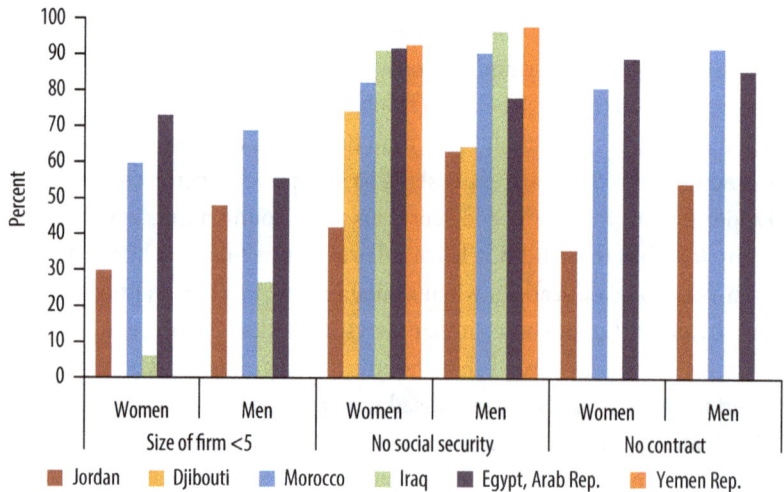

Source: Household surveys (appendixes A and C).

jobs in the informal sector, perhaps due partly to the high incidence of women in the public sector. This broad trend is true for Iraq, Jordan, and Morocco, in which informality is defined as working in businesses with fewer than five workers. The trend also holds true for informal workers in the private sector who lack contracts and social security benefits (figure 3.16). In some MENA countries, lower levels of informality for women also may reflect the fact that, unless driven by necessity, women do not participate if they are unable to secure job benefits. In fact, women in the private sector tend to have much lower levels of education than women in the public sector and are more likely to live in rural regions. Moreover, in countries whose wage data are available, there is evidence that women are paid less than men when they work in similar occupations (box 3.3). This unequal pay dampens their incentive to participate in the labor market.

Unequal Access to Entrepreneurship Opportunities

Women face not only unequal pay and occupational choices but also limited self-employment opportunities through entrepreneurship. As noted earlier, relative to the rest of the world, female-owned and -managed firms in MENA are rare. To a large extent, this gap is due to the Region's business environment, which is not conducive to entrepreneurship in general. The World Bank/IFC Doing Business Surveys reveal that all firms in MENA (regardless of the owners' gender) perceive the business environment as unfair. Both genders cited corruption and anticompetitive practices as the most pervasive constraints (figure 3.17).

Female-headed firms noted few obvious gender-based differences in the constraints to entrepreneurship. This perception may reflect the views of firms that already are well established. It says nothing of the barriers to set up a business. In this regard, gender-neutral barriers could have gender-differentiated effects. For example, cumbersome and costly procedures for opening a business and uncertain chances of recovering assets from a failed venture may be more difficult for women to overcome. Although the data do not enable examination of the views of women who failed to establish businesses, research in Tunisia concluded that the main difficulty for the majority of women entrepreneurs in Tunisia is getting specific information on starting a new business (Drine and Grach 2010). In fact, a recent analysis of existing literature concludes that aspects of the business regulatory environment are estimated to disproportionately affect women in their decisions to become entrepreneurs and their performance in running formal businesses. As the World Bank's Doing Business 2011 report argues, ". . . one possible barrier is that women may have less physical and 'reputational' collateral than men" (Klapper and Parker 2011; World Bank 2010).

Finally, while a survey of business lawyers in the Region suggests that business and investment laws are not necessarily gender biased, laws in other areas can influence their implementation and interpretation, and can be reinforced by gender-based perceptions and attitudes (World Bank 2007). As described above, family laws and regulations can influence economic rights, because women sometimes are considered "legal mi-

BOX 3.3

Explaining the Pay Gap in Egypt

In the MENA countries for which wage information is available, salaried women are concentrated in the public sector and, on average, have more education than men. They also tend to be younger, more urban, and single compared to men. All of these factors are associated with higher rates of pay.

How, then, is it that women are paid less than men? In Egypt, after accounting for the above factors, there is a significant unexplained wage gap between men and women amounting to a 32 percent difference in pay (figure B3.1). Most research in this area ascribes these unexplained gaps to discrimination against women.

FIGURE B3.1

How a Pay Advantage for Women Becomes a Deficit

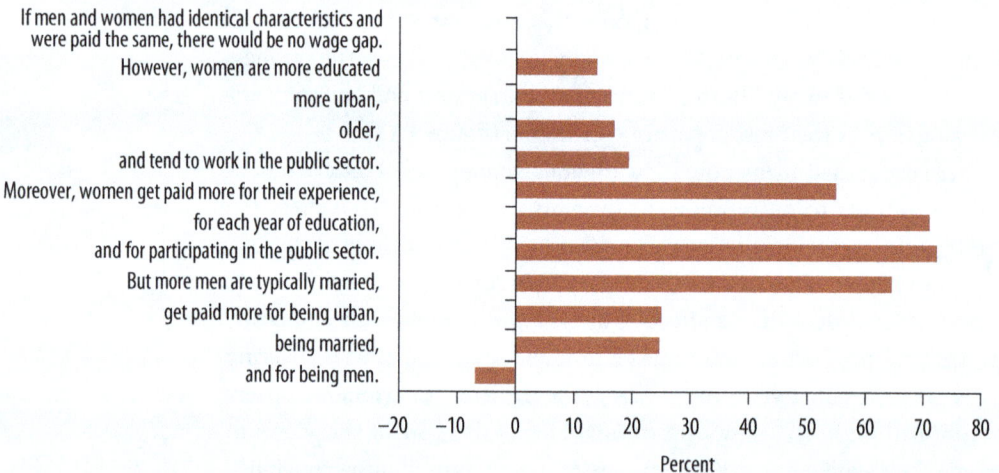

However, it is likely that such standard analysis often unjustly compares women and men. Some occupations are so deeply segmented that finding an appropriate reference group for both women and men is not possible. For example, construction workers tend to be men, so there is not a large enough sample of women to be able to make a gender-based comparison of wage differences in the industry. In Egypt, even when these differences are taken into account, the overall unexplained wage gap is still approximately 22 percent.

nors." Women entrepreneurs consistently cite the requirement to obtain a male relative's permission to travel as a hurdle that inhibits their mobility and ability to conduct business efficiently.

The constraints on female entrepreneurship and the lack of jobs in the private sector, combined with the unsustainability of the social contract,

FIGURE 3.17

Businesses Reporting Each Constraint as a "Major" or "Severe" Obstacle

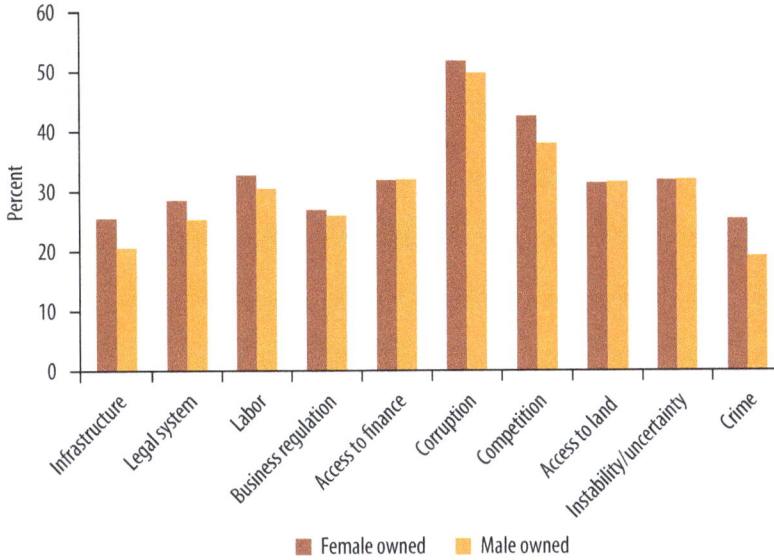

Source: Own calculations based on Business Environment Surveys (appendixes A and C).

especially for the oil-poor countries of the Region, imply an urgent need for reform. These reforms must boost job creation, while reducing policy distortions that have limited private sector development. Without such a concerted effort, the aspirations of young people in the Region, especially women, will remain unmet.

Note

1. For example the average cost of household electricity in Saudi Arabia is approximately $0.02/kw, whereas in Washington, DC, it is $0.13/kw. Similarly, the average cost of gasoline in Saudi Arabia is approximately $0.60/gallon, whereas in the United States, it is close to $4/gallon.

References

Abdelhamid, Doha, and Laila El Baradei. 2010. "Reforming the Pay System for Government Employees in Egypt." *International Public Management Review* 11 (3): 59–87.

Assaad, Ragui. 1997. "The Effects of Public Sector Hiring and Compensation Policies on the Egyptian Labor Market." *World Bank Economic Review* 11 (1): 85–118.

Birks, John S., and Clive A. Sinclair. 1980. *International Migration and Development in the Arab Region.* Geneva: International Labour Office.

Drine, Imed, and Mouna Grach. 2010. "Supporting Women Entrepreneurs in Tunisia." UNU-WIDER Working Paper 2010/100, UNU-WIDER, Helsinki. http://wider@wider.unu.edu.

IFC (International Finance Corporation). 2011a. *Education for Employment: Realizing Arab Youth Potential*. Washington, DC: The World Bank Group.

———. 2011b. *Strengthening Access to Finance for Women-Owned SMEs in Developing Countries*. Washington, DC: The World Bank Group.

IMF (International Monetary Fund). Ca. 2008. *Public Sector Wage Data*. Fiscal Affairs Department. Washington, DC: International Monetary Fund.

———. 2011. "Economic Transformation in MENA: Delivering on the Promise of Shared Prosperity." Note prepared by the Staff of the IMF for the May 27, 2011 summit of the Group of Eight in Deauville, France.

Klapper, Leora F., and Simon C. Parker. 2011. "Gender and Business Environment for New Firm Creation." *World Bank Research Observer* 26 (2): 237–57.

Population Council. 2009. *SYPE (The Survey of Young People in Egypt)*. New York, NY. http://www.popcouncil.org/projects/234_SurveyYoungPeopleEgypt.asp.

Said, Mona. 2001. "Public Sector Employment and Labor Markets in Arab Countries: Recent Developments and Policy Implications." In *Labor and Human Capital in the Middle East: Studies of Labor Markets and Household Behavior*, ed. D. Salehi-Isfahani. Reading, U.K.: Ithaca Press.

Salehi-Isfahani, Djavad. 1999. "Labor and the Challenge of Restructuring in Iran." *Middle East Report* 28 (210): 34–7.

———. 2002. "Population, Human Capital, and Economic Growth in Iran." In *Human Capital: Population Economics in the Middle East*, ed. Ismail Serageldin. London: I.B. Tauris.

———. 2005. "Human Resources in Iran: Potentials and Challenges." *Iranian Studies* 38 (1): 117–47.

———. 2011. "Iranian Youth in Times of Economic Crisis." *Iranian Studies* 44 (6): 789–806.

UNESCO (United Nations Education, Cultural and Scientific Organisation). 2000–10. *UIS (Institute for Statistics)*. Paris.

WEF (World Economic Forum). 2010. *The Global Competitiveness Report 2010–2011*. Geneva. http://www.weforum.org/reports.

World Bank. 2004. *Unlocking the Employment Potential in the Middle East and North Africa: Toward a New Social Contract*. MENA development report, Washington, DC.

———. 2007. *Environment for Women's Entrepreneurship in the Middle East and North Africa Region*. Orientations for development series, Washington, DC.

———. 2009. *From Privilege to Competition: Unlocking Private-Led Growth in the Middle East and North Africa*. MENA development report, Washington, DC.

———. 2010. *Doing Business 2011: Making a Difference for Entrepreneurs*. Washington, DC: World Bank.

———. 2011a. *Education Statistics (EdStats)*. Washington, DC: World Bank. http://data.worldbank.org/data-catalog/ed-stats.

———. 2011b. *Reclaiming Their Voice: New Perspectives from Young Women and Men in Upper Egypt*. Washington, DC.

Yousef, Tarik M. 2004. *Employment, Development and the Social Contract in the Middle East and North Africa*. Washington, DC: World Bank.

CHAPTER 4

Time for Reform Is Now

Aspirations Are Changing

Women's Voices in the Arab Spring

Our demands are somehow similar to men['s], starting with freedom, equal citizenship, and giving women a greater role in society. . . . Women smell freedom at Change Square, where they feel more welcomed than ever before. Their fellow [male] freedom fighters are showing unconventional acceptance [of] their participation and they are actually for the first time letting women be, and say, what they really want.

—Faizah Sulimiani, 29, female protest leader, Yemen
(Rice and others 2011)

I grew up in a world where we believed we could not do anything. Generations believed we could do nothing, and now, in a matter of weeks, we know that we can.

—Mariam Abu Adas, 32, online activist, Jordan, who helped create a company to train young people to use social media (Slackman 2011)

We want women from today to begin exercising their rights. Today on the roads is just the opening in a long campaign. We will not go back.

—Wajeha al-Huwaidar, female activist, Saudi Arabia, speaking out on a campaign to secure women's rights to drive (Murphy 2011)

In recent months, young people in the Middle East and North Africa increasingly are voicing their aspirations and calling for change. A key part of this call for change is access to greater economic opportunities. This demand is no surprise as the economies of the Region go through a demographic transition that is increasing the number of young people in

FIGURE 4.1

Average Years of Total Schooling for Females, Ages 15 and Above, 1960–2010

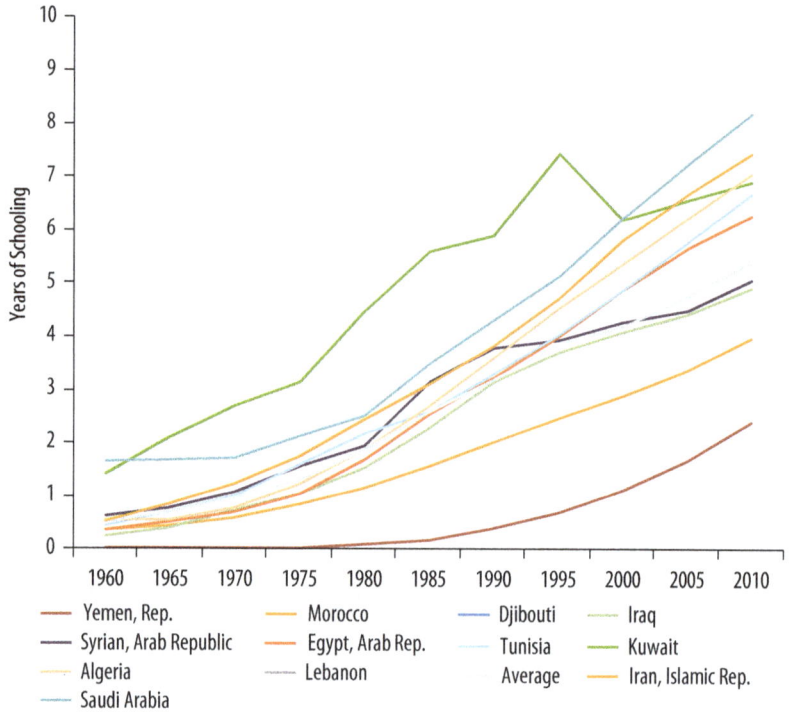

Source: Barro and Lee 2010.

the population and will continue to do so. Youth in most MENA countries are facing high rates of unemployment. The challenge is even greater for young women. Across the Region, young women are more educated than ever before, are having fewer children, and are looking for work. Yet, young women face the highest unemployment rates among all cohorts.

Some governments in the Region are responding by increasing spending on subsidies and public sector wages and expenditures. However, addressing the aspirations and needs of their youth will require comprehensive reforms that boost job creation without overburdening already strained budgets. These reforms will have to put private-sector-led growth front and center in the job creation strategy for women and men.

Women in the MENA Region are obtaining increasing amounts of education (figure 4.1). As they become more educated, women are more likely to participate in the labor market. Education changes aspirations, because increased skills enable women to make increasingly substantial contributions in the formal labor market. Over and above the monetary benefits of work, women may feel a sense of purpose and recognition of their talents and productivity. In countries across the Region, the probability that a woman will participate in the labor market increases with her education irrespective of marital status, age, and location (figure 4.2).

FIGURE 4.2

Female Labor Force Participation and Education

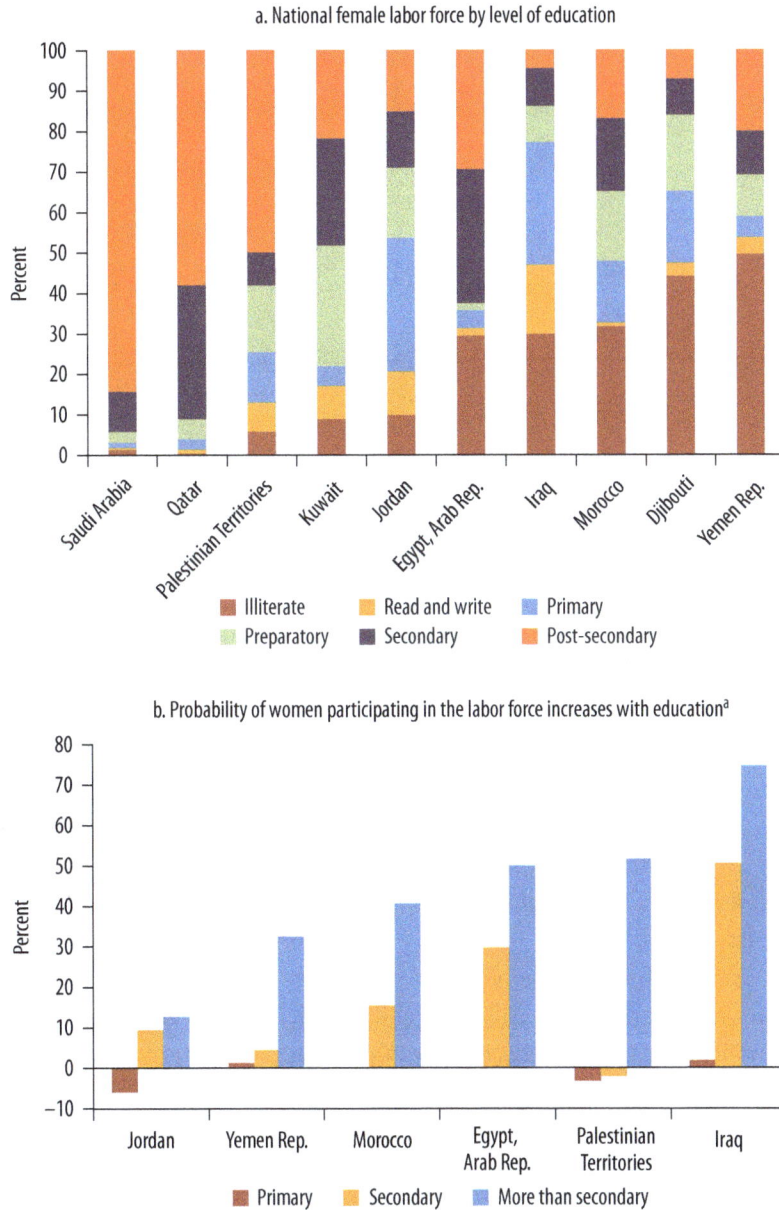

a. National female labor force by level of education

Legend: Illiterate, Read and write, Primary, Preparatory, Secondary, Post-secondary

b. Probability of women participating in the labor force increases with education[a]

Legend: Primary, Secondary, More than secondary

Source: Author estimates based on household surveys and official national statistics (appendixes A and C).

a. Refers to a probit model on labor force participation of women in which the reference group is uneducated women. The model controls for age, marital status, urban/rural effects, household composition, and Regional effects.

FIGURE 4.3

Tunisia: Female Labor Force Participation Rates, by Age and Education

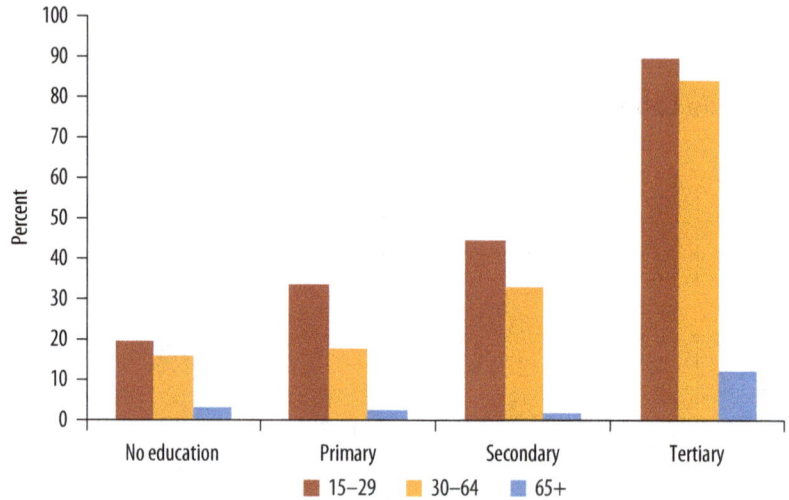

Source: Author estimates; Tunisia Labor Force Survey 2010 (appendixes A and C).

The relationship between education and female labor force participation rates is particularly strong in Tunisia (figure 4.3). Excluding women still in school, almost 90 percent of young women with a tertiary education participate in the labor force. For those with less than primary education, less than 20 percent work or are looking for a job (in either the formal or informal sector). As women grow older, the participation rate falls off slightly, especially for women over 30, as they are more likely to have children and therefore more likely to stay at home. The pattern of lower labor force participation among the less educated is true also for women over 65. Thus female participation in the labor force in Tunisia increases with education, and reduces with age, and the latter may be driven in part by attitudinal and legislative change that favors the younger cohorts (figure 4.3)."

As women stay in school longer and pursue careers in greater numbers, they also tend to delay childbirth and have fewer children.[1] For the past few decades, fertility rates have been declining across the Region (figure 4.4). This downward trend has been complemented by the upward trend in education. The effects of lower fertility and more female education on women's labor force participation in the formal economy have yet to fully materialize. However, it is only a matter of time before women begin to seek work outside the home in larger numbers, compounding the need for more abundant job creation in the Region.

FIGURE 4.4

Fertility Rates, 1960–2005 (Births per Woman)

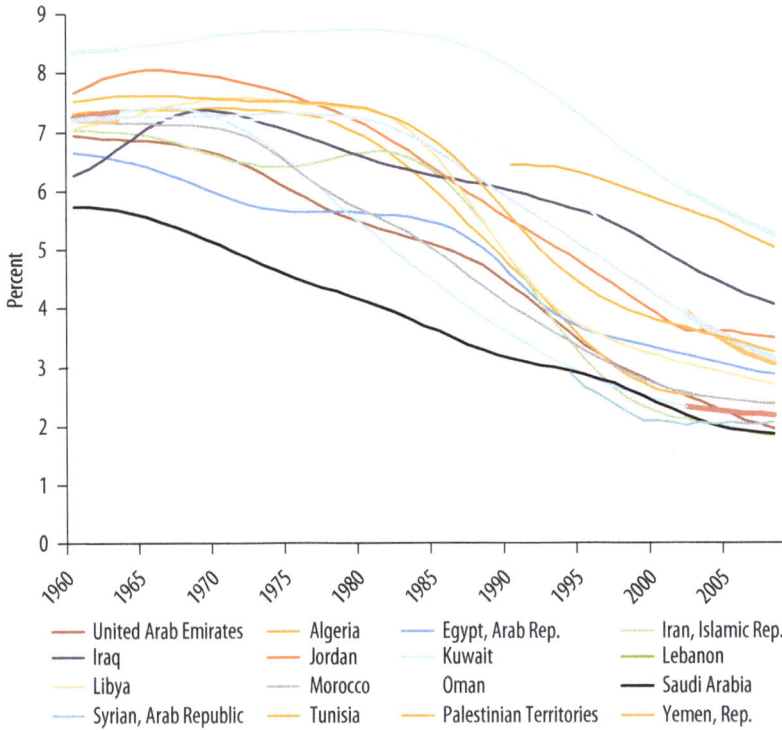

— United Arab Emirates	— Algeria	— Egypt, Arab Rep.	⋯ Iran, Islamic Rep.
— Iraq	— Jordan	— Kuwait	— Lebanon
— Libya	— Morocco	Oman	— Saudi Arabia
— Syrian, Arab Republic	— Tunisia	— Palestinian Territories	— Yemen, Rep.

Source: WDI 2011 (World Bank multiple years).

A Demographic Gift?

MENA is undergoing a demographic transition. The high population growth of the previous decades is reflected in a youth bulge, as is evident from the age structure of the population (figure 4.5). In most MENA countries, 15–29 year olds constitute approximately one-third of the population. As the bulk of the population moves into the working age group by 2050, younger cohorts will continue to be a significant proportion of the population. As a result, MENA faces labor force pressures on an unprecedented scale (Yousef 2004). Over the next few decades, this trend will only accelerate.

The immediate consequence of this demographic structure is the scale of job creation that will be required and will have to be sustained. Consider what would happen if current rates of employment for women and men in the Region remained constant over the next 4 decades (figure 4.6). In 2010, 30–40 million men of working age in the MENA Region were

FIGURE 4.5

Demographic Transition: MENA's Age Structure, 2010 and 2050
population in millions

a. MENA male and female population by age, 2010

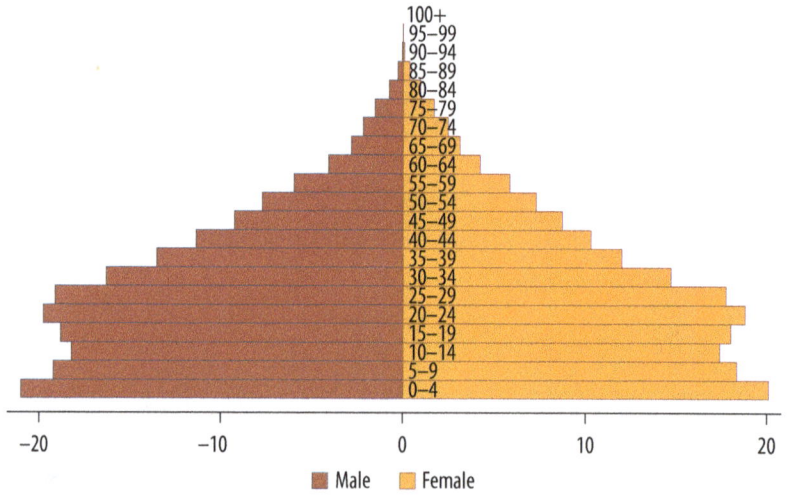

b. MENA male and female population by age, 2050

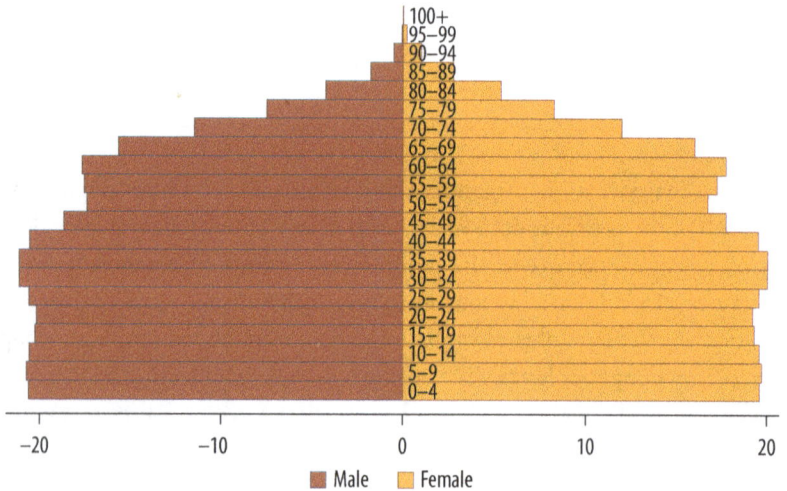

Source: UN DESA 2010.

not employed, and the number was much larger for women of working age. By 2050, 50 million men of working age would be without jobs, and the corresponding number for women would be a staggering 145 million.

FIGURE 4.6

Need for Jobs Will Increase over Time, 1950–2100

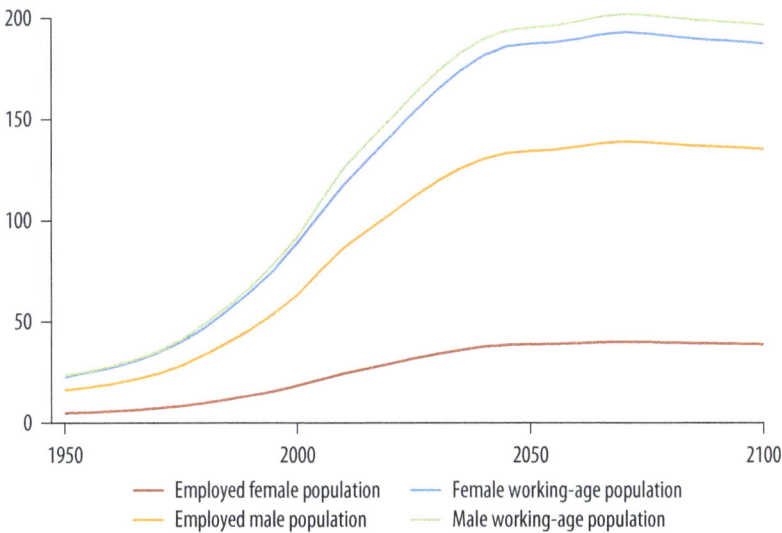

Sources: UN DESA 2010, 2050; WDI 2011 (World Bank multiple years).

In a Region in which both women and men believe that scarce jobs should be prioritized for men, young women are disproportionately affected. Unless major reforms are undertaken to boost job creation, this pool of educated, unemployed youth will expand, and with it, the ever-mounting frustrations from the sheer lack of economic opportunities. This lack of jobs and pent-up frustration will be especially true for the young women of the MENA Region.

Social Contract No Longer Sustainable

The recent popular movements in the Region signal a breakdown of the prevailing social contract, which no longer is sustainable in its implications for fiscal health and sustainable growth. In the past, some of these countries responded by taking steps toward diversification and private sector development. However, recent policy measures are increasing the fiscal strain, especially in oil-poor MENA countries. Early in 2011, the Egyptian government announced a 15 percent increase in the salaries and pensions of the country's 6 million state employees (Birnbaum 2011). Although most other countries will at least partly offset greater spending on social protection with cuts elsewhere, the net effect is a widening of fiscal deficits and reduced space for growth-oriented spending (appendixes B, table B.3).

FIGURE 4.7

GCC Primary Nonoil Balance, 2000–11
percent of nonoil GDP

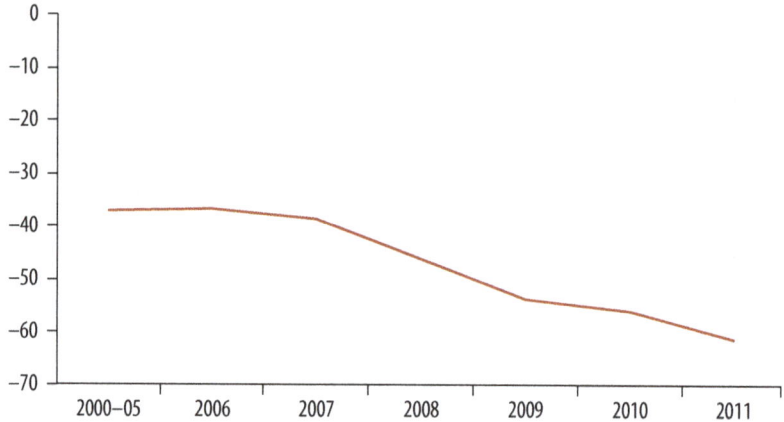

Sources: IMF 2011.

Even in the oil-rich MENA countries, which are benefiting from an increase in oil prices, government spending and nonoil deficits have risen persistently (figure 4.7). Assessments of fiscal sustainability reflect this trend. For example, in Saudi Arabia, the per-barrel price of oil that would enable the government to continue to finance its current programs (also known as the breakeven oil price) rose from US$30 in 2005 to US$80 in 2011. New concessions granted during 2011 also tilted toward public sector jobs and pay, thus adding to the fiscal burden. For example, in Bahrain, civil service pay and allowance raises were announced in 2011, amounting to an additional 2.5 percent of GDP. In the 2011 Kuwaiti budget, 90 percent of increased spending was to go to fuel subsidies and salary increases for a variety of public employees. Although the capital component of GCC government spending is increasing (to approximately one-quarter of the total), the bulk of budgeted spending goes to salaries, transfers, and subsidies.

Note

1. Economic historians have labeled the benefits to growth from a more rapid labor force growth and a low dependency ratio of working to nonworking population that follow fertility transitions as a "demographic gift" (Bloom and Williamson 1998) and a "window of opportunity" (Barlow 1994). Salehi-Isfahani 2002 and 2005, Tunali 1996, and Yousef 1998 show how the changing age structure can play a positive role in the MENA countries.

References

Barlow, Robin. 1994. "Population Growth and Economic Growth: Some More Correlations." *Population and Development Review* 20 (1): 153–65.

Barro, Robert J., and Jong-Wha Lee. Barro-Lee Dataset (2011). http://www .barrolee.com/main.htm.

Birnbaum, Ben. 2011. "Egyptian Leaders Announce 15% Pay Raises." *The Washington Times*, February 7. http://www.washingtontimes.com/news/2011/ feb/7/egyptian-leaders-announce-15-pay-raises/.

Bloom, David E., and Jeffrey G. Williamson. 1998. "Demographic Transitions and Economic Miracles in Emerging Asia." Working Paper 6268, NBER (The National Bureau of Economic Research), Cambridge, MA.

IMF (International Monetary Fund). 2011. "Economic Transformation in MENA: Delivering on the Promise of Shared Prosperity." Note prepared by the Staff of the IMF for the May 27, 2011 summit of the Group of Eight in Deauville, France.

Murphy, Brian. 2011. "Saudi Women Tap Road Rage against Driving Ban." *AP News*, May 24.

Rice, Xan, Katherine Marsh, Tom Finn, Harriet Sherwood, Angelique Chrisafis, and Robert Booth. 2011. "Women Have Emerged as Key Players in the Arab Spring." *The Guardian*, April 22. http://www.guardian.co.uk/world/2011/ apr/22/women-arab-spring.

Salehi-Isfahani, Djavad. 2002. "Population, Human Capital, and Economic Growth in Iran." In *Human Capital: Population Economics in the Middle East*, ed. Ismail Serageldin. London: I.B. Tauris.

———. 2005. "Human Resources in Iran: Potentials and Challenges." *Iranian Studies* 38 (1): 117–47.

Slackman, Michael, 2011. "Bullets Stall Youthful Push for Arab Spring." *The New York Times*, March 18. http://www.nytimes.com/2011/03/18/world/ middleeast/18youth.html?pagewanted=all.

Tunali, Insan. 1996. "Labor Market Implications of the Demographic Window of Opportunity." *The Forum*, 3(2).[[AQ: Please confirm the edit in this reference and provide the page range, if appropriate.]]

UN DESA (Department of Economic and Social Affairs). 2010. *Population Division, Population Estimates and Projections Section*. http://www.un.org/esa/ population/; http://www.unpopulation.org.

———. 2050. *Population Division, Population Estimates and Projections Section*. http:// www.un.org/esa/population/; http://www.unpopulation.org.

World Bank. Multiple years. *WDI (World Development Indicators)*. Washington, DC. data.worldbank.org/data-catalog/world-development-indicators.

Yousef, Tarik M. 2004. *Employment, Development and the Social Contract in the Middle East and North Africa*." World Bank, Washington, DC.

CHAPTER 5

Opening the Door to Women: Policy Directions

A Roadmap to Reform

This report has reviewed the gender challenges in the Middle East and North Africa (MENA) Region, highlighting both the similarities and differences across countries. MENA countries generally are characterized by common religious beliefs, relatively high per capita incomes, and relatively high endowments of oil resources. However, among the countries, these characteristics vary significantly. At the extremes, Djibouti and the Republic of Yemen have relatively low incomes, whereas Kuwait and Qatar are among the wealthiest countries in the world. Meanwhile, although MENA holds an estimated 60 percent of the world oil reserves (Saudi Arabia alone holds 20 percent of the world's proven oil reserves), Jordan, Lebanon, and Morocco have almost no oil endowments.

Against this backdrop, for policies to be effective, they must be tailored to each country's circumstances and germane to its stage of development. Countries with egregious gender gaps in human development need to make significant efforts to address these challenges. Meanwhile, countries with large oil endowments tend to have limited economic diversification, larger public sectors, and limited scope for private sector development (PSD). A reliable revenue stream from oil has enabled governments in these countries to defer economic reforms, whereas most oil-poor countries have more urgent needs to foster PSD and promote export diversification.

The overarching challenge in achieving gender equality in the Region is how to improve women's agency and economic participation. To achieve these, explicit efforts are necessary to create opportunities for women in the public sphere, while relaxing legal, social, and institutional barriers to participation. As evidenced in this report, even at the low rates of female labor force participation, women face disproportionately high levels of unemployment. In a Region in which chronic unemployment is prevalent, especially among youth, efforts to create more jobs for all are critical to expand women's access to economic opportunities. Therefore, MENA governments must engage in comprehensive and coordinated reform to jointly foster private-sector-led job creation, increase the employability of young women and men, and facilitate greater participation of women in the political realm. As these reforms progress, the countries will benefit from higher levels of productivity; a more dynamic private sector; a more fulfilled, involved, and dynamic workforce; and, ultimately, more inclusive societies.

In the past, MENA governments repeatedly have responded to unemployment, rises in the cost of living, and other social grievances by expanding public sector employment and creating or increasing subsidies. These measures are like a patchwork of Band-Aids, which offer a short-term solution to problems but fail to address the underlying structural issues. Instead, they compound the distortions in the economy and, like Band-Aids, can be painful to remove. The fiscal toll of such policies also is becoming increasingly difficult for MENA countries to maintain. Even in the Gulf Cooperation Council countries, which presently enjoy fiscal surpluses, such policies impose a persistent and growing burden on outlays that will become unsustainable in the long run as oil revenues taper off. Instead, reforms need to be structural and target underlying market and institutional failures. The recent popular calls for reform in many MENA countries reiterate the urgency to move decisively toward a fair and inclusive economic model, one that can generate jobs at a sufficiently rapid pace to provide opportunities for a growing workforce of young women and men.

Depending on country context and priorities for reform, countries in the Region may want to undertake complementary and coordinated efforts on multiple fronts. These include:

- *Closing the remaining gender gaps in human development.* Djibouti and the Republic of Yemen, and some regions within MENA countries lag behind the Region in the level of human development. This dimension therefore must be addressed in conjunction with efforts to increase female labor force participation and women's agency.

- *Increasing women's economic opportunities by removing constraints to their participation in the formal labor market and nurturing entrepreneurship.* Many MENA countries still face skills shortages and mismatches between what is learned in school and what private employers demand, overregulation of labor markets, and limited support for female entrepreneurs. Reforms in these areas are an urgent priority.

- *Closing gender gaps in voice and agency by fostering women's participation in politics and protecting their rights—at home and in the wider society.* While countries in the Maghreb—notably Algeria, Morocco, and Tunisia—have advanced the cause of women's agency and made reforms to their legal systems, the pace of reform in many other countries in the Region has lagged behind. Hand in hand with addressing skills shortages and restrictive business regulations, the lagging countries must prioritize reforms to promote women's legal rights and freedoms. Without accompanying legal reforms, the impact of job creation initiatives on women's employment and agency could be limited.

- *Supporting evidence-based policymaking by making national statistical data freely available and by rigorously evaluating policies and programs.* Policies must be predicated on evidence. With the exceptions of Iraq, Palestinian Territories, and the Republic of Yemen, data access is a major issue across the Region. As a result, identifying country-specific gender gaps and formulating nuanced policy interventions are challenges. Countries must invest in learning what works within their social and economic contexts. Systematic learning from rigorously evaluated policy pilots can provide invaluable lessons. Apart from recent exceptions in the Arab Republic of Egypt, Jordan, Morocco, and Tunisia, the Region has a vast knowledge gap in learning from rigorous evaluation. This knowledge gap is especially true of policies related to employment generation because, as the report highlights, there are multiple contributing factors.

Policies to Address the Region's Challenges

Drawing on evidence and examples from the international arena and the analyses in the report, the following section proposes key policy directions to alleviate each different constraint on women's economic and civic participation in the Region.

Closing the Remaining Gender Gaps in Human Development

The MENA Region as a whole already has made great strides in most aspects of human development. As noted above, at the national level, severe human development challenges remain in some countries. In others, strong indicators of human development and gender equality at the national level may mask deficiencies in human development for certain regions or groups of people. Accordingly, progress is still needed on the following fronts.

Expanding access to and quality of service delivery in health care, clean water, and sanitation

Between 1990 and 2008, many countries in the Region experienced declines in excess mortality. However, in Djibouti, girls less than 5 years of age evidenced no improvement in mortality rates, and excess female mortality during reproductive years actually increased. In Algeria, excess mortality rose in the 1990s and has shown no improvement over the last decade. Moreover, despite gradual improvement over time, the Republic of Yemen still has the second highest excess female mortality in the Region.

Broad-based, gender-neutral investments to improve the distribution and quality of health care and of water supply and sanitation can significantly reduce female and child mortality. For instance, expanding the provision of clean water in the United States in the beginning of the twentieth century paid off dramatically in lower infant and child mortality (World Bank 2012a, chapter 7).

At the same time, gender-targeted interventions to address remaining gaps also may be necessary. For instance, Turkey has reduced maternal mortality through improving health care delivery combined with focusing on expectant mothers. Given the effects of social norms on mobility, efforts also need to be made to bring health care closer to homes, or to locate health care in places with access to reliable transportation. In Bangladesh, a successful program that ran from 1978 to 1997 brought health services to the doorstep by training local women to distribute oral rehydration, immunizations, and family planning services (Lewis and Lockheed 2007, 187).

Improving access to education and its quality

MENA countries exhibit a diverse set of educational challenges. Many countries have invested heavily in education and generally have prioritized gender equality. Nevertheless, early dropout rates among girls remain high in Djibouti, Morocco, and the Republic of Yemen. Enrollment ratios in primary school remain well below 100 in both Djibouti and the Republic of Yemen. Although the Region as a whole does not exhibit significant inequality in access to schooling, disparities remain both among and within countries in the Region. At the same time, low education quality—resulting from poor facilities, overcrowded classrooms, and absentee teachers—contributes to poor educational outcomes, such as high repetition and drop-out rates and low achievement levels. High enrollment rates may mask low levels of actual educational attainment, which in turn contribute to the skills shortages and mismatches endemic in many countries in the Region. Since the reasons for poor educational outcomes are context specific, policy approaches must be designed to fit the country and address local conditions. This tailoring may take the form of efforts to lower student–teacher ratios, increase teacher attendance rates, or introduce tests to monitor cognitive and learning outcomes at various levels.

"Thinking equal" within the home

The decision to send a girl child to school or to seek health care for her is influenced by both economic constraints and social norms. Certain incentive-based approaches can be effective in encouraging equal treatment of girls and boys within the household. A widely used intervention of this kind is the conditional cash transfer (CCT) program, which provides financial incentives to households to keep the girls in school, or to ensure regular and timely health care for the women. CCTs have been introduced in a number of MENA countries, especially among the rural poor. Evidence from Morocco suggests that while cash transfers can be effective in improving educational outcomes, making transfers conditional on attendance may not be cost effective (box 5.1).

Additional interventions could be put in place to overcome the restrictions induced by social norms that inhibit girls' access to schooling or health care. Providing transportation facilities or subsidies to girls to be able to access school or health facilities more easily, or interventions such as having more female teachers and building girls' bathrooms in schools, may make it easier for parents to continue to send their girls to school.

Ultimately, identifying the appropriate mix of policies is strongly dependent on country context. Rather than relying on experience elsewhere, it is preferable to conduct carefully designed trials of proposed interventions on a small scale before scaling them up to a national or Regional level.

Expanding Economic Opportunities for Women

The very low rates of female labor force participation in MENA countries partly reflect women's preferences and the demands of family life, but they also reflect the lack of opportunities for those who want to work. This dearth is starkly reflected in the dramatically high unemployment rates for young women, particularly for those with high levels of education. These women want to work but cannot find suitable employment. Improving women's access to economic opportunities will enhance their roles in the public sphere and tap their productive potential, boosting the creativity and dynamism of the economy. Arguably, the economic empowerment of women can be a powerful lever to strengthen their voice and agency in other spheres. To achieve economic empowerment, efforts are necessary, on one hand, to expand the scale and type of job opportuni-

BOX 5.1

(Un)conditional Cash Transfers in Morocco

Experiments in countries such as Indonesia and Mexico have found that giving parents conditional cash transfers (CCTs) for sending their children to school can significantly boost school attendance rates.

Between 2008 and 2010, the Moroccan Ministry of Education conducted a pilot cash transfer program, called Tayssir, in 260 rural primary school sectors in the five poorest regions of Morocco. The program, which lasted for two full academic years, was designed to measure the impact of cash transfers on children's enrollment, attendance, and academic achievement in primary school. Three aspects of the program are particularly relevant: (a) transfers were given to either mothers or fathers; (b)

transfers increased by grade level; and (c) in some schools, all families who enrolled in the program were given unconditional cash transfers (regardless of whether their child attended school). In other schools, transfers were given to parents only if their child had missed four or fewer days of school in the previous month.

Preliminary results from household and school surveys designed to evaluate the impact of the Tayssir program show that (a) cash transfers improved school attendance and educational outcomes; (b) giving transfers to mothers was slightly more effective than giving transfers to fathers; and (c) making transfers conditional on attendance was not cost effective in the Moroccan context.

Source: Benhassine and others 2011.

Note: A school sector consists of a "central" school and several smaller "satellite" schools, which are administered by the headmaster of the central school.

ties; and on the other, to facilitate greater choice and mobility as well as to ensure compatibility with family life.

Creating jobs for all

Young people of both genders face considerable challenges in finding jobs in the MENA Region. As discussed extensively throughout the report, the problems of unemployment and economic exclusion apply to young men as well as women. For many years, most MENA countries have fostered large public sectors to absorb excess labor, but this policy is unsustainable both fiscally and in light of the massive increase in numbers of young jobseekers. For the supply of jobs to increase in line with the growth of the working-age population, private firms must be encouraged to hire and grow. Hence, policies to foster private sector growth and job creation are paramount and must be tailored to the country context. In some contexts, such as the Palestinian Territories, the employment chal-

BOX 5.2

The Palestinian Territories: A Unique Context

In the last decade, the Palestinian Territories has witnessed some of the highest unemployment rates in the world. In 2009, overall unemployment rates were above 20 percent in the West Bank and well above 35 percent in Gaza. Over the last decade, female labor force participation rates in the Palestinian territories have been consistently below 16 percent—among the lowest in the world. It is of great concern that, although female labor force participation has been on the rise since 2003, unemployment among women also has increased sharply. These parallel increases suggest that widespread male unemployment is pushing women to look for work; but with fewer jobs to go around, women find it increasingly difficult to find work.

In the unique landscape of the Palestinian Territories, mobility constraints for women and men extend well beyond those imposed by social norms and legal restrictions. Extensive internal and external barriers to physical mobility form the most significant constraints to growth and private sector job creation. Under these conditions, the single most important reform would be to ease restrictions and lift the closure regime that has constrained growth, investment, and, consequently, the job creation that is essential for a young and highly educated population. In the absence of vibrant employment-generating growth, social assistance will remain a critical element of Palestinian policy for the foreseeable future.

lenge is compounded by other significant constraints to growth and private investment (box 5.2).

• *Fostering growth and job creation in the private sector*—Over the last three decades, MENA countries have made efforts to move from a model of state-led growth to one relying more on the private sector. However, the current economic structures do not yet exhibit the sort of dynamism and growth potential found in high-growth economies. In some economies, this lack of dynamism may be driven by structural features, for example, a Dutch disease effect in the oil-rich countries. However, slow growth also is deeply rooted in the implicit social contract under which many countries in the Region long have operated. As a result, the majority of the population has maintained a status quo, whereas an elite has enjoyed privileged economic and political opportunities. As the 2009 World Bank report, "Privilege to Competition: Unlocking Private-Led Growth in the Middle East and North Africa," demonstrates, such an arrangement has created economies dominated by noncompetitive markets with barriers to entry and exit and protective labor regulations (World Bank 2009). The latter, in turn, have increased the costs of hiring labor while deterring the competitiveness of the private sector.

Although many MENA governments have tried to improve their overall business environments and employment policies to promote growth, stability, and jobs, these efforts have fallen short of expectations and have been unable to elicit the commensurate response of private sector growth and employment.

Clearly, the policy environment needs to explicitly encourage private sector firms to invest and grow. Examples of other countries' best-practice reforms that have been effective in this regard include (a) tax incentives and tax holidays for start-up companies and (b) investment promotion for high-growth and high-value services such as tourism.

Policies also should support the creation, expansion, and competitiveness of new firms and sectors within the domestic and international markets. Fostering links between educational institutions and the private sector could lead to productive partnerships in research, development, and training. Contests that enable private sector firms to bid openly for public contracts can be particularly useful to elicit private sector needs and priorities. Incentivizing innovations and entrepreneurship will increase economic competitiveness while drawing more women into the labor force.

Given the considerable gender-based occupational and educational segregation in the Region, women's employment will be increased fastest if governments promote the growth of "female-friendly" industries that employ large numbers of female citizens. High-value service sectors, such as information and communication technology (ICT) in particular, have demonstrated an ability to pull women into the workforce. While manufacturing varies widely in the use of female labor, sectors such as garments and food processing are particularly "female friendly."[1] As with all best-practice industrial policy, conditionality, sunset clauses, built-in program reviews, and monitoring and periodic evaluation are desirable (Rodrik 2008).

• *Reducing legal barriers to private sector growth and job creation*— The cost of setting up a business in some MENA countries is unusually high. In these countries, it is so difficult to fire employees that firms are reluctant to hire them in the first place. This is a particular problem for young people with no work experience on whom firms must "take a chance" in hiring. Governments could foster private sector growth by reducing regulations on investment, employment, and business registration. Beginning after 2005, Egypt undertook reforms intended to lower the barriers to entry for small businesses (box 5.3).

Surveys show that the greatest barriers faced by MENA firms are uncertainty about government policy, concerns about the consistency and fairness of regulation, and the presence of anticompetitive practices

Doing Business in Egypt

The 2005 Doing Business report ranked Egypt as the worst performer in the MENA Region regarding the ease of doing business. Within two short years, Egypt improved from 165 to 126 in the rankings, making it the top reformer worldwide. Along with broad-based reforms in tax and customs administration, Egypt made efforts to simplify regulatory functions, including creating one-stop shops (OSS)

for business registration in several key locations such as Cairo and Alexandria.

According to the IFC, by the end of 2007: "the number of days needed to start a business in Alexandria [had been] reduced by 30 percent. Costs fell by eight percent, and procedures were reduced by about 30 percent . . . company registrations started to increase, growing by almost 15 percent, in 2007."

Source: Hamdy and Sader 2008.

(Hamdy and Sader 2008, 89). MENA governments must demonstrate efforts to improve the transparency and accountability of regulatory policy, and, furthermore, to ensure that regulations are enforced consistently across all public and private sector firms.

Lengthy, complex, and costly procedures such as are required to register and license businesses may impact women disproportionately, as often they have more time constraints. Women may be subject to more interference, or open to exploitation, during their interactions with government officials, who can consider them a soft target for corruption and speed payments. Thus, streamlining procedures and improving transparency can greatly improve business outcomes for women (Simavi, Manuel, and Blackden 2010).

Creating jobs is a necessary but not sufficient step to increase female economic participation. It also is critical to break down the legal and social barriers that discourage employers from hiring female candidates and discourage women who want to work from accepting available jobs. From the analysis above and other research on labor markets in the Region, there clearly are many such barriers. Targeted and coordinated measures will help to remove them. The following are a number of suggested programs and policies (many from MENA countries) that have a successful track record in this regard.

• *Redressing skills mismatches*—Throughout the Region, firms complain about the shortage of job candidates with suitable skills. Notwithstanding the Region's impressive rates of educational attainment, questions remain about the quality of school and university education, and its relevance to the modern workplace.

The education system must be reformed to better respond to market signals and equip young people with the skills demanded by the private sector. Youth are being trained predominantly in traditional disciplines useful for public sector jobs, but of limited interest to private sector employers. To make graduates more attractive to firms, initiatives to encourage young people to seek training and experience in the nontraditional fields in demand by the private sector, including medicine, engineering, law, business administration, and ICT, could be vital. To ensure sustainability and skills matching, the active participation of the private sector in design and implementation is key. Elsewhere in the world, providing scholarships and prizes to girls is one approach that has been very successful in boosting educational outcomes (box 5.4). Admissions quotas for tertiary studies have a direct positive effect on the enrollment of girls in nontraditional fields and have been introduced in a number of MENA countries. However, in certain cases, these quotas can be distortionary and work against women. In Kuwait and Oman, for example, young

BOX 5.4

Incentives for Success

Scholarship programs are one method of encouraging girls to work harder in school and pursue nontraditional subjects. However, some argue that scholarship programs may encourage cheating and adversely affect the motivation of weaker students.

Evidence from a randomized experiment conducted in two districts in Kenya suggests that these criticisms are unfounded. Merit-based scholarships were offered to girls in a number of randomly selected primary schools in each district. The scholarships were awarded to the top 15 percent of girls based on their scores in a district examination, and covered one year's school fees, a textbook allowance,

and a certificate presented at a recognition ceremony.

The results of the experiment showed that the scholarship had a number of unexpected benefits. As expected, the test scores of all girls in the selected schools improved, even those of girls who were unlikely to win. Teacher attendance also increased. Perhaps as a result, some evidence suggested that the test scores of boys improved as well, even though boys were not eligible for the scholarships. These results suggest that scholarships offered to girls can have positive spillover effects on the quality of education for all students, as well as encourage more girls to study nontraditional subjects.

Source: Kremer and others 2009.

BOX 5.5

How Effective Are Active Labor Market Policies?

For the past half-century, the effectiveness of active labor market policies (ALMPs) has been a matter of vigorous debate. There have been numerous impact evaluation studies of individual ALMPs, mostly in Europe and the United States. Job search assistance programs generally have favorable impacts, especially in the short run. Evidence on the effectiveness of wage subsidies in raising the employment of the subsidized groups is generally positive, although not uniformly so. Training programs can show mixed results. In a few cases, the estimated impacts are zero or even negative; but, in sum, subsidies are found to have a modest likelihood of improving post-program employment rates.

In MENA, there is little systematic analysis of the effectiveness of ALMPs (mostly training), and most programs remain largely un-assessed. A recent World Bank study finds that most programs are not designed to accommodate the needs of female participants. There is a need for increased program targeting, as well as flexible schedules (offering classes during nights/weekends and offering different schedule alternatives), combined with child care opportunities. Most important, to inform policy, these programs must be rigorously evaluated.

Source: World Bank 2010a.

---

women now need higher grade-point averages than do young men to enroll in subjects such as engineering because the number of female applicants is so high relative to the quota (Kelly and Breslin 2010).

Universities could consider curricula reform to expose students to specialized fields such as information technology. Such changes can be made in consultation with the private sector, making use of partnerships such as cadetship programs, or exchanges of employees and instructors between educational institutions and firms.

Finally, employers often report that young jobseekers lack the "soft skills" (comportment and interview, presentation, and teamwork skills) that are necessary to succeed in the modern workplace. Employability and soft skills training for young people may ease the transition from school to work. However, evidence of the effectiveness of these ALMPs for soft skills is very limited (box 5.5). Initial results from the Jordan NOW pilot suggest that soft-skills training alone has a limited effect on employment.

• *Boosting female employment by combating negative stereotypes and creating an enabling environment for hiring women*—Women in the MENA Region are employed overwhelmingly in the public sector.

This skewed outcome can be explained in part by the pay gap described above. However, another reason is that private employers find women more "costly" to employ than men.

Firms fear that maternity may interrupt women's employment, costing the firm maternity benefits and replacement labor costs. While all MENA countries guarantee women paid maternity leave, approximately half of the countries mandate that the employers pay the benefits. This policy makes women relatively more expensive than men, discouraging firms from hiring them or lowering the rate of pay that firms offer women. For instance, Egypt has legislation that triggers the mandatory provision of childcare services at a minimum number of female employees. These laws discourage firms from expanding their female employment capacity beyond that point. This disincentive could be removed by reforming the laws to set the minimum as the number of total employees (women and men). More broadly, moving to a shared social security system, in which all employers and employees contribute to a national maternity fund, would reduce the relative cost to employers of hiring women of child-bearing age. Recent reforms in Jordan are a model of how establishing a successful national maternity fund can be done (box 5.6).

Furthermore, policies need to be designed to dispel common prejudices and social norms about female employees. In MENA countries, some employers have misconceptions about the reliability, productivity, and commitment of women and young people in the workplace. It is important to combat these misconceptions and improve the confidence of private sector firms in the employability of youth and women. Given the difficulty that firms in many MENA countries have in firing unsuitable workers, internships and short-term incentives to firms can provide young people with workplace experience while giving firms the opportu-

BOX 5.6

Jordan's Innovations in Shared Social Security

Jordan's parliament recently passed a broad social insurance reform law, which extends coverage to microfirms and adds unemployment, health, and maternity benefits to the package. Until recently, the full cost of the maternity benefit including 10 weeks of paid maternity leave was borne by the employer. This cost created disincentives for employers to hire women and may well have contributed to the very low level of female participation in Jordan's private sector. The reform entails financing maternity benefits through a 0.75 percent levy on payroll taxes on all workers, regardless of gender. Both employers and employees contribute to a "Maternity Fund," which is managed by the Social Security Corporation (SSC).

nity to screen them before hiring. In Jordan, for instance, a recently completed pilot provided a "job voucher" to young female graduates, effectively subsidizing firms that take a chance on hiring them (box 5.7).

• ***Removing regulatory barriers and easing credit access for female entrepreneurs***—As an alternative to paid employment, more needs to be done to encourage women to start their own businesses. As well as generating income for their families, female entrepreneurs set a positive example for other women and may be more likely to hire female employees.

MENA countries' female entrepreneurship rates are the lowest in the world (Chamlou, Klapper, and Muzi 2008). As business owners, MENA women face many disadvantages. Registering a business often is more difficult for women than for men, in part because, in some countries, a

---

BOX 5.7

Jordan: New Work Opportunities for Women (Jordan NOW)

The Jordan New Work Opportunities for Women (NOW) pilot was designed explicitly to support a rigorous impact evaluation. The pilot randomly assigned 1,347 female community college graduates of the 2010 cohort to one of three labor market interventions: a 3-week soft-skills training course for 300 women, a 6-month job voucher offer for 300 women, a dual training and job voucher offer for 300 women, and a control group for 499 women. The job voucher offered a firm a 6-month wage subsidy conditional on hiring a graduate.

Early results from the midline survey indicated that employers responded to clear financial incentives: the job vouchers induced a 39 percent rise in female employment. Moreover, 57 percent of women expected to keep their jobs after their vouchers expired. In contrast, the training program received extremely positive feedback from trainees, yet had no significant effects on employment. A detailed survey was then undertaken to verify and understand the long-term impacts of the pilot. While the pilot succeeded in its objective of increasing female labor force participation and helping young women accrue work experience, the majority of the jobs did not translate into permanent employment. The pilot highlighted critical constraints to young job seekers in Jordanian labor market regulations: the minimum wage and the requirement to register workers in social security limited the willingness of many firms to retain these young graduates after the wage subsidy expired.

To identify other effective alternatives to facilitate the school-to-work transition, an extension of the pilot is underway which involves an employee screening and matching intervention that develops signaling mechanisms for jobseekers, reduces the search costs for employers, and connects jobseekers with employers.

woman requires permission from a male guardian. In contexts in which women have limited or no rights to family capital for collateral, accessing credit also can be a challenge. An IFC MENA survey of women entrepreneurs in five countries (Bahrain, Jordan, Lebanon, Tunisia, and the United Arab Emirates) showed that 50–75 percent of women had applied for external financing for their businesses, but the majority was not successful. The difficulties included high interest rates, collateral requirements, lack of track record, and complexity of the application process (IFC 2011b).

Microfinance is an oft-cited example of a policy that can support female entrepreneurs. However, recent studies of its effectiveness for female entrepreneurs have found that outcomes are limited and typically weaker for women than men (box 5.11) (Banerjee and others 2010; De Mel, McKenzie, and Woodruff 2009; Karlan and Zinman 2009). Rather, policies must make business registration easier and less expensive, and help women access credit by enabling them to register their assets and enter contracts on their own terms.

As discussed earlier, reforming regulations to allow collateralization of movable as well as immovable assets could improve access to finance for women, who often are excluded from land ownership (Simavi, Manuel, and Blackden 2010). Mandating joint titling of assets of spouses is another policy approach to enhance women's access to collateral. Lack of credit history can be another barrier for women applying for loans for businesses. Lowering the threshold of loans covered by credit bureaus is instrumental in helping women build credit histories (Pearce 2011). As a remedy, the Syrian Arab Republic established a credit bureau that offers information from microfinance organizations that are used by women. Recently, Jordan lowered the minimum loan amount offered by its credit bureau by one-third, and the Republic of Yemen's credit bureau abolished any minimum loan threshold (World Bank 2011b). In Syria, approximately one-third of microcredit borrowers are women, whereas, in Jordan and Syria, female borrowers comprise up to 84 percent and approximately 96 percent of all borrowers, respectively (Pearce 2011). Another option is to provide small and medium entrepreneurs with training and advice on business skills and legal and regulatory procedures.

Encouraging and Assisting Women to Participate in the Labor Force

In addition to creating jobs and advancing women's legal rights, policymakers need to encourage more women to work and improve their employability. For women to participate more fully in the formal labor market, governments need to help them balance their family responsibilities and also make the workplace a safer environment. At the same time, to be competitive candidates for jobs, women need to acquire skills that are relevant to the private sector.

• *Fostering a healthy balance between work and family life*—Finding ways to make work and family life more compatible is an important policy priority. Flexible work hours and provisions for maternity and child care are important issues to be addressed. Jobs that provide more flexibility in these dimensions would enable women to make contributions in the public sphere without feeling that they are compromising their roles within their families.

In the last century in OECD countries, many married women first entered the workforce in a part-time or casual capacity. Flexible work hours and arrangements to work from home make it less costly for women to combine work with family responsibilities. In the US, "flex-work" has enabled many female workers to continue working after marriage (Goldin 2006; Jaumotte 2003). Flexible work arrangements are well suited to occupations in which physical presence is not required and output is easy to

---

BOX 5.8

Bringing Jobs to Women's Doorsteps: Desicrew's Innovative Business Model

Desicrew is a rural business process outsourcing (BPO) company in India that uses an innovative business model to bring young rural women into the workforce. Rural BPOs shift back office tasks from urban locations to small towns and villages, creating high-skill employment outside of major urban centers. Employees enter data, manage databases, transcribe interviews, or aggregate information from the internet for corporate clients. Given the lower costs of living in rural areas, the wages attract rural youth while generating large cost savings for clients.

Approximately two-thirds of Desicrew's employees are women. As they do not have the option to work in a city, for many of them, these jobs are unique new opportunities. Parents are unwilling to let their daughters move outside their immediate area due to a combination of safety concerns and cultural restrictions. To convince parents to allow their daughters to work, the company undertook an extensive information campaign, stressing the benefits of well-paid regular employment and the safety and prestige of working in a company that is seen as modern and urban.

Desicrew's experience suggests that rural outsourcing can play an important role in empowering women, improving their self-esteem and confidence, and strengthening their bargaining power within the household.

Source: Ranger 2010; Desicrew. India. http://desicrew.in/index.html.

monitor, such as call centers and data entry (box 5.8). However, it is important to ensure that increased flexibility does not substitute for job security, benefits, or work quality; and that casual contracts are not exploited by firms to evade unduly restrictive dismissal laws and other employee entitlements and protections.[2] In Tunisia, labor legislation passed in 2006 allows female employees in the public sector the option of part-time work at two-thirds of their full-time salaries while retaining full rights to advancement, promotion, holiday, and retirement and social coverage. However, because this option is limited to women, it has been criticized for not being extended to men (UN OHCHR 2010).

For young women looking for paid work, volunteering and temporary work opportunities provide an opportunity to build skills and networks and thereby boost their employability. The Teach for America program is an excellent example of a service-based volunteer program suitable for highly educated young people. The program offers college graduates in the United States the opportunity to gain teaching experience in disadvantaged areas, expand their breadth of experience, and utilize their talents. Entry into the program has become very competitive, reflecting the value of the experience to young people.

The high cost (or unavailability) of child care is a major reason why women in general choose not to work. Many developed countries have encouraged women to enter the workforce by providing fully or partially subsidized child care. Although there is some evidence that subsidized child care provision can enable women to continue their employment after childbirth, there also are examples suggesting that affordable child care by itself may not translate into higher female labor force participation (Blau and Currie 2006; Lefebvre and Merrigan 2009; Nicodemo and Waldmann 2009). It is important that childcare subsidies and tax policies are crafted carefully so that women gain net income from working.[3]

On the other hand, tax policies can be tweaked to encourage women to work. While the US government provides only small child care subsidies and no maternity leave benefits, tax incentives make it attractive for mothers to return to work after pregnancy. These incentives include the Child Care Tax Credit and the Earned Income Tax Credit (EITC). According to several rigorous studies, the EITC has substantially increased the labor supply of women. For example, Meyer and Rosenbaum (2000) found that the employment of single mothers in 1996 was 7 percentage points higher because of the EITC. Thus, the US experience suggests that, to encourage women with children to work, incentive-based schemes may be more effective than direct subsidies for child care (a common policy in many European countries).[4]

- ***Enhancing women's freedom to pursue employment and entrepreneurial activities***—Restrictive labor laws that inhibit women's full par-

FIGURE 5.1

Women's Employment Restrictions Pervasive in MENA

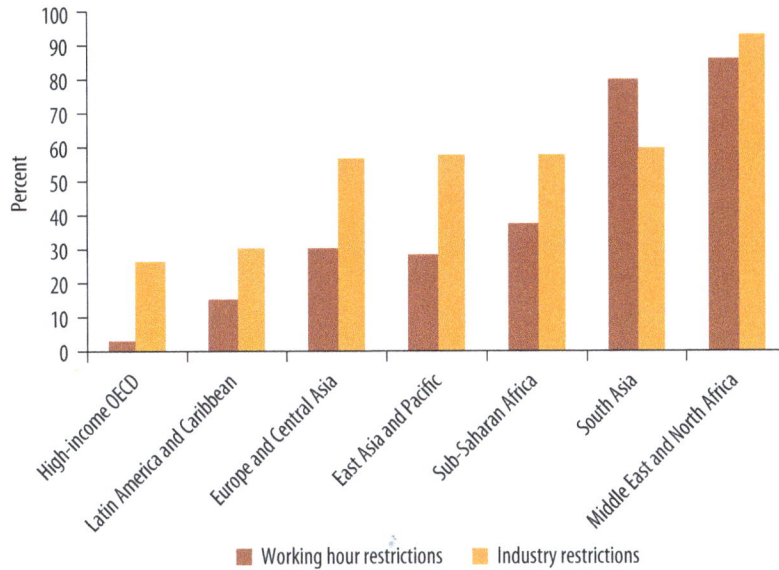

Source: Women Business and the Law database 2012.

ticipation in the labor market need to be reformed. Many MENA countries prohibit women from working at night and in certain industries (figure 5.1 and box 5.9) (World Bank 2012b). Relaxing such prohibitions would increase the employment opportunities available to women.

In many countries in the Region, a woman explicitly or implicitly requires the permission of the head of household or guardian to apply for a passport, travel outside of the country, and work outside of her home. Legislative change is of primary importance. Pending legislation, there are pragmatic ways to ease such mobility restrictions. Clauses in marriage contracts that guarantee women the right to work already are used in some countries (such as the Islamic Republic of Iran) to circumvent restrictions. Among the amendments to Egypt's Family Code in 2000, a new form of marriage contract was introduced that provides a blank space for stipulations. Examples of such stipulations are enabling female spouses to formalize property rights over the matrimonial home and its furnishings; prohibiting polygamy; and permitting women to seek unilateral divorces through a marriage registrar without the requirement for a court judgment. The initial proposal by women's groups was for a template marriage contract containing nine stipulations to which the couple could agree at the time of marriage. However, in the final reform, the proposal was watered down. Nevertheless, similar template marriage contracts still could be piloted at venues such as marriage registries, civil courts, and religious courts.

BOX 5.9

The Burden of Proof: Conditions for Women to Work in Saudi Arabia

Saudi Arabia's Manpower Commission is the agency responsible for implementing the labor laws. The commission lists five conditions that must be met before a woman can be employed:

1. The woman is in need of work.
2. The woman has the permission of her legal guardian.
3. The work she is performing suits her "female" nature and is such as to not deter her from her responsibilities toward her home and marriage and would not cause harm to the society.
4. The woman is to work in an area completely separate from men.
5. The woman is to maintain a decent appearance and wear the hijab according to Shari'a.

Source: World Bank 2011a.

Women ought to be able to be travel for their work, or change jobs, without their guardians having to repeatedly give written permission. One solution recently implemented in Saudi Arabia is for women to be issued an identification card with a one-time written permission from her guardian that allows her open travel. The card, issued by a local agency of the Ministry of Interior, is attached to the woman's passport, and clears her to travel until her passport expires. A similar procedure could be implemented to enable women to change employers without their guardians having to give renewed permissions.

• *Creating a safer, protected work environment, especially for young women*—Many families in MENA countries rightly are concerned about the risks that women face in the workplace. In some countries, harassment remains a serious problem and discourages women from working, particularly in the private sector. An initial step is to introduce legislation sanctioning harassment in the workplace. Algeria, Iraq, Morocco, and Tunisia have enacted legislation that criminalizes sexual harassment in the workplace and enables women to prosecute claims in court. Implementation and enforcement of these laws remain issues (as they do elsewhere in the world). Notwithstanding, promoting greater sensitivity in the workplace and improving monitoring and reporting mechanisms are essential, for example, by strengthening the capacity of the labor inspectorates within a country.

One approach to combat harassment is to provide firm-level training on how to maintain a gender-friendly work environment and thereby make private sector work attractive to women. The Gender Equity Model in Egypt (GEME) seeks to make working conditions in private firms more gender friendly. Participating firms undergo a training and certification program, at the end of which firms successfully completing the program receive a government-endorsed Gender Equity Seal. However, the program has suffered from low uptake. Consequently, serious modifications are required to extend the program to small and medium enterprises. Another new initiative recently launched in Egypt is HarassMap, a mobile-phone-based reporting system of cases of harassment, which is raising awareness of the problem and warning women of harassment trouble spots (http://www.harassmap.org). Crowdsourcing in this anonymous way is an innovative approach to measure the endemic problem of sexual harassment in Egypt. Using this system, women may be less afraid to report such events to family or the police out of fear of stigmatization, blame, or retribution.[5]

Steps also could be taken to improve women's ability to travel safely to and from work. In surveys from MENA countries, people identify the lack of safe, reliable transportation as a significant constraint on women's ability to work. Addressing this deficiency would be relatively inexpensive and could greatly increase the work opportunities available to women. In India and Mexico, public buses and trains designate spaces reserved for women to safely travel to and from work. The private sector also can directly ease mobility constraints for women. For example, some Indian firms provide corporate buses to take women from their homes directly and safely to the workplace.

Women working in the informal sector (such as domestic and agricultural workers) often are not covered by the labor protections offered to formal sector workers. Lack of formalized protection puts these women at risk of harassment, job loss, and nonpayment of salaries. Extending formal sector rights to informal workers (including regular payment of salaries, minimum wages, sick leave, and maximum work hours) would reduce these risks but also could limit informal sector employment opportunities. These tradeoffs are especially important in countries in which, in the absence of opportunities in the formal sector, women depend on informal activities for income.

Closing Gender Gaps in Voice and Agency

To be truly equal, women must have the opportunity to participate fully in public affairs, and have equal rights in the society and in the home.

Increasing women's representation in political life

While most countries in the Region guarantee constitutional equality for women and men, MENA's rates of female representation in parliaments are among the lowest in the world. To better represent the interests of women in the public sphere, MENA countries need to actively promote women's political and civic participation. While surveys from the Region indicate a lack of confidence in women's leadership capacities, studies from elsewhere in the world make clear that, despite being less experienced in politics than men, women perform just as well as men.[6,7] Increasing women's political representation has the potential to change deep-seated discriminatory norms: exposure to women leaders results in lower rates of electoral and psychological bias against women (Beaman and others 2009).

Across the world, countries are instituting formal mandates for women to be represented in politics through quotas in political bodies. Quotas need not be a permanent measure. Evidence exists that, even after their withdrawal, their positive effects on women's political participation remain (box 5.10) (Bhavnani 2009). However, to reduce the chances that women are not used simply as proxies for men, it would be desirable for quota legislation to be accompanied by close monitoring of both de jure and de facto compliance.

An alternate approach, which has met with considerable success in the recent Constituent Assembly elections in Tunisia, is to require equal representation by women and men on party lists. While the requirement that parties supply equal numbers of female and male candidates did not result in equal numbers of seats won, Tunisia elected a higher share of female

---

BOX 5.10

Temporary Quotas, Permanent Results

In 1997 and 2002 studies of ward-level elections in Mumbai, Bhavnani (2009) found that reserving seats for women not only increased their rate of success after the quotas were removed, but also increased the number of women who stood for office.

More important, quotas seem to have made the electorate more willing to vote for women. The share of votes polled by all female candidates rose from a mere 3.3 percent in 1997 to 15.0 percent in 2002.

Taken together, these findings suggest that quotas work partly by encouraging capable women to run for office and partly by teaching parties that women can win elections.

members to the assembly than any other parliamentary body in the MENA Region.

Women's influence in other decision-making institutions remains low throughout the Region. Few women hold leadership positions in workers' unions, and women's participation in Arab trade unions "is almost always limited to women's issues" (Kawar 2002). Female representation on company boards also is low.

Enhancing women's roles in decision making at local and community levels

Even in the absence of systemic changes to the electoral system, women's civic participation can be enhanced by strengthening their roles in local associations such as village development committees, self-help groups, and community health providers' groups.

One encouraging example comes from Afghanistan's National Solidarity Program (NSP). This government program creates elected gender-balanced Community Development Councils, and empowers them to select, design, and manage village-level microprojects. An impact evaluation of the NSP found that, in addition to improving villagers' access to services, the program has increased the engagement of women across a number of dimensions of community life. At the same time, through the program, senior women in the village have gained increased respect, and men have become more open to female participation in local governance (Beath and others 2010).

Safeguarding women's legal rights within the home

Head of household laws and guardianship laws that impinge on women's mobility and decision-making choices should be repealed. Citizenship laws that prevent women married to non-nationals from passing on their nationality to their husbands or their children also should be reformed, because these laws have economic implications for the whole family in lost access to benefits such as housing and education. Creating intraregional linkages among legislative decision makers, academic institutions, women's networks, and lawyers' associations to study the dynamics of reform and the substantive content of reform can accelerate the process. For example, a project aimed at comparing the Yemeni Personal Code with the Moroccan Family Code has been established based at both the Sana'a University Gender Research and Study Center in the Republic of Yemen and the Sidi Mohammed Ben Abdallah Fez University in Morocco (Yemen Women Union 2009).

Women rely on household assets for financial security and as collateral for credit. As discussed, access to collateral is an important prerequisite to enable female entrepreneurs to borrow for their businesses. Yet, many women in the Region still lack any ownership rights to household property because they are women. One solution is to introduce a community of property regime for monogamous marriages. This regime is already an option for families in Algeria, Morocco, and Tunisia. Nonetheless, it sometimes is not sufficient to simply provide this option, because women with limited household bargaining power can be coerced to decline it. Designating the joint regime as the default option makes it more likely that women will have legal ownership rights to household property.

A related issue is the vulnerability that women face in the event of divorce or the death of their spouses. In the West Bank, a government alimony fund offers protection for divorced women whose ex-husbands evade court orders for maintenance payments. Alimony funds are not an entirely new concept. In the 1960s, Iraq established an alimony fund to provide financial support to divorced women. However, since the 1990s, this fund has been practically defunct. In 2004, Egypt established a family security fund to provide alimony and child support to divorcees whose husbands refused to support them. In an earlier incarnation, a government fund had distributed these funds but had found it difficult to collect reimbursement payments from the husbands, especially those working in the private or informal sectors. The new fund's resources were generated by administrative fees levied on the registration of births, marriages, and divorces, supplemented by additional contributions from the government budget. Tunisia set up and supported a similar fund (Law 93-65 of July 5, 1993). A commission set up to evaluate its impacts found that, from the fund's creation in 1998 to 2007, 9,735 families had benefited from it (Euromed Gender Equality Programme 2010c). In 2010, Morocco also legislated a familial mutual assistance fund, to be implemented in 2011, that would guarantee alimony payments to divorced mothers who have custody of their children (Euromed Gender Equality Programme 2010a).

Women also can be pressured to give up their inheritance rights to male relatives. To protect them from pressure from family members, Jordan is drafting legislation to prevent women from handing over their inheritance for 3 months. This approach is innovative, but further study is needed to gauge its effectiveness and replication possibilities. Another Jordanian initiative in the same spirit provides tax breaks for living bequests or gifts to daughters.

Finally, setting a minimum age of marriage—and increasing that minimum age—will help increase women's bargaining power and lower the risk of domestic violence (Jensen and Thornton 2003). Girls who marry early may not have the chance to pursue a full education or make choices about their lives as independent, mature adults before marriage circumscribes their choices. Algeria, Egypt, and Morocco implemented reforms to increase the minimum legal age of marriage for both sexes. However, in some countries, such as Morocco, there is still the option to apply to the court for approval of the marriage of a girl and a boy both less than 18 years old (UNSTAT 2012). Removing this option would close a possible loophole that permits early marriage. The government also could undertake awareness building around the benefits of later marriage because early marriage tends to persist in rural low-income areas.

Finally, domestic violence prevention legislation should be introduced to protect women. Data show that where these laws exist, levels of domestic violence are lower and fewer people find it acceptable (UN Women 2011). Egypt, Jordan, Morocco, and Tunisia all have laws to prevent domestic violence.

Enforcing women's rights and building women's confidence in the legal system

Reforms to laws will not be effective unless they are enforced effectively. On one hand, women need to be aware of their rights; on the other, they need to be confident that their rights will be upheld. Employers and even police and judges can be unaware of new laws and reforms. Gender sensitization training for judges and court personnel also helps improve women's perceptions of the court system and their confidence in it. Influential networks, such as legal and business associations, could be important advocates for policy change and enforce it in their professions.

Given the prevailing social norms and the relative dominance of men in the legal system, promoting the active participation of women in the legal process would improve access to justice and improve women's confidence in the legal system. Female Shari'a court judges have been appointed in Malaysia and in the Palestinian Territories. Other countries need to consider taking steps in the same direction.

It is important to take steps to ensure that courts are more female friendly. The Moroccan government established family sections within district courts as part of its strategy to implement the new Family Code. A female social worker is assigned to every family court, and there is a program for gender-sensitivity training of all family court judges (UN Women 2011). In addition, the use of mediation (offered by Egyptian family courts) and alternative dispute resolution (ADR) mechanisms could increase access to justice for women. Monitoring the quality of such services is key to ensure that they conform to nondiscriminatory principles and international human rights standards.

Other initiatives to improve access to justice include legal aid clinics and mobile courts. One such initiative, the Jordan Center for Legal Aid, was piloted with support from the World Bank and other donors. From

2009 to 2011, the center provided free or reduced-cost legal counseling for 700 people and legal representation to 180 people. The center was housed within offices of another nongovernmental organization that provided social welfare services. This pairing had the unintended effect of enabling women to seek legal advice without attracting attention and hostility from their communities. The Jordan Center for Legal Aid together with the Jordan Bar Association created the first pro bono lawyers' association. This association will help implement a system of "one-stop shops" to provide legal aid and counseling, thus increasing access and quality of service. The Ministry of Social Welfare recently agreed to refer poor women in need of legal assistance to the Justice Center for Legal Aid (World Bank 2010b). The United Nations Population Fund (UNFPA) is supporting the capacity building of legal clinics run by the Yemeni Women's Union in various locations across the country (Yemen Women Union 2009).

Paralegal schemes have been effective in other parts of the world (PEKKA in Indonesia, TIMAP in Sierra Leone). The use of paralegals can offer a lower-cost means to expand legal coverage and provide access to women, especially in rural areas. Paralegals can help women obtain birth certificates, marriage registration documents, and national identification cards, and, in general, raise women's awareness of their rights. Court information kiosks and the translation of laws into local dialects and languages also are useful in making laws more accessible.

The availability of good-quality services to tackle domestic violence can mean that more women turn to them. One-stop crisis centers have been set up in government hospitals in Malaysia. Women receive medical treatment, support, and counseling from social workers and volunteers from women's organizations. In Tamil Nadu, India, 188 all-women police units were created to focus on crimes against women. This change has increased women's willingness to report domestic violence (World Bank 2012a). Departments for the protection of families have been set up in the West Bank. They aim to provide women with counseling and support and referrals to shelters when needed. The departments also intend to develop a task force of female police officers who can provide social and legal counseling to women (Euromed Gender Equality Programme 2010b).

Spreading the word: Expanding the use of social and traditional media to inform women of their rights and to agitate for change

Many of the constraints faced by women who want to participate in the public sphere result in part from social norms. These norms will change over time, but this change can be influenced by the way that the media portray women. Soap operas and chat shows can provide fora that influence views on topics as diverse as women's roles in the workplace and domestic violence. In addition to traditional media such as radio, television, and print, the internet (particularly social networking platforms such as Facebook and Twitter) is a very effective means of reaching target audiences. Such new media can be powerful tools to disseminate information and build awareness of women's rights and capabilities.

A number of innovative programs elsewhere in the world provide examples of how media can be harnessed to shape social norms. The Meena Communication Initiative in South Asia has used a variety of media to raise awareness of gender inequality and the potential of girls. The initiative featured a girl cartoon character who uses her education to help her parents read directions on a package of seeds and detect cheating by a trader (Lewis and Lockheed 2007, 186). In Kenya, an initiative to educate young girls about the high returns to vocational training increased their enrollment in trade-school courses typically dominated by men (World Bank 2012a, 33).

Finally, programs could make use of successful female role models to demonstrate to young girls that women can succeed in the public sphere. A study in India showed that teenage girls who had repeated exposure to women leaders were more likely to express aspirations to marry later, have fewer children, and obtain jobs requiring higher education (World Bank 2012a, 33).

Supporting Evidence-Based Policymaking

Finally, in all countries in the MENA Region, there is a severe shortage of good quality data for analysis and policy design. While such data often are collected by government agencies, they are not always shared freely. This lack of transparency limits the extent to which data can be used for research, policy dialogue, and innovation, especially by the private sector and nongovernmental organizations. Furthermore, to date, very few policy interventions are rigorously evaluated. Thus, the lessons learned cannot be transferred to other contexts.

MENA countries must improve the collection and sharing of detailed survey and administrative data to facilitate economic monitoring and the design of appropriate policies and reforms. Greater transparency and data sharing are essential to improve the success of the Region's reform efforts. Data on how women use the legal system also are lacking. More research is needed to understand how and where women settle disputes, whether in the formal court system or in the informal legal system (family or informal religious councils). For example, Jordan has extensive data on its formal courts that have not been utilized for court-user studies or to provide other gender-disaggregated data. Furthermore, the country lacks research capacity in these areas.

In addition, the Region needs to perform more rigorous monitoring and evaluation of new policies. Many job creation and training initiatives

---

BOX 5.11

Learning What Works . . . and What Doesn't

Recent evidence on the gender impacts of grants to microentrepreneurs is sobering. In Sri Lanka, grants had no effect on the incomes of women, even though women did not invest less in their businesses than did men (De Mel, McKenzie, and Woodruff 2009). These results point to the importance of learning what works, what does not, and why, through rigorous impact evaluations.

In Egypt, a new project aims to improve access to finance to micro- and small enterprises, which account for about 99 percent of all enterprises. As part of this project, post office branches are being used as outlets to offer microenterprise loans to disadvantaged women in some of the poorest 1,000 villages. A randomized impact evaluation—the first such initiative in the world for a government-run microfinance program—has been designed to understand the effectiveness of this program. The lessons learned will inform both the design of future loan products to be offered, and the decision on whether to scale up the post office lending model.

---

are being tried in MENA countries by governments and private sector agents alike (box 5.11; Angel-Urdinola, Semlali, and Stefani Broadmann 2010).

However, there is limited evidence on how well these initiatives work in practice. Rigorous impact evaluation of pilot programs can precisely measure the net benefits and cost effectiveness of interventions. This evidence will help policymakers fine-tune the program in the studied country and can be used to help design similar policies in other countries.

Notes

1. Alesina, Giuliano, and Nunn (2011) go so far as to suggest that, by making agriculture a more or less "male-oriented" activity, agroclimatic conditions of the past largely determined today's attitudes toward gender.
2. Booth, Francesconi, and Frank (2002) found that temporary jobs in the UK tended to be paid less than permanent jobs. However, these jobs also were effective "stepping stones" for jobseekers to find attractive companies and eventually move into permanent employment.
3. Immervoll and Barber (2006, 36) found that, in many OECD countries, childcare costs could substantially erode the financial benefits to women from working. In some OECD countries, low-paid women actually were worse off if they worked and sent their children to child care.
4. Some European countries have programs similar to EITC, including Belgium, Denmark, Finland, Sweden, France, and the Netherlands.

5. Crowdsourcing is a means of leveraging mass collaboration through web tech-
   nologies that facilitate information sharing and collaboration. With crowdsourcing, tasks are performed by a community of people or crowd through an
   open call, rather than by an employee or a group of employees.
6. The body of evidence is based on India's reform to include quotas for women
   in village governments. Since the 73rd Constitutional Amendment of 1992,
   no less than one-third of the total number of seats in democratically elected
   village governments, and no less than one-third of the staff of the office of the
   president of the village government, has been reserved for women.
7. For an overview of the justification for reservations and the main findings from
   India, see Duflo 2005.

References

Alesina, Alberto, Paola Giuliano, and Nathan Nunn. 2011. "On the Origins of
    Gender Roles: Women and the Plough." Working Paper 17098, NBER,
    Cambridge, MA.

Angel-Urdinola, Diego F., Amina Semlali, and Stefani Broadmann. 2010. "Non-
    Public Provision of Active Labor Market Programs in Arab-Mediterranean
    Countries: An Inventory of Youth Programs." Social Protection Discussion
    Paper 1005, World Bank, Washington, DC.

Banerjee, Abhijit, Esther Duflo, Rachel Glennerster, and Cynthia Kinnan. 2010.
    "The Miracle of Microfinance? Evidence from a Randomized Evaluation."
    Working Paper, Jameel Poverty Action Lab, Boston, MA.

Beaman, Lori, Raghabendra Chattopadhyay, Esther Duflo, Rohini Pande, and
    Petia Topalova. 2009. "Powerful Women: Does Exposure Reduce Bias?" *The
    Quarterly Journal of Economics* 124 (4): 1497–540.

Beath, Andrew, Fotini Christia, Ruben Enikolopov, and Shahim Ahmad Kabuli.
    2010. *Randomized Impact Evaluation of Phase-II of Afghanistan's National Solidar-
    ity Programme (NSP): Estimates of Interim Program Impact from First Follow-up
    Survey.* World Bank, Washington, DC.

Benhassine, Najy. 2011. "Impact Evaluation of Conditional Cash Transfer Pro-
    gram in Morocco." Unpublished notes, World Bank, Washington, DC.

Bhavnani, Rikhil R. 2009. "Do Electoral Quotas Work after They Are With-
    drawn? Evidence from a Natural Experiment in India." *American Political
    Science Review* 103 (1): 23–35.

Blau, David, and Janet Currie. 2006. *Preschool, Day Care, and Afterschool Care:
    Who's Minding the Kids?* Handbook of the Economics of Education. Amster-
    dam: Elsevier.

Booth, Alison L., Marco Francesconi, and Jeff Frank. 2002. "Temporary Jobs:
    Stepping Stones or Dead Ends?" *The Economic Journal* 112: F189–213.

Chamlou, Nadereh, Leora Klapper, and Silvia Muzi. 2008. *Environment for Wom-
    en's Entrepreneurship in the Middle East and North Africa Region.* Orientations
    for Development Series. Washington, DC: World Bank.

De Mel, Suresh, David J. McKenzie, and Christopher Woodruff. 2009. "Measur-
    ing Microenterprise Profits: Must We Ask How the Sausage Is Made?" *Jour-
    nal of Development Economics* 88 (1): 19-31.

Desicrew. India. http://desicrew.in/index.html.

Duflo, Esther. 2005. "Why Political Reservations?" *Journal of the European Economic Association* 3 (2–3): 668–78.

Euromed Gender Equality Programme. 2010a. *Enhancing Equality between Men and Women in the Euromed Region 2008–2011: National Situation Analysis Report: Women's Human Rights and Gender Equality: Morocco*. Brussels.

_____. 2010b. *Enhancing Equality between Men and Women in the Euromed Region 2008–2011: National Situation Analysis Report; Women's Human Rights and Gender Equality: Occupied Palestinian Territory*. Brussels.

_____. 2010c. *Enhancing Equality between Men and Women in the Euromed Region 2008–2011: National Situation Analysis Report; Women's Human Rights and Gender Equality: Tunisia*. Brussels.

Goldin, Claudia. 2006. "The Quiet Revolution That Transformed Women's Employment, Education, and Family." *American Economic Review*, Papers and Proceedings 96 (May): 1–21.

Hamdy, Sherif, and Frank Sader. 2008. *Simplifying Business Start-up Procedures in Egypt: The Alexandria Project Experience Memoirs*. IFC (International Finance Corporation), Washington, DC.

IFC (International Finance Corporation). 2011b. *Strengthening Access to Finance for Women-Owned SMEs in Developing Countries*. Washington, DC: The World Bank Group.

Immervoll, Herwig, and David Barber. 2006. "Can Parents Afford to Work? Childcare Costs, Tax-Benefit Policies and Work Incentives." Discussion Paper 1932, Institute for the Study of Labor, Bonn, Germany. www.iza.org/en/webcontent/publications/papers/.

Jaumotte, Florence. 2003. "Labor Force Participation of Women: Empirical Evidence on the Role of Policy and Other Determinants in OECD Countries." *OECD Economic Studies* 37 (2): 51–108.

Jensen, Robert, and Rebecca Thornton. 2003. "Early Female Marriage in the Developing World." *Gender and Development* 11 (2): 9–19.

Karlan, Dean, and Jonathan Zinman. 2009. "Expanding Microenterprise Credit Access: Using Randomized Supply Decisions to Estimate the Impacts in Manila." Economic Growth Center Discussion Paper Series 976, Yale University, Hartford, CT.

Kawar, Mary. 2002. "An Overview of Women's Participation in Employers and Worker Organisations in an Era of Economic Restructuring of the Arab Region." *Al-Raida* XIX (97–98) (Spring/Summer). 28–29,

Kelly, Sanja, and Julia Breslin. 2010. *Women's Rights in the Middle East and North Africa: Progress amid Resistance*. New York, NY: Freedom House; Lanham, MD: Rowman & Littlefield.

Kremer, Michael, Edward Miguel, and Rebecca Thornton. 2009. "Incentives to Learn." *Review of Economics and Statistics* 91 (3): 437–56.

Lefebvre, Pierre, and Philip Merrigan. 2009. "Dynamic Labour Supply Effects of Childcare Subsidies: Evidence from a Canadian Natural Experiment on Low-Fee Universal Child Care." *Labor Economics* 5 (16): 490–502.

Lewis, Maureen A., and Marlaine E. Lockheed. 2007. *Exclusion, Gender, and Schooling: Case Studies from the Developing World*. Washington, DC: Center for Global Development.

Meyer, Bruce D., and Dan T. Rosebaum. 2000. "Making Single Mothers Work: Recent Tax and Welfare Policy and Its Effects." Working Paper 7491, NBER, Cambridge, MA.

Nicodemo, Catia, and Robert Waldmann. 2009. "Child-Care and Participation in the Labor Market for Married Women in Mediterranean Countries." Discussion Paper 3983, Institute for the Study of Labor, Bonn, Germany.

Pearce, Douglas. 2011. "Financial Inclusion in the Middle East and North Africa: Analysis and Roadmap Recommendations." Working Paper 5610. World Bank, Middle East and North Africa Region Financial and Private Sector Development Unit, Washington, DC.

Ranger, Martin. 2010. "Desicrew: Rural Outsourcing in India." http://martin rangerimages.com/blog/stories/desicrew-rural-outsourcing-in-india/.

Rodrik, Dani. 2008. "Normalizing Industrial Policy." Lee, Henry, William C. Clark, and Michael Devereux. "Biofuels and Sustainable Development." Working Paper 2008-0132, Weatherhead Center for International Affairs, Harvard University, Cambridge, MA.

Simavi, Sevi, Clare Manuel, and Mark Blackden. 2010. *Gender Dimensions of Investment Climate Reform: A Guide for Policy Makers and Practitioners.* Washington, DC: World Bank.

UN OHCHR (United Nations Office of the High Commissioner for Human Rights). 2010. *Concluding Observations of CEDAW Committee on Tunisia.* UN OHCHR (Office of the High Commissioner for Human Rights), Geneva. http://daccess-dds-ny.un.org/doc/UNDOC/GEN/G10/463/92/PDF/G1046392.pdf?OpenElement.

UNSTAT (United Nations Statistics Division). 2012. New York, NY. http://data.un.org/DocumentData.aspx?q=minimum+age+of+marriage&id=294.

UN Women (United Nations Entity for Gender Equality and the Empowerment of Women). 2011. *Progress of the World's Women: In Pursuit of Justice.* New York. http://www.unwomen.org/publications/progress-of-the-worlds-women-in-pursuit-of-justice/.

World Bank. 2009. *From Privilege to Competition: Unlocking Private-Led Growth in the Middle East and North Africa.* MENA development report, Washington, DC.

_____. 2010a. *Egypt Gender Assessment Update.* Washington, DC. https://open knowledge.worldbank.org/handle/10986/2192.

_____. 2010b. *Public Sector Governance Reform: Enhancing Delivery of Justice Sector Services to the Poor.* Washington, DC. http://siteresources.worldbank.org/NEWS/Resources/FormatResults2010-MNA-PB-New-Justice-Sector-sector.pdf.

_____. 2011a. "Study on Female-Headed Households and Women in Al-Madinah al-Munawarah." Unpublished. Middle East and North Africa Region, Finance and Private Sector Department, Washington, DC.

_____. 2011b. *Women, Business and the Law 2012: Removing Barriers to Economic Inclusion.* Washington, DC: World Bank.

_____. 2012a. *World Development Report 2012: Gender Equality and Development.* Washington, DC.

_____. 2012b. Women, Business and the Law database. http://wbl.worldbank.org/.

Yemen Women Union. 2009. "A Comparison between Moroccan and Yemeni Family Law." Seminar, Sana'a, December 12–16.

Technical Notes for Figures

Figure O.1   MENA's Progress in Female Literacy, 1985–2010

Data sources	World Development Indicators (WDI) 2011
Regions	World Bank's country classification (except MENA. See appendix C)
Variables	Female literacy rate
Data construction methodology	Data in year 1985 is the average of available data from 1981–85.
	Data in year 2010 is the average of available data from 2006–10.
	Regional data (EAP, ECA, LAC, SA, and SSA) were aggregated using population-weighted average methodology.

$$Annual\ growth\ rate\ = exp\left[\frac{\log(data2010) - \log(data1985)}{25}\right]-1$$

Figure O.2   MENA's Progress in Women's Health and Education, 1985–2010 (Average Annual Growth Rates in Key Indicators)

Data sources	World Development Indicators (WDI) 2011
Regions	World Bank's country classification (except MENA. See appendix B)
Variables	– Female life expectancy – Ratio of female to male primary
Data construction methodology	Data in year 1985 is the average of available data from 1981–85.
	Data in year 2010 is the average of available data from 2006–10.
	Regional data (EAP, ECA, LAC, SA, and SSA) were aggregated using population-weighted average methodology.

$$Annual\ growth\ rate\ = exp\left[\frac{\log(data2010) - \log(data1985)}{25}\right]-1$$

Figure O.3   Female and Male Labor Force Participation across MENA

Data sources	Bahrain: Labour Market Regulatory Authority (LMRA) for national population labor statistics 2011
	Djibouti: Governance Survey 2010
	Egypt: Labor Market Panel Survey (ELMPS) 2006
	Iraq: Household Socio-Economic Survey (IHSES) 2007
	Jordan: Labor Market Panel Survey 2010
	Kuwait: Annual Statistical Abstract and "Unemployment in Kuwait: Facts and Figures" 2009
	Morocco Household and Youth Survey (MHYS) 2009–10
	Oman labor statistics: Official estimates for national population 2009
	Qatar: Labor statistics and 2010 Census estimates for national population.
	Saudi Arabia: Saudi manpower survey estimates for national population 2009
	United Arab Emirates: Official estimates for national population based on Labor Force Survey 2009
	Palestinian Territories-Palestinian Central Bureau of Statistics Labor Force Survey (LFS) 2006
	Yemen: Household Budget Survey (HBS) 2005–06
Variables	Labor force participation rates for men and women, ages 15–64
Data construction methodology	Labor force participation rate is the sum of employed and unemployed individuals, as a % of the total economically active population, here defined as the population ages 15–64.

Figure O.4   Gender Gap in Unemployment for Young Women

Data sources	World Development Indicators (WDI) 2011
Variables	– Unemployment, youth female – Unemployment, youth male
Data construction methodology	Latest data available were used. Specifically:

	Available year	
	Unemployment rates, youth male	Unemployment rates, youth female
Algeria	2004	2004
Bahrain	2001	2001
Egypt	2007	2007
Iran	2008	2008
Jordan	2009	2009
Kuwait	2005	2005
Lebanon	2007	2007
Morocco	2009	2009
Qatar	2007	2007
Saudi Arabia	2008	2008
Syria	2007	2007
Tunisia	2005	2005
U.A.E.	2008	2008
Palestinian Territories	2008	2008

Figure O.5   **Women in Legislatures** (Lower or Single Houses)

Data sources   International Parliamentary Union 2011 (http://www.ipu
                        .org/wmn-e/classif.htm)

Variables   Women in national parliaments (lower of single houses)

Data construction   Countries' data were used.
methodology

Figure O.6   **Female Labor Force Participation, 1980–2009**

Data sources   World Development Indicators (WDI) 2011

Variables   – Female labor force participation (% of female population
                          ages 15+)
                        – Male labor force participation (% of male population
                          ages 15+)

Data construction   Regional data (MENA, rest of the world, Muslim majority
methodology   countries) were aggregated using population-weighted
                        average.

                        Latest data available were used.

	Available year	
	Female labor force participation	Male labor force participation
Bangladesh	2009	2009
Indonesia	2009	2009
Malaysia	2009	2009
Pakistan	2009	2009
Turkey	2009	2009

Figure O.7   **Public Sector Wage Gap: Difference in Average Hourly Earnings for Salaried Workers in the Public and Private Sectors**

Data sources   Egypt Labor Market Panel Survey (ELMPS) 2006

                        Iraq Household Socio-Economic Survey (IHSES) 2007
                        Palestinian Territories.

                        Palestinian Labor Force Survey (PLFS) 2006

                        Yemen Household Budget Survey (HBS) 2005–06

Variables   – Hourly earnings for salaried public workers
                        – Hourly earnings for salaried private workers

Data construction   By country and gender, the measure graphed is the
methodology   difference between the average hourly earnings of the
                        public and private salaried workers divided by the private
                        average.

Figure O.8   Demographic Transition: MENA's Male and Female Age Structure, 2010 and 2050

Data sources	United Nations Dept. of Economic and Social Affairs Population Div., Population Estimates and Projections Section (UN DESA) 2010–50
Variables	– Male population – Female population
Data construction methodology	Regional data (MENA men, MENA women) were aggregated using population-weighted average method.

Figure O.9   Necessity to Create Jobs for Women and Men, 1950–2100

Data sources	World Development Indicators (WDI) 2011
Variables	– Employed female population – Employed male population – Female working-age population (ages 15–64) – Male working-age population (ages 15–64)
Data construction methodology	Regional data (MENA) were aggregated using population-weighted average method.

$$Employment\ Rate = (1 - Unemployment\ Rate) \times Labor\ Force\ Participation\ Rate$$

$$Employed\ Population = Employment\ Rate \times Working\ Age\ Population$$

Assumptions:

– Female working-age population and male working-age population grow as UN predicts.

– Female and male unemployment rates and labor force participation rates continue to stay at the 2010 levels.

Figure O.10   GCC Primary Nonoil Balance

Data sources	International Monetary Fund (IMF)
Variables	Nonoil primary balance
Data construction methodology	GCC data over time were used.

Figure 1.1   MENA's Progress in Women's Literacy, 1985–2010

See Figure 1.

Figure 1.2   MENA's Progress in Women's Health and Education, 1985–2010 (Average Annual Growth Rates in Key Indicators)

See Figure 2.

Figure 1.3   Skewed Sex Ratios at Birth and Excess Female Mortality in MENA and the Rest of the World, 1990 and 2008 (Girls Missing at Birth and Excess Female Deaths after Birth, 000s)

Data sources	Staff calculations based on data from WHO 2010 and UN DESA 2009
Regions	World Bank's country classification
Variables	Girls missing at birth
Data construction methodology	Girls missing at birth are estimated through comparisons of the sex ratio at birth in countries around the world to those in comparable populations with no discrimination. This measure also computes excess female (male) mortality by comparing the mortality risks of women relative to men in every country and every age with those seen in developed economies today—the "reference population."

Figure 1.4   Female-to-Male Enrollment Ratios: MENA Countries, 1975–2010

Data sources	World Development Indicators (WDI) 2011
Variables	– Ratio of female to male primary enrollment (%) – Ratio of female to male secondary enrollment (%) – Ratio of female to make tertiary enrollment (%)
Data construction methodology	Latest data available were used. Specifically:

	Available year		
	Ratio of female-to-male primary enrollment (%)	Ratio of female-to-male secondary enrollment (%)	Ratio of female-to-male tertiary enrollment (%)
Algeria	2009	2005	2009
Bahrain	2009	2009	N/A
Djibouti	2009	2009	2009
Egypt	2007	2004	2004
Iran	2009	2009	2009
Iraq	2007	2007	2004
Jordan	2008	2008	2008
Kuwait	2009	2009	2004
Lebanon	2009	2009	2009
Libya	2006	2006	2003
Morocco	2009	2007	2009
Oman	2009	2003	2003
Saudi Arabia	2009	2009	2009
Syria	2009	2009	N/A
Tunisia	2008	2008	2008
U.A.E.	2009	2009	2009
Palestinian Territories	2009	2009	2009
Yemen	2008	2005	2007

Figure 1.5   More Women Than Men Attend University in Many MENA Countries, 2011

Data sources   World Development Indicators (WDI) 2011

Variables   – School enrollment, tertiary, female (% gross)
                      – School enrollment, tertiary, male (% gross)

Data construction   Latest available data were used. Specifically:
methodology

	Available year	
	School enrollment, tertiary, female (% gross)	School enrollment, tertiary, male (% gross)
Algeria	2009	2009
Bahrain	N/A	N/A
Djibouti	2009	2009
Egypt	2004	2004
Iran	2009	2009
Iraq	2004	2004
Jordan	2008	2008
Kuwait	2004	2004
Lebanon	2009	2009
Libya	2003	2003
Morocco	2009	2009
Oman	2003	2003
Saudi Arabia	2009	2009
Syria	N/A	N/A
Tunisia	2008	2008
U.A.E.	2009	2009
Palestinian Territories	2009	2009
Yemen	2007	2007

Figure 1.6   Per Capita Wealth Positively Related to Female Health Outcomes

Data sources   World Development Indicators (WDI) 2005–09

Variables   – Female life expectancy at birth (years)
                      – Per capita GDP at current prices (US$)

Data construction   Variables are averaged over 2005–09 and converted into
methodology   logarithmic scale.

Figure 1.7   Boys and Girls Drop Out of School for Different Reasons: Evidence from Iraq, Ages 11–24

Data sources   Iraq Household Socio-Economic Survey 2006–07

Variables   Reason for dropping out of school

Data construction   Proportion of boys and girls, by reason, aged 11–24, of all
methodology   who dropped out of school was used.

Figure 1.8   Female Labor Force Participation across Regions, 1980–2009

Data sources	World Development Indicators (WDI) 2011
Regions	World Bank's country classifications. MENA includes all income levels.
Variables	Female labor participation rate (% of female population aged 15+)
Data construction methodology	Latest data available were used.

Figure 1.9   Female Labor Force Participation Rate, 1980–2009

Data sources	World Development Indicators (WDI) 2011
Regions	World Bank's country classifications
Variables	Female labor participation rate (% of female population aged 15+)
Data construction methodology	Latest data available were used.

Figure 1.10   Female and Male Labor Force Participation across MENA, 1980–2009

See Figure 3.

Figure 1.11   Unemployment in MENA and Rest of the World

Data sources	Team calculations based on World Development Indicators (WDI) 2010
Regions	World Bank's country classifications (except MENA. See appendix B)
Variables	– Unemployment, female (% of female labor force)
	– Unemployment, male (% of male labor force)
	– Unemployment, youth female (% of female labor force ages 15–24)
	– Unemployment, youth male (% of male labor force ages 15–24)
Data construction methodology	Regional data (World, MENA, and LMI) were aggregated using population-weighted average.
	Latest data available were used.

Figure 1.12   Tunisia: Unemployment and Participation Rates by Governorate, Women Aged 15–64

Data sources	Tunisia Labor Force Surveys 2010.
Variables	– Unemployment rates – Labor force participation rates
Data construction methodology	Country data were used.

Figure 1.13   Tunisia: Unemployment and Participation Rates by Governorate and Education Level, Women Aged 15–64

Data sources	Tunisia Labor Force Survey 2010
Variables	– Unemployment rates by education level – Labor force participation rates by education level
Data construction methodology	Country data were used.

Figure 1.14   Distribution of Female-Owned Firms by Size

Data sources	Business Enterprise Surveys for Algeria 2007, Egypt 2008, Jordan 2006, Lebanon 2006, Morocco 2007, Oman 2003, Saudi Arabia 2005, Syria 2009, Palestinian Territories 2006, and Yemen 2010
Variables	– Firm size is measured by the number of permanent workers in the firm. – Firms are classified as being owned by a woman if any of the principal owners of the firm is female.
Data construction methodology	Firms owned by women were classified as micro (fewer than 10 workers), small (10–49 workers), medium (50–99 workers), and large (100+ workers). Figure shows the share of female-owned firms by size for each country.

Figure 1.15   Share of Female Workers by Gender of Owner

Data sources	Business Enterprise Surveys for Algeria 2007, Egypt 2008, Jordan 2006, Lebanon 2006, Morocco 2007, Oman 2003, Saudi Arabia 2005, Syria 2009, Palestinian Territories 2006, and Yemen 2010
Variables	– Firms are classified as owned by a woman if any of the principal owners of the firm is female. – Female workers are the number of permanent full-time production and nonproduction workers who are female. – Total permanent full-time workers are the number of permanent, full-time employees that the establishment employed.
Data construction methodology	Share of female workers is calculated as % of total permanent full-time workers.

Figure 1.16   Women in Legislatures (Lower or Single Houses)

See Figure 5.

Figure B2.1a   Oil and the Export-Driven Demand for Female Labor

Data sources	UN COMTRADE 2007
	UNIDO INSTAT4 2009
	World CIA Factbook
	World Development Indicators (WDI) 2011
Variables	– Export-driven potential demand for female labor
	– Proven oil reserves per capita
Data construction methodology	The construction of the export-driven potential demand for female labor follows Do and others (2010). Proven oil reserves per capita divides proven oil reserves levels (in million barrels) by 2011 population. All variables are in logarithmic scale.

Solid line depicts fitted values. Dashed lines are the bounds of the 95 percent confidence interval obtained from the following regression:

Ordinary least square regression	Export-driven potential demand for female labor (log)
Per capita proven oil reserves (log)	−0.022***
	(0.003)
Constant	3.586***
	(0.049)
Number of observations	110
Adjusted R squared	0.303

1. All variables are in logarithmic scale so that coefficients are elasticities. Standard errors (in parentheses) account for heteroskedasticity. Results are robust to adding control variables (such as population, wealth) and to removing potential outliers.

2. Robust standard errors in parentheses. ***, ** and * indicate statistical significance as 1%, 5%, and 10% levels, respectively.

Figure B2.1b   Export-Driven Demand for Female Labor over Time

Data sources	UN COMTRADE 2007
	UNIDO Industrial Statistics database 2009 (INDSTAT4 2009)
	World Development Indicators (WDI) 2011
Variables	Export-driven potential demand for female labor
Data construction methodology	See explanation for box 2.1 figure a.

Figure 2.1   Change in Female Labor Force Participation (Relative to OECD Average)

Data sources	UN COMTRADE 2007
	UNIDO Industrial Statistics database 2009 (INDSTAT4 2009)
	World CIA Factbook
	World Development Indicators (WDI) 2011
Variables	– Female labor force participation
	– Region dummies: World Bank's country classifications (except MENA. See appendix B)
	– Dummy variable if a country is Muslim majority
	– Proven oil reserves per capita
Data construction methodology	Proven oil reserves per capita divides proven oil reserves levels (in million barrels) by 2011 population. Proven oil reserves per capita and female labor force participation are in logarithmic scale in the regression.
	Values graphed are coefficients converted to elasticities (to measure % changes relative to the OECD average) from the following regression:

	Female labor force participation (log)		
Ordinary least squares regression	Coefficient	Std. error	% change relative to OECD average^
MENA	−0.63	0.11	−0.47
EAP	0.14	0.10	0.00
ECA	0.17	0.05	0.19
SA	−0.21	0.13	−0.19
LAC	−0.14	0.05	−0.13
SSA	0.24	0.05	0.28
Per capita proven oil reserves (log)	0.01	0.01	0.00
Dummy for Muslim majority country	−0.14	0.06	−0.14
Number of observations			175.00
R^2			0.56

Note: Robust standard errors; ^ = only coefficients significant at 11 or less % are reported.

Figures B2.2a and B2.2b   Respondents from Egypt and Indonesia who agree with the statements: "When jobs are scarce, men should have more right to a job than women" and "Consider work rather or very important"

Data sources	World Values Survey (WVS) 2005
Variables	– Percent of female respondents agreeing with the statement (% of total female respondents)
	– Percent of male respondents agreeing with the statement (% of total male respondents)
	– Percentage point difference (% male agree—% female agree)

Figure 2.2   Respondents from MENA and around the World Who Disagree with the Following Statements about Women, Work, Education, and Politics

Data sources	World Values Survey (WVS) 2005
Variables	– Percent of female respondents disagreeing with the statement (% total female respondents)
	– Percent of male respondents disagreeing with the statement (% of total male respondents)
Data construction methodology	Group data (MENA women, MENA men, world women, world men) were aggregated using population-weighted average method.

Figure 2.3   In Iraq and Morocco, Women Spent Far More Time Than Men on Household Chores and Child Care

Data sources	Iraq Household Socio-Economic Survey 2007 (IHSES 2007)
	Morocco Household and Youth Survey (MHYS) 2009–10
Variables	Individual-level variable on time spent on household chores and child care as a fraction (%) of total time (excluding sleep, bathing/personal care and eating). For Morocco the variable is for individuals aged 15–29 years; for Iraq the variable is for individuals older than 10 years.
Data construction methodology	Data from the Time Use module was used to calculate at the individual level the ratio of the time spent on household chores /child care and the total amount of time (excluding sleep, bathing/personal care, and eating).

Figure 2.4   Percent Who Agree That "Being a Housewife Is Just as Fulfilling as Working for Pay"

Data sources	World Values Survey (WVS) 2005
Variables	– Percent of unmarried female respondents agreeing to the question (% total female respondents)
	– Percent of married female respondents agreeing to the question (% total female respondents)
Data construction methodology	Countries' data were used.

Figure 2.5   Labor Force Participation of Women by Marital Status (Aged 15–64)

Data sources	Djibouti Governance Survey 2010
	Egypt Labor Market Panel Survey (ELMPS) 2006
	Iraq Household Socio-Economic Survey (IHSES) 2007
	Yemen Household Budget Survey (HBS) 2005–06
	Jordan Labor Market Panel Survey 2010
	Morocco Household and Youth Survey (MHYS) 2009–10
Variables	– Labor Force participation rates for men and women ages 15–64
	– Marital status is defined as either being married or not. Unmarried individuals include never married, divorced, and widows ages 15–64.
Data construction methodology	Labor force participation of married and unmarried women by country

Figure 2.6   Labor Force Participation of MENA Female Immigrants to the United States

Data sources	Staff calculations based on the 5% US Census in 2000 and ACS surveys 2001–09
Variables	Labor force participation (LFP) rates for women ages 18–64
Data construction methodology	LFP of married and unmarried women by country of birth was used.

Figure 2.7   Marital Gap in Labor Force Participation of Emigrants from MENA

Data sources	Staff calculations based on the 5% US Census in 2000; ACS surveys 2001–09; and Enquête emploi en continu, Institut National de Statistiques et d'Etudes Economiques 2009
Variables	Labor force participation (LFP) rates for women ages 18–64
Data construction methodology	LFP rates of women who migrated after 18 years old, before 18 years old, and born in country of MENA ancestry were used.

Figure 2.8   Marital Gap in Labor Force Participation of Emigrants from Other Regions

Data sources	Staff calculations based on the 5% US Census in 2000; ACS surveys 2001–09; Enquête emploi en continu, Institut National de Statistiques et d'Etudes Economiques 2009
Variables	LFP rates for women ages 18–64
Data construction methodology	LFP rates of women who migrated after 18 years old, before 18 years old, and born in the United States of non-MENA ancestry or born in France of non-MENA and non-French ancestry

Figure 2.9   Timeline of Legal Reforms in Selected Countries, 1931–2004

Data sources	Women, Business and Law (WBL) team calculations for inputs into the World Development Report (WDR) 2012
Variables	Dates of legislation, various countries
Data construction methodology	Key legislation dates related to women's agency were used.

Figure 2.10   Most Common Restrictions for Married Women in Five Regions

Data sources	Women, Business and the Law database (World Bank 2012)
Variables	Restrictions include:

Sign a contract	Open a bank account	Register a business	Travel outside the home	Travel outside the country	Get a job	Apply for passport	Convey citizenship to children	Choose where to live	Be head of household

Data construction methodology	Number of restrictions by Region were counted.

Figure 3.1   Public Employment as a Share of Total Employment

Data sources	Bahrain: Labour Market Regulatory Authority (LMRA) for national population. Average for the first quarters of 2008–10
	Djibouti Governance Survey 2010
	Egypt Labor Market Panel Survey (ELMPS) 2006
	Iraq Household Socio-Economic Survey (IHSES) 2007
	Oman: Official estimates for national population; average for 2005–09, table 9-2.
	Qatar: Estimates for national population from the Statistic Authority—Census April for 2010
	Yemen Household Budget Survey (HBS) 2005–06
	UAE: Official estimates for national population based on Labor Force Survey 2009
	Jordan Labor Market Panel Survey 2010
	Morocco Household and Youth Survey (MHYS) 2009–10
Variables	From household surveys: Salaried public sector workers as a % of total workers
	Bahrain: Public sector employment as share of total employment for Bahraini population
	UAE: Share of federal and local government workers as share of total employed national population
	Oman: Government employment is the sum of Omani workers in civil service, Diwan of Royal Court, Royal Court Affairs, and public corporations. Total employment is equal to government employment plus total Omanis working in the private sector.
	Qatar: Workers in government or government establishments as share of total employed population
Data construction methodology	Share of public sector employment as share of total employment was used.

Figure 3.2   Public Sector Wage Bill as a Percent of GDP and Total Expenditure, 2008

Data sources	IMF Fiscal Affairs Dept., Employment and Wages database 2010
Variables	Compensation of public employees as a % of GDP. Where available, general government figures were used; otherwise, central government figures were used.
	Compensation of public employees as a % of public expenses. Where available, general government figures were used; otherwise, central government figures were used.
Data construction methodology	Country-level data were averaged by Region according to the World Bank standard regional classification. Number of observations for each Region was: Middle East and North Africa (MNA)—10, East Asia and Pacific (EAP)—5, Eastern Europe and Central Asia (ECA)—17, Latin America and Caribbean (LAC)—10, South Asia (SA)—5, and Sub-Saharan Africa (SSA)—36.

Figure 3.3   Public Sector Wage Gap: Difference in Average Hourly Earnings for Salaried Workers in Public and Private Sectors

See Figure 7.

Figure 3.4   Public Sector Employment as Share of Total Employment

Data sources	Bahrain: Labour Market Regulatory Authority (LMRA) for national population. Average for the first quarters of 2008–10
	Djibouti Governance Survey 2010
	Egypt Labor Market Panel Survey (ELMPS) 2006
	Iraq Household Socio-Economic Survey (IHSES) 2007
	Oman: Official estimates for national population; average for 2005–09, table 9-2
	Qatar: Estimates for national population from the Statistic Authority—Census April for 2010
	Yemen Household Budget Survey (HBS) 2005–06
	UAE: Official estimates for national population based on Labor Force Survey 2009
	Jordan Labor Market Panel Survey 2010
	Morocco Household and Youth Survey (MHYS) 2009–10
Variables	From household surveys: Salaried public sector workers as a % of total workers
	Bahrain: Public sector employment as share of total employment for Bahraini population
	UAE: Share of federal and local government workers as share of total employed national population
	Oman: Government employment is the sum of Omani workers in civil service, Diwan of Royal Court, Royal Court Affairs, and public corporations. Total employment is equal to government employment plus total Omanis working in the private sector.
	Qatar: Workers in government or government establishments as share of total employed population
Data construction methodology	Share of public sector employment as share of total employment for males and females

Figure 3.5   Incidence of Job Benefits in Public and Private Sectors

Data sources	Egypt Labor Market Panel Survey (ELMPS) 2006
	Iraq Household Socio-Economic Survey (IHSES) 2007
	Yemen Household Budget Survey (HBS) 2005–06
	Jordan Labor Market Panel Survey 2010
	Morocco Household and Youth Survey (MHYS) 2009–10
Variables	Social Security
	Legal contract
	Health insurance
	Paid sick leave
Data construction methodology	Variables take on values of 1 or 0 based on whether individuals have affiliations with social security programs through their work, have a legal job contract, receive health insurance at work, or have paid sick leave from work.

Figure 3.6   Share of Workers with Post-Secondary Education

Data sources	Egypt Labor Market Panel Survey (ELMPS) 2006
	Iraq Household Socio-Economic Survey (IHSES) 2007
	Yemen Household Budget Survey (HBS) 2005–06
	Jordan Labor Market Panel Survey 2010
	Morocco Household and Youth Survey (MHYS) 2009–10
	Djibouti Governance Survey 2010
Variables	Educational attainment for all working individuals
	Post-secondary education includes university and technical degrees beyond secondary education.
Data construction methodology	Percent of all workers with educational attainment beyond secondary school is calculated for each country.

Figure 3.7   Female Unemployment Rates by Education Level

Data sources	Labor Force Survey 2006. Palestinian Central Bureau of Statistics
	Iraq Household Socio-Economic Survey (IHSES) 2007
	Yemen Household Budget Survey (HBS) 2005–06
	Jordan Labor Market Panel Survey 2010
	Morocco Household and Youth Survey (MHYS) 2009–10
	Saudi Arabia: 2009 Saudi manpower survey estimates for national population
Variables	Unemployed population at each level of education
	Labor force at each level of education
	Educational attainment
Data construction methodology	Unemployment rates are calculated for individuals at each level of education.

Figure 3.8   Subsidies as Share of GDP, 2009

Data sources	IMF and other sources. See details below.
Data construction methodology	**Lebanon:** No food or gas subsidies. These data refer to subsidies to the electricity company, a fraction of which can be considered consumer subsidies. **Syria:** For 2009, IMF estimates an implicit energy subsidy of 4.9% of GDP (–1.3% implicit prices subsidy of 6.2% in compensatory measures). The data reported are mostly food subsidies (1.4% comes from the Price Stabilization Fund, or PSF, which subsidizes mainly bread and sugar). There also are substantial agricultural producer subsidies via administered domestic prices for wheat, sugar beets, and cotton. **Iraq:** Direct fuel subsidies are zero. Data reported are basically food subsidies under the Public Distribution System (Source: IMF). Indirect fuel subsidies are estimates by IMF of approximately 1.5% of GDP in 2009. **Kuwait:** The data refer to the explicit subsidy number as calculated by the IMF for 2006–07 and is the last detailed estimate. When many implicit subsidies are counted, their total subsidy estimate is actually 32% of GDP (a great part of this amount was in social security expenses for that year). The benchmark figure used to add both implicit and explicit subsidies is 20% of GDP.

Figure 3.9   Labor Force Participation and Marriage: Marginal Effects Relative to Single Women

Data sources	Labor Force Survey 2006. Palestinian Central Bureau of Statistics
	Iraq Household Socio-Economic Survey (IHSES) 2007
	Yemen Household Budget Survey (HBS) 2005–06
	Jordan Labor Market Panel Survey 2010
	Morocco Household and Youth Survey (MHYS) 2009–10
	Djibouti Governance Survey 2010
Variables	Labor force participation
	Marital status
Data construction methodology	LFP rates are calculated for women according to their marital status for each country.

Figure 3.10   Public Expenditure on Education, 2000–10

Data sources	UNESCO Institute for Statistics (UIS)
Variables	Public expenditure on education as % of GDP
Data construction methodology	Country-level data are averaged by region according to the World Bank standard regional classification.

Figure 3.11   Share of Firms Identifying Labor Constraints as Biggest Constraint to Doing Business

Data sources	World Competitiveness Report, 2010–11. Extracted from Country Economic Profiles
Variables	Share of firms identifying the following as the most problematic factors for doing business: Inadequately educated workforce, poor work ethic in national labor force, restrictive labor regulations. From a list of 15 factors, respondents were asked to select the 5 most problematic for doing business in their country and to rank them from 1 (most problematic) to 5.
Data construction methodology	Bars in the figure show the responses weighted according to their rankings.

Figure 3.12   Countries in Which Fields of Study Are Male- Female-Dominated

Data sources   EdStats 2011

Variables   – Enrollment in education, tertiary, female
                      – Enrollment in education, tertiary, total
                      – Enrollment in humanities and art, tertiary, female
                      – Enrollment in humanities and art, tertiary, total
                      – Enrollment in social sciences, business, and law, tertiary, female
                      – Enrollment in social sciences, business, and law, tertiary, total
                      – Enrollment in science, tertiary, female
                      – Enrollment in science, tertiary, total
                      – Enrollment in engineering, manufacturing, and construction, tertiary, female
                      – Enrollment in engineering, manufacturing, and construction, tertiary, total
                      – Enrollment in agriculture, tertiary, female
                      – Enrollment in agriculture, tertiary, total
                      – Enrollment in health and welfare, tertiary, female
                      – Enrollment in health and welfare, tertiary, total
                      – Enrollment in services, tertiary, female
                      – Enrollment in services, tertiary, total

Data construction   Field of studies is female-dominated when female enrollment is more than 50% of total
methodology   enrollment.

                      Field of studies is male-dominated when female enrollment is equal to or less than 50%
                      of total enrollment.

                      Available years and available MENA countries in each field of study were used.

Field of Studies	Available Countries (latest data)
Agriculture	Algeria 2006, Iran 2009, Iraq 2004, Jordan 2008, Lebanon 2009, Morocco 2009, Oman 2005, Saudi Arabia 2009, Palestinian Territories 2009
Education	Algeria 2006, Bahrain 2010, Iran 2009, Iraq 2004, Jordan 2008, Lebanon 2009, Morocco 2009, Oman 2005, Qatar 2004, Saudi Arabia 2009, Palestinian Territories 2009
Engineering, manufacturing, and construction	Algeria 2006, Bahrain 2010, Djibouti 2010, Iran 2009, Iraq 2004, Jordan 2008, Lebanon 2009, Morocco 2009, Oman 2005, Qatar 2004, Saudi Arabia 2009, Palestinian Territories 2009
Health and welfare	Algeria 2006, Bahrain 2010, Iran 2009, Iraq 2004, Jordan 2008, Lebanon 2009, Morocco 2009, Oman 2005, Qatar 2004, Saudi Arabia 2009, Palestinian Territories 2009
Humanities and art	Algeria 2006, Bahrain 2010, Djibouti 2010, Iran 2009, Iraq 2004, Jordan 2008, Lebanon 2009, Morocco 2009, Oman 2005, Qatar 2004, Saudi Arabia 2009, Palestinian Territories 2009
Science	Algeria 2006, Bahrain 2010, Djibouti 2010, Iran 2009, Iraq 2004, Jordan 2008, Lebanon 2009, Morocco 2009, Oman 2005, Qatar 2004, Saudi Arabia 2009, Palestinian Territories 2009
Services	Algeria 2006, Bahrain 2010, Djibouti 2010, Iran 2009, Iraq 2004, Jordan 2008, Lebanon 2009, Morocco 2009, Saudi Arabia 2009, Palestinian Territories 2009
Social sciences, business, and law	Algeria 2006, Bahrain 2010, Djibouti 2010, Iran 2009, Iraq 2004, Jordan 2008, Lebanon 2009, Morocco 2009, Oman 2005, Qatar 2004, Saudi Arabia 2009, Palestinian Territories 2009

Figure 3.13 Occupational Segregation: Industrial Distribution of Employment by Gender for Three Gulf Countries

Data sources	Kuwait: 2009 Annual Statistical Abstract and on "Unemployment in Kuwait: Facts and Figures"
	Saudi Arabia: 2009 Saudi manpower survey estimates for national population
	Qatar labor statistics 2010 Census estimates for national population
Variables	Economically active population 15+ by occupation and sex
Data construction methodology	Countries' data were used.

Figure 3.14 Egypt: Share Acquiring Job-Relevant Skills

Data sources	Survey of Young People in Egypt (SYPE) 2009
Variables	Percent acquiring job-relevant skill
Data construction methodology	Share of young people 15–29 years who say "Yes" to have acquired specific types of job-relevant skills was measured.

Figure 3.15 Type of Private Sector Worker by Gender

Data sources	Egypt Labor Market Panel Survey (ELMPS) 2006
	Iraq Household Socio-Economic Survey (IHSES) 2007
	Yemen Household Budget Survey (HBS) 2005–06
	Jordan Labor Market Panel Survey 2010
	Morocco Household and Youth Survey (MHYS) 2009–10
	Djibouti Governance Survey 2010
Variables	Private sector employment
	Self-employed individuals
	Salaried workers
	Unpaid family workers
Data construction methodology	Private sector workers are either self employed, salaried workers, or unpaid family workers. The shares of each type were calculated for all female and male workers in each country.

Figure 3.16   Informal Workers

Data sources	Egypt Labor Market Panel Survey (ELMPS) 2006
	Iraq Household Socio-Economic Survey (IHSES) 2007
	Yemen Household Budget Survey (HBS) 2005–06
	Jordan Labor Market Panel Survey 2010
	Morocco Household and Youth Survey (MHYS) 2009–10
	Djibouti Governance Survey 2010
Variables	Size of establishment in which individuals work
	Whether the individual has social security coverage
	Whether the individual has a labor contract
Data construction methodology	According to the literature, informality is defined in three ways. The productivity definition classifies as informal those who work in establishments with fewer than 5 workers. The social protection definition classifies as informal workers who do not have social security coverage. Finally, the legalistic definition classifies as informal workers who do not have a legal contract.

Figure 3.17   Share of Businesses Reporting Each Constraint as a "Major" or "Severe" Obstacle

Data sources	Business Enterprise Surveys for Algeria 2007, Egypt 2008, Jordan 2006, Lebanon 2006, Morocco 2007, Oman 2003, Saudi Arabia 2005, Syria 2009, Palestinian Territories 2006, and Yemen 2010
Variables	– Firms were classified as woman-owned if any of the principal owners of the firm was female.
	– Share of businesses that reported each of the identified constraints as major or severe on a scale of 0 to 4, where 0 implies no constraint and 4 is a severe constraint.
Data construction methodology	Aggregate constraint indices were constructed for the following categories:

1. Land: Includes access to land and cost of land
2. Crime: Includes crime/theft/disorder
3. Uncertainty: Includes macroeconomic uncertainty, political instability, and regulatory policy uncertainty
4. Access to finance: Includes access to and cost of finance
5. Competition: Includes anticompetitive practices
6. Legal system: Includes legal system/dispute resolution/access to courts tribunals
7. Corruption: Includes corruption as a constraint to entrepreneurship
8. Infrastructure: Includes telecommunications, electricity, water, and transport
9. Labor: Includes labor regulations and availability of skilled workers
10. Business regulations: Includes tax rates, tax administration, business licensing, and customs and trade regulations.

Figure 4.1   Average Years of Total Schooling for Females, Age 15 and Above, 1960–2010

Data sources	Barro-Lee 2010. Paper by Robert J. Barro and Jong-Wha Lee, http://www.barrolee.com/main.htm
Variables	Average years of total schooling, 15+. Total is the average years of education completed among people over age 15.
Data construction methodology	Countries' data over time were used.

Figure 4.2   Female Labor Force Participation and Education

Data sources	Bahrain labor statistics: Labour Market Regulatory Authority (LMRA) for national population 2011
	Djibouti Governance Survey 2010
	Egypt Labor Market Panel Survey (ELMPS) 2006
	Iraq Household Socio-Economic Survey (IHSES) 2007
	Jordan Labor Market Panel Survey 2010
	Kuwait: 2009 Annual Statistical Abstract and on "Unemployment in Kuwait: Facts and Figures"
	Morocco Household and Youth Survey (MHYS) 2009–10
	Oman labor statistics, 2009: Official estimates for national population
	Palestinian Central Bureau of Statistics: Labor Force Survey 2006
	Saudi Arabia: Saudi manpower survey estimates for national population 2009
	United Arab Emirates: Official estimates for national population based on Labor Force Survey 2009
	Qatar labor statistics 2010 and Census estimates for national population
	Yemen Household Budget Survey (HBS) 2005–06
Variables	Female labor force by level of education
Data construction methodology	**Panel A:** Graphs the share of national female labor force by level of education
	Panel B: Refers to a probit model that estimates the probability of female labor force participation as a function of the level of education, in which the reference group is uneducated women. The model controls for age, marital status, urban/rural effects, household composition, and effects. See regression results in table A2.4.

Figure 4.3   Tunisia Female Labor Force Participation by Age and Education

Data sources	Tunisia Labor Force Survey 2010
Variables	Female labor force participation
Data construction methodology	Countries' data were used.

Figure 4.4   Fertility Rates, 1960–2005 (Births per Woman)

Data sources	World Development Indicators (WDI) 2011
Variables	Fertility rates
Data construction methodology	Countries' data over time were used.

Figure 4.5   Demographic Transition: MENA Age Structure, 2010 and 2050

See Figure 8.

Figure 4.6   Necessity to Create Jobs Will Increase over Time

See Figure 9.

Figure 4.7   GCC Nonoil Primary Balance, 2000–11

See Figure 10.

Figure 5.1   Women's Employment Restrictions Pervasive in MENA

Data sources	Women, Business and Law database (WBL) (World Bank 2012b)
Variables	Dummy variables for whether women can work at night and whether women can work in the same industries as men
Data construction methodology	Percentage of countries in which each variable equals 1 was used.

Tables

TABLE B.1

Determinants of Human Development Outcomes

Panel A: Education	Female adult literacy		Primary enrollment male/female ratio		Secondary enrollment male/female ratio		Tertiary enrollment male/female ratio	
	(1)	(2)	(3)	(4)	(5)	(6)	(7)	(8)
MENA (1: yes, 0: no)	0.097	***−0.235	−0.025	**−0.076	−0.003	**−0.116	0.120	***−0.158
	(0.120)	(0.088)	(0.037)	(0.034)	(0.070)	(0.056)	(0.117)	(0.051)
Current per capita GDP (2005)		***0.365		***0.72		***0.160		***0.396
		(0.043)		(0.019)		(0.025		(0.022)
Adjustment R-squared	0.00	0.61	0.00	0.27	0.00	0.44	0.01	0.73
Number of observations	85	85	146	146	143	143	119	119

Panel B: Health	Female adult literacy		Primary enrollment male/female ratio		Secondary enrollment male/female ratio		Tertiary enrollment male/female ratio	
	(1)	(2)	(3)	(4)	(5)	(6)	(7)	(8)
MENA (1: yes, 0: no)	**0.074	−0.007	***−1.210	−0.209	**−0.331	−0.079	−0.807	0.058
	(0.035)	(0.031)	(0.273)	(0.277)	(0.149)	(0.153)	(0.653)	(0.495)
Current per capita GDP (2005)		***0.114		***−0.870		***−0.355		***−1.093
		(0.015)		(0.142)		(0.073)		(0.146)
Adjustment R-squared	0.02	0.49	0.10	0.48	0.03	0.42	0.02	0.63
Number of observations	160	160	54	54	149	149	92	92

Note: All variables are in logarithmic scale so that coefficients are elasticities. Standard errors (in parentheses) account for heteroskedasticity. Results are robust to adding control variables (such as population, wealth) and to removing potential outliers. All regressions are population weighted, include a constant. Variables are in logarithm (except for the MENA dummy variable), so that coefficients are elasticities. Data restricted to non-OECD countries. For data sources and variable definitions, see data source in Appendix C.

TABLE B.2

Main Manufacturing Exports: MENA Countries

Country	Largest export sector		Second largest export sector	
	Sector name	Share of exports (%)	Sector name	Share of exports (%)
Oil-rich countries				
Algeria	Manufacture of refined petroleum products	89.1	Manufacture of beverages	4.1
Iran	Manufacture of refined petroleum products	93.0	Manufacture of other textiles	3.1
Iraq	Manufacture of refined petroleum products	98.4	Manufacturing n.e.c.	0.3
Kuwait	Manufacture of refined petroleum products	94.2	Manufacture of basic chemicals	1.6
Libya	Manufacture of refined petroleum products	97.4	Manufacture of basic chemicals	1.9
Oman	Manufacture of refined petroleum products	89.3	Manufacturing n.e.c.	3.9
Saudi Arabia	Manufacture of refined petroleum products	94.1	Manufacture of basic chemicals	3.3
United Arab Emirates	Manufacture of refined petroleum products	79.9	Manufacture of motor vehicles	3.3
Yemen	Manufacture of refined petroleum products	66.9	Production, processing, and perservation of meat, fish, fruit, vegetables, oils, and fats	21.1
Oil-poor countries				
Egypt	Manufacture of refined petroleum products	53,2	Spinning, weaving, and finishing of textiles	16.9
Jordan	Manufacture of basic chemicals	46.8	Manufacture of other chemical products	7.4
Lebanon	Manufacturing n.e.c.	18.5	Manufacture of refined petroleum products	13.4
Morocco	Manufacture of basic chemicals	42.7	Manufacture of wearing apparel, except fur apparel	15.7
Syria	Manufacture of refined petroleum products	76.7	Spinning, weaving, and finishing of textiles	5.1
Tunisia	Manufacture of refined petroleum products	26.4	Manufacture of wearing apparel, except fur apparel	19.3

Note: n.e.c. = not elsewhere classified.

TABLE B.3

General Government Fiscal Balance
percent of GDP

	Average						Projected
	2000–05	2006	2007	2008	2009	2010	2011
Oil exporters	7.9	15.1	12.3	12.0	−1.8	2.5	6.9
Algeria	6.6	13.5	4.4	7.7	−6.8	−2.7	5.0
Bahrain[2]	1.4	2.7	1.9	4.9	−6.6	−7.8	1.6
Iran, Islamic Rep.	2.0	0	2.4	−0.2	−1.9	0.6	4.0
Iraq	...	15.5	12.4	−1.2	−21.8	−10.8	−4.4
Kuwait[2]	27.2	35.4	39.8	19.8	23.5	17.4	22.3
Libya	12.6	33.1	28.6	30.3	7.0	9.2	...
Oman[2]	8.4	13.8	11.1	13.8	−1.2	6.2	14.2
Qatar	8.8	8.6	10.8	10.3	15.2	12.8	13.8
Saudi Arabia	7.7	24.6	15.8	34.4	−4.7	7.7	12.8
United Arab Emirates[3]	4.5	18.1	15.4	16.5	−12.6	−1.3	6.5
Yemen	0.0	1.2	−7.2	−4.5	−10.2	−4.0	−6.4
Oil importers	−5.7	−4.3	−4.7	−3.2	−5.1	−4.5	−6.2
Djibouti	−1.8	−2.4	−2.6	1.3	−4.6	−0.5	−0.1
Egypt[2]	−9.9	−8.2	−7.3	−6.8	−6.9	−8.1	−9.7
Jordan	−3.1	−3.4	−5.5	−5.4	−8.5	−5.4	−6.8
Lebanon[2]	−15.3	−10.4	−10.8	−9.5	−8.2	−7.2	−10.5
Morocco[2]	−5.2	−1.8	0.3	1.5	−2.1	−4.2	−4.9
Syrian Arab Republic	−2.1	−1.1	−4.0	−2.9	−2.9	−4.8	−6.8
Tunisia	−2.6	−2.9	−2.8	−0.7	−2.6	−1.2	−4.3
Memorandum							
MENA[1]	3.0	8.6	6.4	8.6	−3.4	0.6	3.3
GCC	9.3	22.4	17.5	24.7	−0.8	7.2	12.6
Maghreb[1]	3.1	10.4	6.0	8.2	−2.9	−0.9	0.1
Mashreq	−8.7	−7.0	−7.0	−6.4	−6.5	−7.4	−9.2

Source: IMF. Various years, its data not a publication.
Notes:
1. 2011 data exclude Libya.
2. Central government.
3. Consolidated accounts of the federal government and the emirates Abu Dhabi, Dubai, and Sharjah.

TABLE B.4

Marginal Effect on Probability of Labor Force Participation

| | Probability of Labor Force Participation | | | | | |
| | Egypt | | Jordan | | Morocco | |
Variables	Female	Male	Female	Male	Female	Male
Primary	−0.0127	−0.0103	−0.0590**	0.128***	0.0130	0.0495***
	(0.0191)	(0.00765)	(0.0239)	(0.0214)	(0.0172)	(0.0187)
Secondary	0.294***	−0.000898	0.00171	0.0913***	0.152***	0.0193
	(0.0159)	(0.00667)	(0.0273)	(0.0101)	(0.0247)	(0.0209)
More than secondary	0.498***	0.00276	0.317***	0.129***	0.405***	0.0760***
	(0.0171)	(0.00730)	(0.0323)	(0.0120)	(0.0547)	(0.0253)
Age	0.0483***	0.0220***	0.0283***	0.0156***	0.0155***	0.0397***
	(0.00318)	(0.00144)	(0.00426)	(0.00284)	(0.00303)	(0.00369)
Age squared	−0.0563***	−0.0308***	−0.000375***	−0.000282***	−0.000178***	−0.000565***
	(0.00406)	(0.00175)	(5.79e−05)	(3.40e−05)	(3.90e−05)	(4.48e−05)
Married	−0.300***	0.0773***	−0.263***	0.100***	−0.161***	0.190***
	(0.0209)	(0.0133)	(0.0255)	(0.0228)	(0.0194)	(0.0293)
Divorced	−0.107***	0.0172	−0.00901	−0.118*	0.00163	0.0244
	(0.0319)	(0.0201)	(0.0382)	(0.0607)	(0.0318)	(0.0638)
Widow	−0.188***	0.0334***	−0.119***	0.0478	−0.0507***	0.0958*
	(0.0177)	(0.0110)	(0.0185)	(0.0346)	(0.0194)	(0.0557)
Urban	−0.0654***	−0.000849	−0.0212	0.0232**	0.0106	−0.0625***
	(0.0125)	(0.00541)	(0.0134)	(0.00994)	(0.0139)	(0.0171)
Camp						
Region effects	Yes	Yes	Yes	Yes	Yes	Yes
Household composition	Yes	Yes	Yes	Yes	Yes	Yes
Observations	10439	10015	6061	6048	3339	3112
Pseudo R²	0.185	0.193	0.265	0.238	0.214	0.144

Notes:
1. Robust standard errors in parentheses.
2. *** p<0.01, ** p<0.05, * p<01.

Probability of Labor Force Participation

	Iraq		Palestinian Territories		Yemen		Djibouti	
	Female	Male	Female	Male	Female	Male	Female	Male
	0.0182***	0.0506***	−0.0349***	0.280***	0.0137***	0.0722***	0.202***	0.125***
	(0.00552)	(0.00885)	(0.00930)	(0.0170)	(0.00473)	(0.00833)	(0.0548)	(0.0263)
	0.506***	0.0616***	−0.0228**	0.142***	0.0439***	0.0537***	0.153***	0.0279
	(0.0187)	(0.00769)	(0.0102)	(0.00463)	(0.00848)	(0.00778)	(0.0538)	(0.0309)
	0.747***	0.0652***	0.516***	0.167***	0.324***	0.0562***	0.156	−0.103*
	(0.0179)	(0.00654)	(0.0160)	(0.00494)	(0.0270)	(0.00836)	(0.109)	(0.0584)
	0.0135***	0.0189***	0.0234***	0.0185***	0.00583***	0.0218***	0.0103	−0.000357
	(0.00129)	(0.00155)	(0.00141)	(0.00123)	(0.000736)	(0.00173)	(0.0108)	(0.00443)
	−0.000154***	−0.000314***	−0.000274***	−0.000314***	−5.95e−05***	−0.000286***	−0.000203	−4.86e-05
	(1.70e−05)	(1.93e−05)	(0.00002)	(0.00001)	(9.50e−06)	(2.12e−05)	(0.000133)	(3.91e−05)
	−0.100***	0.0928***	−0.179***	0.129***	−0.0350***	0.110***	−0.311***	0.0432
	(0.00966)	(0.0115)	(0.00812)	(0.00950)	(0.00540)	(0.0131)	(0.0538)	(0.0466)
	0.0328	0.0304	−0.0473***	0.0157	0.00152	−0.0764*	0.0785	−0.0100
	(0.0263)	(0.0299)	(0.0123)	(0.0293)	(0.00723)	(0.0444)	(0.0949)	(0.101)
	−0.0234**	0.0235	−0.103***	−0.0700	−0.00452	−0.0127	−0.207***	−0.159
	(0.0107)	(0.0217)	(0.00662)	(0.0524)	(0.00564)	(0.0383)	(0.0732)	(0.154)
	−0.135***	0.000487	−0.0650***	−0.000165	0.0150***	−0.0223***	0.0337	−0.151
	(0.00604)	(0.00504)	(0.00567)	(0.00499)	(0.00322)	(0.00647)	(0.150)	(0.118)
			−0.0706***	−0.0447***				
			(0.00583)	(0.00780)				
	Yes	Yes	Yes	Yes	Yes	Yes	Yes	Yes
	Yes	Yes	No	No	Yes	Yes	Yes	Yes
	32762	29829	30639	32330	23822	20550	1071	1014
	0.305	0.175	0.272	0.134	0.209	0.149	0.221	0.176

TABLE B.5

Marginal Effect on Probability of Being Unemployed

| | Probability of Being Unemployed | | | | | |
| | Egypt | | Jordan | | Morocco | |
Variables	Female	Male	Female	Male	Female	Male
Youth (15 to 29 years)	0.167***	0.0189***	0.221***	0.0485***	0.126***	0.0288*
	(0.0175)	(0.00477)	(0.0279)	(0.0130)	(0.0468)	(0.0159)
Primary	0.148**	−0.00265	0.172	−0.00619	0.0947	−0.0106
	(0.0655)	(0.00618)	(0.135)	(0.0230)	(0.0789)	(0.0161)
Secondary	0.418***	0.0226***	0.285*	−0.0234	0.137**	0.0240
	(0.0355)	(0.00613)	(0.160)	(0.0206)	(0.0651)	(0.0177)
More than secondary	0.397***	0.0482***	0.170**	−0.0246	0.0400	−0.0133
	(0.0408)	(0.00967)	(0.0738)	(0.0213)	(0.0764)	(0.0246)
Married	−0.123***	−0.0576***	−0.00140	−0.125***	−0.114**	−0.139***
	(0.0217)	(0.00889)	(0.0353)	(0.0187)	(0.0485)	(0.0216)
Divorced	−0.0542***	−0.00130	−0.0377	−0.0185	−0.113**	−0.0186
	(0.0203)	(0.0170)	(0.0552)	(0.0470)	(0.0557)	(0.0588)
Widow	−0.0676***	−0.0167**	−0.00313		−0.0416	
	(0.0160)	(0.00766)	(0.0715)		(0.0855)	
Urban	−0.00365	0.00854**	−0.0478*	0.00745	0.116**	0.0482***
	(0.0118)	(0.00373)	(0.0246)	(0.00864)	(0.0492)	(0.0137)
Region effects	Yes	Yes	Yes	Yes	Yes	Yes
Household composition	Yes	Yes	Yes	Yes	Yes	Yes
Observations	3305	9050	1,451	5,319	542	2503
Pseudo R²	0.360	0.228	0.196	0.083	0.181	0.186

Note:
1. Robust standard errors in parentheses.
2. *** p<0.01, ** p<0.05, * p<01.

Probability of Being Unemployed							
Iraq		Palestinian Territories		Yemen		Djibouti	
Female	Male	Female	Male	Female	Male	Female	Male
0.140***	0.0485***	0.175***	0.0144*	0.102***	0.0201***	0.266***	0.162***
(0.0166)	(0.00739)	(0.0127)	(0.00865)	(0.0205)	(0.00353)	(0.0621)	(0.0545)
0.0302	−0.0103	0.118***	0.0613**	0.0161	−0.000268	0.0880	0.0846
(0.0226)	(0.00846)	(0.0427)	(0.0276)	(0.0253)	(0.00308)	(0.0679)	(0.0595)
0.0408	−0.0208**	0.207***	−0.0223	0.0946**	0.000852	−0.0931	−0.0465
(0.0270)	(0.00920)	(0.0619)	(0.0283)	(0.0406)	(0.00333)	(0.0658)	(0.0508)
0.0500	−0.00749	0.303***	−0.0775***	0.0226	0.00837	−0.520***	−0.340***
(0.0317)	(0.0114)	(0.0370)	(0.0254)	(0.0238)	(0.00563)	(0.0986)	(0.0700)
−0.0598***	−0.118***	−0.0796***	−0.116***	−0.0332**	−0.0342***	−0.139*	−0.350***
(0.0112)	(0.00897)	(0.0120)	(0.00959)	(0.0140)	(0.00508)	(0.0729)	(0.0565)
0.0216	−0.0334	0.0686*	0.0887*	−0.0349***	−0.00948***	−0.244*	−0.0277
(0.0381)	(0.0262)	(0.0404)	(0.0521)	(0.0121)	(0.00258)	(0.125)	(0.172)
−0.00132	−0.0227	−0.0401	0.00247			−0.263*	−0.227
(0.0265)	(0.0284)	(0.0327)	(0.0776)			(0.148)	(0.198)
0.0809***	0.00586	0.00718	−0.0188***	0.0132	0.00407**	0.0232	0.0579
(0.0142)	(0.00517)	(0.0126)	(0.00658)	(0.0178)	(0.00204)	(0.331)	(0.128)
Yes	Yes	Yes	Yes	Yes	Yes	Yes	Yes
Yes	Yes	No	No	Yes	Yes	Yes	Yes
5,228	27,085	6,681	29,281	1732	17648	403	815
0.191	0.107	0.209	0.071	0.241	0.231	0.204	0.149

Data Sources

	Source	Comments
Country classification	http://data.worldbank.org/about/country-classifications/country-and-lending-groups	The flagship follows the World Bank's country classification based on geographic locations and/or income level (2010 gross national income per capita). One exception is its classification of the Middle East and North Africa Region (see below).
Middle East and North Africa Region	http://data.worldbank.org/about/country-classifications/country-and-lending-groups	The flagship defines 19 MENA countries: Algeria, Bahrain, Djibouti, Egypt, Iran, Iraq, Jordan, Kuwait, Lebanon, Libya, Morocco, Oman, Qatar, Saudi Arabia, Syria, Tunisia, United Arab Emirates, Palestinian Territories, and Yemen.
World Values Survey (WVS)	http://www.wvsevsdb.com/wvs/WVSData.jsp	Wave 2005–07.
World Development Indicators (WDI)	http://data.worldbank.org/data-catalog/world-development-indicators	Data averaged over 5-year intervals over 1960–10.
EdStats	http://go.worldbank.org/ITABCOGIV1	Data averaged over 5-year intervals over 1960–2010.
The Pew Forum of Religion and Public Life	http://pewforum.org/uploadedfiles/Orphan_Migrated_Content/Muslimpopulation.pdf	2009 estimates of Muslim population in the world.
World CIA Factbook	https://www.cia.gov/library/publications/the-world-factbook/rankorder/2178rank.html	2010 estimates of proven oil reserves.
LABORSTA (ILO)	http://laborsta.ilo.org/	Data on public sector and total employment for 2005–08.
IMF Fiscal Affairs Dept.	http://www.imf.org/external/pubs/cat/longres.aspx?sk=24193.0	Clements and others 2010.

	Source	Comments
Household surveys	Djibouti Governance Survey 2010	
	Egypt Labor Market Panel Survey (ELMPS) 2006	
	Iraq Household Socio-Economic Survey (IHSES) 2007	
	Jordan Labor Market Panel Survey 2010	
	Morocco Household and Youth Survey (MHYS) 2009–10	
	Tunisia Labor Market Survey 2000 and 2010	
	Yemen Household Budget Survey (HBS) 2005–06	
Bahrain labor statistics	Labour Market Regulatory Authority (LMRA) for national population http://blmi.lmra.bh/2011/03/mi_data.xml	Central Informatics Organisation (CIO), Kingdom of Bahrain.
Oman labor statistics	Official estimates for national population http://www.mone.gov.om/book/SYB2010/2-population.pdf	2009.
Qatar labor statistics	Estimates for national population from the Statistic Authority—Census April/2010 http://www.qix.gov.qa/portal/page/portal/qix/subject_area/Statistics?subject_area=183	Census April/2010.
United Arab Emirates	Official estimates for national population based on Labor Force Survey 2009 http://www.uaestatistics.gov.ae/ReportPDF/DSS_SS_LF%20Main%20Indicators%202008-2009.xls	2009.
Kuwait labor statistics	http://cso.gov.kw	Official estimates for national population based on the 2009 Annual Statistical Abstract and on "Unemployment in Kuwait: Facts and Figures."
Saudi Arabia labor statistics	2009 Saudi manpower survey http://www.cdsi.gov.sa/english/index.php?option=com_docman&task=doc_download&gid=831&Itemid=113	Various tables.
World Bank Doing Business	http://www.doingbusiness.org/Data	Doing Business provides objective measures of business regulations and their enforcement across 183 economies.
UNESCO Institute for Statistics (UIS)	EdStats http://databank.worldbank.org/ddp/home.do?Step=12&id=4&CNO=1159	Used for estimates of spending on education across countries and Regions.
World Competitiveness Report 2010–11.	http://www3.weforum.org/docs/WEF_GlobalCompetitivenessReport_2010-11.pdf	

	Source	Comments
Business Environment Surveys	https://www.enterprisesurveys.org/	Algeria 2007; Egypt 2004, 2007, and 2008; Jordan 2006; Lebanon 2006; Morocco 2004, 2007; Oman 2003; Saudi Arabia 2005; Syria 2009; Palestinian Territories 2006; and Yemen 2010.
Barro-Lee 2010	Paper by Robert J. Barro and Jong-Wha Lee http://www.barrolee.com/main.htm	Cross-country data on years of education of women.
UNIDO Industrial Statistics Database (INDSTAT4 2009)	http://www.unido.org/index.php?id=1000309	Total employment and female employment in each manufacturing sector used to construct a measure of industry-specific needs for female labor.
UN COMTRADE 2007	http://comtrade.un.org/	International trade flows are used to construct measures of industrial structure for each country.
Penn World Tables 7.0—Heston and others 2011	http://pwt.econ.upenn.edu/php_site/pwt_index.php	Other macroeconomic variables are not available in World Development Indicators (WDI) or Barro Lee 2010.

www.ingramcontent.com/pod-product-compliance
Lightning Source LLC
Chambersburg PA
CBHW080611270326
41928CB00016B/3007